210903017

W9-AVI-381

COMING CLEAN

COMING CLEAN

The True Story of a Cocaine Drug Lord
and His Unexpected Encounter

Jorge L. Valdés, Ph.D.
with Ken Abraham

To order additional copies of this book, contact:
Xlibris Corporation
1-888-795-4274
www.Xlibris.com
Orders@Xlibris.com
46636

CONTENTS

PART FOUR—1987-1995

Ours is a Jesus who bleeds . . . which is to say, a Jesus made of flesh and blood like us. The blood on his face, side, hands, and feet are the signs of his humanity; not the abstract [humanity] of the philosophers and theologians, but the flesh and blood humanity of those who dare to kiss his wounds.

—Roberto S. Goizueta
Caminemos con Jesus: Toward a Hispanic/
Latino Theology of Accompaniment
Orbis Books, 1995

ONE

THE STRUGGLE

From my chair on the platform I watched nervously as the gang members gathered inside the storefront church. The Blue Island section of inner-city Chicago was notorious for gang activity. Local thugs had torched the original church building; this new "sanctuary" was a simple affair of beige-painted cement blocks and dry wall. Overhead, panels of flickering fluorescent lights alternated with acoustic tiles in the dropped ceiling.

Several young Hispanic men slouched on the blue folding chairs lined in rows before me. With arms folded across their chests, they transmitted a clear message: "Go ahead. Impress me—if you can."

Many of the young men and women wore clothing or symbols identifying their particular gang affiliation. Most of them—male and female alike—bore scars on their faces, hands, or arms, marking them as veterans in Chicago's gang wars. And they had come to hear me—Jorge Valdés, once one of the most powerful drug lords in the world, a man who brought tons of cocaine into America and who could make a million dollars on any given day, and often did.

That was the old Jorge. Now, as I peered out at the tough-looking audience, I worried. *What does the new Jorge Valdés have to say to these kids—or to anyone else, for that matter?*

I saw anger on some of the faces. The cynicism in their eyes had for many years been in mine as well. No doubt many of these young people were angry at the hand life had dealt them. Most, I knew, were involved with drugs in some way. Many were users, hooked on the cocaine I had once imported; others were dealers, risking their lives daily to make a few bucks for themselves and a lot of money for somebody else.

I once believed that the cocaine I sold in massive amounts was merely a luxury item for the rich and famous. That was a devil's lie. These kids knew firsthand the trickle-down effect of the merchandise I'd sold to their mothers and fathers, thereby destroying many of their families. Some of their parents were dead, and most of the rest were divorced. Some of the kids had been born addicted to drugs. Most of them lived in poverty. Many had already served time in prison.

Because of me.

Because of the all-consuming, overpowering destructiveness of my products. What could I possibly tell them in a single hour that would make up for my role in the awful tragedies that consumed their lives?

I knew that, despite their tough appearance, many of these young men and women were hurting inside. For some, the hurt would come out in hatred and revenge; for others, in determination—"I'll get what I want whatever the cost." I could relate to that insatiable lust for power, and for money and all it could buy.

I knew, too, the powerful magnetic pull of the illusions of grandeur dangling before their eyes. *Why pursue anything else when I can make big money selling drugs? I'm not hurting anyone. I'm not holding my customers' noses and making them snort coke. They want what I have to offer!*

Oh yes, I could empathize with these young people, but I was still worried. This wasn't the usual Sunday morning church crowd. Would they listen to me? Would they hear the truth I wanted so desperately to tell them? Or would they shrug it off, just as I had rejected the words of so many who offered me a better way?

It was almost time to start. I deliberately submerged my anxiety beneath the victory I'd struggled to reach earlier in the day.

I had awakened before sunrise to prepare my heart and mind for this event. I'd had only five hours of sleep, but my rest had been peaceful. That in itself was new for me. As a drug lord I had slept fitfully, often with a nine-millimeter Beretta pistol at my bedside, wondering, *Is this the night my life will end?* The least little sound would bring me bounding to my feet, pistol in hand, to search the darkness for the paid killers I knew would eventually come.

In my heyday as a drug lord I had been fearless. With steel guts I had survived a plane crash in the jungle and endured unrelenting torture at the hands of Central American thugs—torture that affected my health for years but never overcame my determination to withhold information from my torturers. Years later, however, imagined assaults haunted the darkness of my nights.

Through a change I never thought possible, I survived that time of emotional torture and lost my fear of being killed. Since I was no longer protected by a platoon of bodyguards, armed with an arsenal, I was now an easy target for anyone seeking revenge. And I realized that simply revealing some of the things I knew could someday cost me my life or, worse, put the lives of my wife and children in jeopardy. But I no longer feared death.

This morning I had wrestled with a different fear: the fear of being inadequate for the awesome task ahead of me, fear that somehow I might disappoint the One responsible for my transformed life. I knew that addressing the gang members would be a thrilling opportunity but a painful experience.

People often say to me these days, "Jorge, if God can change you, he can change anyone." I knew that was true. But what if the rough edges of my story inadvertently glorified my past instead of pointing to the God who redeemed me from it?

There in my library, I dropped to my knees.

I prayed for wisdom; I prayed for strength; I prayed for the gang members who would hear me that night. Though I'd become a disciplined and enthusiastic student of the Bible and theology for the past several years, earning both a master's and a doctor's degree in New Testament studies, I knew that the young people I'd be speaking to that night weren't interested in theological points or philosophical issues. They were too busy trying to survive. They weren't concerned about making it to heaven; they simply wanted to make it through the night.

Perspiration trickled down my face. A passion was stirring in my heart to help hurting people where they lived, far away from the quiet halls of higher learning. *God, is this your will for me?* I prayed. *Am I to take the gospel to the gangs and to the streets?* Perhaps this evening would provide an answer for me as well as for my audience.

It was to be the first time that this group of Hispanic gangs would assemble peaceably (we hoped) in one room. Peter Contreras, the pastor of this inner-city church for more than twenty years, had earned a reputation as a good Samaritan in the Blue Island neighborhood. Oftentimes, he had taken in kids who had been stabbed or shot and left to die on the church's doorsteps.

If Pastor Contreras said something was worthwhile, the people of his parish took note. So for three months he had worked energetically to get the word out about my speaking engagement. He and his staff had used every method imaginable to challenge the inner-city community, including the gang members, to come hear not just a message about immorality, money, and drug excesses, but also a message of hope.

Many people were intrigued with what they'd heard about me. Some wanted to know how a poor Cuban kid could grow up to be the U.S. head of a powerful Colombian drug cartel and what one newspaper labeled "the mastermind of the largest drug conspiracy in the history of Central America." Others were enamored with the enormous amounts of money I had made—and lost. Still others wanted to know how someone like me could possibly change.

For all these reasons and more, the rival gangs would be there—and the atmosphere would be electric. One spark could set off an explosion that would rock this neighborhood.

O God, I prayed, *how often do these kids come together, except to fight, maim, or kill one another?* I stopped cold. *Kill one another.* That's exactly what my fellow

Hispanics were doing. Some did it with guns, others with drugs, but the end result was the same: My people were dying.

Please God, I prayed. *Let me help put a stop to this senseless killing.* The immensity of the mission God had set before me was overwhelming.

Even as I prayed, God was fighting a tug of war with the enemy within me. The Holy Spirit gently but firmly tugged one way, assuring me I was forgiven, that old things had passed away, that my life was new. But with taunting reminders of my sinful past, the enemy of my soul continued to jerk me the other way. The battle raged on. Great drops of perspiration ran down my face.

"O God!" I cried out. "I'm so sorry for all I've done. How could I have been so wretched? How could I have been such a selfish, immoral, egotistical pig? How could I have hurt so many innocent people? How can you ever use someone like me?"

Now I was yelling at the top of my lungs. "What do you want from me? Why me, Lord? Why did you save me? What have I ever done for you except to desecrate your name and your people? Why do you care about someone like me, someone who lived such a horrible life?"

In the midst of my questions, God's Holy Spirit suddenly won the tug of war. A tremendous sense of peace enveloped me, and I was sure of his presence and his love.

I picked up my Bible and read again, "I have not given you a spirit of fear, but of power." As the sun peeked through my window, my heart was strangely warmed. I realized afresh that it was not my goodness—nor my awfulness—that God would use; he simply wanted my availability. He would do the rest.

Tears of joy washed my face as I committed myself again to speak that night to these kids.

I was ready. The struggle was over.

Later that evening, when I stood up on the platform, I began by telling the gang members, "I was everything you have ever wanted to be . . . and never will be. But today I am everything you need to be."

The large and rowdy crowd grew quiet. A few of them nudged each other, as if to say, "Yeah, right!"

"I've had everything you're looking for," I continued. "I've achieved everything you're dreaming about. And I've also experienced your worst nightmares. But today my life is filled with more love than I ever thought possible."

The story I told them—the story of my coming clean from a life of horrendous corruption—is the story I want to tell you now.

PART ONE

1956-1978

Why at this moment in our lives, a moment that was supposed to be so full of joy with a new life in a new land, why had it all taken such a terrible twist? . . .

It was the beginning of an awful conviction, a deepening and despairing realization that I would know for many years: There was no God.

TWO

FLEEING FIDEL

I was born a fighter—fighting for my life.

Soon after my birth on February 29, 1956, in Santiago de las Vegas, Cuba—a small, rural town on the outskirts of Havana—I contracted acute diphtheria, an often fatal disease causing inflammation of the heart and nervous system. My mother took me to the town clinic, but after a week of treatment the doctors said they could do nothing further. My condition continued to worsen. My mother prayed fervently and took me to a hospital many miles from home where other doctors treated me. Finally, after nearly a month, I fought my way back to health.

I was the Cuban version of a Gerber baby, with long, dark, curly hair. I was actually photographed for baby food advertisements in Cuba, but my modeling career was cut short by another fight, one with international ramifications.

In 1959, a young Cuban lawyer and son of a sugar cane planter, Fidel Castro Ruz, and his band of revolutionaries wrenched power from the oppressive, iron-fisted government of dictator Fulgencio Batista.

Two years later, Castro began expropriating all American-owned businesses in Cuba. The United States responded by cutting off diplomatic relations with the Castro government. Later that same year, the Kennedy administration armed a group of Cuban exiles and, with the help of the American CIA, attempted an invasion at the Bay of Pigs, an inlet on the Cuban coast. Midway through the operation, the U.S. reneged on its commitment to back up the invaders. The attack was an abysmal failure, with nearly twelve hundred exiles taken prisoner.

Following the Bay of Pigs fiasco, Castro announced that Cuba had become a communist country; he allied himself with the Soviet Union and implemented a Marxist-Leninist economic program. For my parents, Hidalgo and Angela Teresa Valdés, Castro's announcement could mean only one thing: The communists would soon strip them of everything they had worked so hard to obtain.

My father earned an excellent income from the furniture factory he owned. Although we were by no means wealthy, we lived comfortably in a large house with a spacious patio, adorned by a fabulous array of tropical flowers lovingly tended by my mother. We owned a car and most other conveniences common to moderately affluent middle-class families in Cuba at that time.

Beyond the potential loss of material possessions, my father and mother hated the thought of their children growing up in a repressed society, indoctrinated by Castro's pablum, which was already being force-fed to school-age children by the revolution's new "educators." They began forging a plan to willingly leave everything behind, flee to America, and begin a new life at age forty.

I awakened early on the morning of October 11, 1966, roused from my sleep by my mother's urgent prodding. "Jorge, wake up. Hurry! Today we are going to America!" I was ten years old, my brother, J.C., was nine, and my sister, Maria, was five.

Mom's excitement was contagious. "Your aunt and uncle are waiting for us in Miami. We'll meet them there and live with them until we can afford our own place. America is a place where all your dreams can come true!"

At the airport, my brother, sister, and I trailed our parents closely as we made our way through various security checks. Suddenly, at one counter, I saw my mother's face go pale. An official shook his head and began arguing with my father. My father began arguing with my mother, and before long she broke down crying. I couldn't understand much of what was going on, but apparently there was an error on Mom's passport—it listed her as being fifty-five years old—and the authorities would not permit her to leave Cuba until it was corrected. The rest of the family could go, but Mother must stay behind.

"No, no!" my father said. "If you cannot go, none of us will go."

"Bebo, don't be foolish," my mother implored. "All that matters is our children. Go, please, go!"

"I will not!"

My mother suddenly turned to me. "Jorge," she said, placing the hands of J.C. and Maria in mine. "Take your brother and sister, and go. I don't want you to stay here any longer."

I couldn't believe my ears, but Mother was insistent. "Hurry, Jorge. Run! You must get on that plane." She began to push us through the gate area into a long corridor leading to the tarmac.

I was virtually in shock as we children numbly made our way down the corridor, and the pain and bewilderment of that moment was seared into my memory forever.

"Oh, Teresa!" The pain in my dad's voice behind me was unmistakable. "All right," I heard him say. "We can't let them go alone. I will go. But you must follow as soon as you can. Please."

"I will, I will," Mother promised. "Just go!"

My father's footsteps echoed down the corridor as he came running to join us.

I turned to see my mother standing in the gate area, waving good-bye. Emotional pain ripped through me. It felt like the end of the world. We all cried, including my father.

But there was no time for prolonged good-byes. We scurried into the plane and hastily found our seats just before the airliner began to move. I stared blankly out the windows as the plane's huge engines roared for takeoff. Confusing thoughts surged through my mind. Why at this moment in our lives, a moment that was supposed to be so full of joy with a new life in a new land, why had it all taken such a terrible twist? We had left behind nearly all our earthly possessions: our house, our car, our food, our money, our toys, everything but the clothes we were wearing. We were leaving our homeland—and our mother.

It was the beginning of an awful conviction, a deepening and despairing realization that I would know for many years: There was no God. The God of the Bible, the God that Mom prayed to all the time, did not exist. If he did, why would he have allowed this to happen to my family? Why didn't he care for us? Surely, the communists had been right. Christianity was a cruel, sick joke.

The seeds of a new and controlling determination were planted within me that day: *I must become tough. I must be my own god.*

Arriving in Miami, we were hustled off the plane and directed into immigration lines like a herd of cattle. We were part of a massive influx of Cuban refugees seeking freedom from Castro's fast-closing fist, so the airport was teeming with people, many of whom could not speak or read En glish and who no doubt felt as frightened and insecure as I did.

Following a brief check of our travel papers, we were vaccinated—which made me sick for days—then released from the immigration area. Then what a welcome sight it was in this foreign place to see the warm, smiling faces of our waiting relatives, though most of them were unfamiliar to me, having left Cuba when I was younger. I embraced them and listened excitedly as they gave us an instant course on the wonders of life in America.

But as we drove to my relatives' apartment, I began to have second thoughts about this land of opportunity. From what I saw through the car window, the neighborhoods were noisy, filthy, and depressing.

Our relatives lived in a one-bedroom apartment in a cramped section of Miami known as Little Havana. Under the same roof lived my aunt—Mom's sister—and another uncle and his wife and two children. Mom's grandmother was there also. Our relatives welcomed the four of us into their home, and we were deeply grateful, but it felt as though we were living on top of one another. Nine of us slept on the floor. *Welcome to America.*

Everything about the swirling city life around me felt strange, not just the unfamiliar language. American affluence in particular both awed and intrigued me. One day my cousin Albert drove by in a beautiful Pontiac Le Mans, candy apple red with white interior. As I gazed in wonder at the American status symbol, I thought, *What will it take for me to have something like that one day?* I was quickly becoming attracted to American extravagances—all of which seemed out of reach.

My dad found a job as a stock boy in a department store warehouse. It was quite a step down for a man who had owned a factory, but Dad never complained. Realizing that I had to help support our family, I got a job delivering morning newspapers before school. I earned only a few dollars a week, but every penny helped.

Each day after I delivered my newspapers, J.C. and I walked about ten blocks to Silver Bluff Elementary School. We couldn't understand En glish very well, and other kids mocked us constantly. We had little money for school lunches and often little food in our cupboards at home, so we were hungry most of the day.

School soon became a battleground for J.C. and me. Almost every day we became embroiled in another fistfight. We fought with just about anyone who looked at us wrong or called us names. We threatened some of the richer kids, "Give us your lunch money or we'll beat you up!"

My father was too proud to accept welfare or any other assistance from the government. He simply worked hard and hoped to pay his own way. Sometimes we'd hear a knock on the door, announcing a visit from our friends Gloria and Manolo Magluta. This generous couple had fled Cuba earlier than we had, and they now owned a small bakery in Miami. After a day's work Gloria and Manolo would occasionally bring leftover cake trimmings for us to eat. Saturated with sugar, the trimmings may not have been the most nutritious diet, but they temporarily stilled the hunger pangs in our stomachs.

The worst of our situation was being separated from our mother. As the oldest child I tried to be strong for my brother and sister as well as for my father. But each night the four of us cried ourselves to sleep.

At last, in December, just before Christmas, we got word that our mother was coming to America! Finally, everything was going to be all right. The United States truly would be the land of opportunity.

When Mom stepped off the plane in Miami, our excitement was immediately cut short. Her steps were faltering, and she looked ill.

While still in Cuba, Mom had been diagnosed as having a tumor in her throat, which severely impaired her breathing. Now she could barely function. Consequently, after school I did most of our cleaning, dusting, and mopping. Twice a week, I walked twelve blocks to a self-service laundry, lugging our dirty clothes. I was the only ten-year-old boy doing his family's laundry, and I drew curious but compassionate smiles from many of the women there.

When I wasn't doing housework, I worked odd jobs in the neighborhood, trying to earn money to help our family survive. One of my uncles gave me a broken-down lawn mower, and for about five dollars I had it repaired and painted it myself. The Jorge Valdés Lawn Service was up and running. I convinced J.C. to join me, and I enlisted several other neighbor boys who needed money and were willing to work hard. I charged my clients three dollars per lawn, out of which I paid one dollar to my brother or whoever did the actual work. Meanwhile, I went inside and talked to the clients and sipped lemonade. With my two-dollar-per-yard profit, I felt like some big-time entrepreneur. Every penny of my earnings went to my parents.

Eventually my family saved enough money to buy a television, which quickly became the focal point of our family life. As in many American households, the TV fostered fascination, wonder, and, of course, a lust to acquire more things. That lust sometimes got me into trouble.

One day on our way home from the beach, still wearing our swimming shorts, my cousin Eddie and I stopped in at a drugstore. Inside we spotted a set of swim fins. I wanted those flippers badly . . . real badly.

"Wow, Eddie! Look at these. I wish we had enough money to buy these fins."

Eddie's eyes sparkled mischievously. "We don't need any money, Jorge."

I caught on immediately to what he was implying. "Why don't you steal one," I told him, "and I'll steal the other." We planned our strategy carefully—Eddie would escape one way, while I made for another aisle. Then we moved decisively. I stuffed the flipper inside my shorts and started walking toward the exit in what I believed was a casual manner.

Near the front door, the store manager noticed something unusual. It's not easy to walk quickly with a swim fin sticking out of one's shorts.

He grabbed me and started yelling, "Hold it right there, you little thief!"

I immediately began spinning a story. "Oh no, sir. I was getting ready to pay for it, honest. It's a gift for my cousin, and I didn't want to tell him 'cause it's his birthday, and—" That's when I saw another employee grabbing Eddie by the neck, the swim fin protruding from his shorts.

The store manager called my father, who said he'd be right there.

I didn't know what to expect when Dad arrived. Would he be angry? Would he slap me across the face? (I almost wished he would.) But he did nothing of the sort. My father looked at me and literally began crying from shame as the manager explained the scheme Eddie and I had tried to pull off. The embarrassment and hurt in my father's eyes were more unbearable than any punishment he could have given me. I never forgot that look.

After living in Miami for about a year, J.C. and I joined the local Boy Scout troop, which was as poor as its members. Most of our tents had holes, our uniforms were old and patched, and we traveled to camping events in an old beat-up bus. On one camping trip we noticed another group of Scouts unloading nearby. They were traveling in big, late-model cars, and their uniforms and equipment looked topnotch. We soon discovered that this troop was from Coral Gables, one of Florida's more affluent cities.

Early in our week at camp, the scouts of Silver Bluff (led by J.C. and me) added a resolution to the Boy Scout Oath—namely, that rich kids should give to poor kids. Then we threatened to whip the tar out of the Coral Gables troop every day unless they gave us all their money, which they did.

We also told them they couldn't come out of their tents after ten o'clock. At night the camp canteen was bustling with activity, serving the hungry Silver Bluff scouts with late-night snacks that we otherwise could not have afforded. We felt like Robin Hood and his merry men. Besides, I thought those rich kids needed to lose some weight.

On the way back to Miami, our troop stopped at a restaurant. By now we were broke, having spent at camp all our money from the Coral Gables kids. "Don't worry," I told our guys. "Order up. I'm paying, and I have plenty of money," I lied, knowing I didn't have a dime on me.

While the Silver Bluff troop gulped down the unexpected feast, I settled on a plan.

From the pay phone in the corner, I called the police and told them where I was. "I've just planted a bomb here," I said, disguising my twelve-year-old voice. "I'm in love with one of the waitresses and she left me, so I'm going to blow up the place!" I hung up the phone, wiped my fingerprints off the receiver, returned to my table, and nonchalantly tackled my meal.

Some of my friends cast furtive looks in my direction as the waitresses started handing out the bills. "Don't worry," I assured the guys as I calmly continued to eat.

Several police cars suddenly roared into the parking lot. The police burst through the doors of the restaurant and stormed inside, shouting, "Clear the building! Everyone out. There's a bomb in here somewhere!"

People scurried for the exits. I calmly took one last sip from my drink, wiped my mouth with my napkin, and then ran to catch up with the other Silver Bluff scouts, already heading toward the bus. We drove away without paying a cent—and I discovered the rush that came with power, respect, and an appearance of wealth.

My father at that time was making eighty cents an hour, and our rent was eighty dollars a month. But my parents were extremely proud and ruled out asking anyone for assistance. Again and again they told us kids, "We came to this country to give you the opportunity to grow up in freedom and to give you an education. We didn't come here to ask anybody for anything or to take anything from anybody."

Our parents' sacrifices meant a lot to us. Nevertheless, I struggled with the contrast between the values Mom and Dad taught me and the values displayed in society. I weighed the conflict in my mind and heart. *Are Mom and Dad right? No, they aren't. Look at the people who are getting ahead. They aren't necessarily the smartest or the hardest workers; more often they're simply the shrewdest or the ones most willing to go after what they want regardless of who they trample on.*

My growing cynicism was bolstered by the fact that, no matter how hard we worked, our financial condition continued to deteriorate. Only two months after an operation for her cancer, Mom went back to work, throwing herself into whatever jobs she could find. She worked in factories, she worked as a seamstress, she even picked tomatoes on her hands and knees on a farm in Homestead. Nothing helped; we just couldn't get ahead.

Finally, in the autumn of 1969, my mother had had enough. When a cousin living in New Jersey called with the news of greater opportunities up north, Mom was convinced we should move. Our grandmother, Dad's mom who had recently joined us from Cuba, would come too.

The long train ride up the eastern coast was exciting, but we received a shock when we stepped off the train in New Jersey. The October weather was cold and dreary; everything seemed dark, damp, ugly, and dirty.

Again we moved in with relatives, my mom's cousin and her husband and daughter. The three of them and the six of us squeezed into a one-bedroom apartment in a poor Hispanic neighborhood in Union City. Again we slept on the floor.

A month later my family moved into our own apartment in the worst neighborhood I'd ever seen. When we moved in, we had to literally scrape mud and crud off the walls.

Beyond the walls of our small apartment was a war zone. Machine guns were being sold upstairs; another apartment housed a shooting gallery where heroin was sold and where junkies came and tested the "product." A prostitution ring operated out of the building as well.

The winter weather made life even worse. By a miracle of her faith, Mom had been able to enroll J.C., Maria, and me in a Catholic school ten blocks away. We normally walked to school, but sometimes the weather was so ferociously cold that my mother hired a taxi to take us. We couldn't do that often, however, because the one-dollar fare was more than we could afford. I dreamed of the day when I would make enough money that this would no longer be a concern. *And instead of riding in a taxi,* I thought, *I'll ride in a limousine.*

Three

To Really Be Somebody

As a teenager, one of my earliest jobs was at a warehouse where many other Hispanics were employed. Because I was bilingual (my English had greatly improved), I was promoted to night manager within a week after being at the warehouse. My organizational skills were being noticed. The promotion also meant a larger income, but I continued to give two-thirds of my earnings to my parents.

During this period in my life, the motivation for all of us, what kept us alive, was the strength of our family and the hope we shared. We honestly believed that if we worked hard enough, we would overcome the odds. And we lived on daydreams. We'd go to a store as a family and stare in awe at the fabulous selection of items. We rarely bought anything, but it was fun to look. We'd drive around the rich neighborhoods and see the houses that we wanted to have one day. Although we struggled just to pay for our apartment and the bare necessities, Mom and Dad instilled in us a strong sense of pride, which motivated me for a long time.

My grammar-school grades were good enough that I earned an acceptance letter from Hudson Catholic High School. I was the happiest person on earth the day I received that letter. Now I really could *be* somebody. My first day at the school, however, I found out exactly what sort of somebody I was to be at Hudson—one who was ostracized. I walked into the school corridor to discover that nobody would speak to me.

Most of the students at Hudson came from affluent white families; there were only two or three other Hispanics besides me. I had a constant, pervasive sense of not belonging. In my classes, in the hallways, in the cafeteria, or in the library, I kept to myself.

Fortunately, one of the teachers at Hudson befriended me. Antonio Fernandez was a member of a Catholic monastic order. He was also Cuban, so Mom and Dad invited him to the house for a meal. Brother Fernandez became my confidant. His example of faith and dedication inspired me to work even harder and to be that much better than everyone else.

When he left the monastic order, I teased him. "So you're a man now."

Brother Fernandez laughed and answered, "I've always been a man, Jorge. I just belonged to a religious order before. It's possible to be a strong man and also a good Christian, you know."

No, I didn't know that.

The turning point in my school life at Hudson came when baseball season rolled around in February. I excelled during tryouts and was selected to be the main backup catcher for the varsity team as well as the starting catcher for the junior varsity. When the coach sent me to get my uniform, I picked number five, after my hero, Johnny Bench, all-star catcher for the Cincinnati Reds.

Making the team brought fringe benefits. Everybody at Hudson accepted me. All the kids wanted to sit with me in the cafeteria. I was learning that in America it's often not *who* you are, but *what* you are that matters to people.

One of my more intriguing friendships in high school was with a fellow Cuban who was also on the baseball team and a hustler in every sense of the word. This classmate had a car, so I often rode home from baseball practice with him. We got to be pretty good buddies, even though he was older than I was. I parted company with him, however, when I discovered he was selling drugs in school, mostly pills—uppers and downers, which were the rage at that time.

I was dead set against drugs, even when kids at school offered them to me for free. As I watched some of the other ballplayers pop a pill before or after a game, I would think, *How can they do this to themselves?* I saw some of my friends with tremendous potential allow their lives to be ruined by drugs. I thought, *I don't want to have anything to do with that stuff.*

In my sophomore year, Hudson High hired a new coach for baseball and basketball, Rocky Pope. Unfortunately, we didn't hit it off together. Maybe Rocky didn't care for my fun-loving approach to the game. I was always laughing and cutting up. Rocky was not amused. He benched me and let my backup become the starting catcher on the varsity team. At the end of my sophomore year, I dropped out of high-school baseball, the game I loved so much, and enrolled in karate class along with J.C.

My brother wasn't thrilled with the sport, but I had found my niche. I enjoyed karate, probably because I enjoyed fighting. I was skinny, but I was scrappy and quick. After a while, my teacher felt I was ready for tournament competition.

Dad drove J.C. and me to our first competitive matches. I won my first three fights easily and proceeded to the championship round. As I was preparing for my match, the black belts standing by encouraged me and really pumped me up. "You can beat him!" they told me. They advised me to start the match by immediately coming out and throwing a hard punch to catch my opponent off guard.

When the signal came to begin, I took my mentors' advice. My opponent barely had time to bow before I slugged him right in the eye! The judges promptly issued me a warning. My opponent recovered and came at me with a vengeance, connecting with hard, painful kicks to my knees. I kicked back at him, hitting him so hard on his instep that his foot bubbled up like a softball and he had to be taken to the hospital. The officials disqualified me for excessive violence. I lost the match, but I won the respect of my fellow karate competitors.

During the summer of my sophomore year, my family visited again with our relatives in Miami. While we were there, my mom found a house she liked. The owners wanted only $19,000 for the property—a steal if you had any money, which we didn't. My father was indecisive, but Mom took me with her to see the real estate agent—her En glish was still rough, so I served as her interpreter—and we made an offer on the house. When my father found out, he was extremely distraught. "I can't leave you two alone for a minute!" he said. "How are we going to afford this?" Indeed it would be another year before we could finally move into the house.

Our anticipation was running high as we drove our packed cars back to Miami in the spring of 1973. Certainly we were thrilled to be moving to a warmer climate, but even more important, we would once again be close to our extended family members. For many Americans, *family* means mom, dad, and the kids, but to us, *family* included grandparents, aunts, uncles, cousins, and all of their extended families and friends. We ate and celebrated together, worked and played together, laughed and cried together, and helped one another through tough times.

I needed only one more credit—an En glish class—to finish my high-school graduation requirements. I enrolled at Miami's Coral Park High School, and I also enrolled in Miami-Dade Junior College. I enjoyed dealing with numbers and had decided I wanted to become an accountant and, perhaps someday, a tax lawyer.

I frequently told my mom I wanted to be a millionaire by the time I was thirty. "And the first thing I'm going to do is to buy you a mansion."

My parents encouraged me: "We know you can do it, Jorge."

Soon after we settled into our Miami house, I began looking for a job with flexible hours so I could continue my schooling. A friend of the family, Eugenio Cruz, worked at a Federal Reserve Bank and helped me get a job there. I worked in the check collection department in the mornings and attended classes in the afternoon.

I felt a tremendous sense of pride when I bragged to my friends that I was working for the federal government. Now that I was in college, my expenses were higher—car maintenance and gas, insurance, and college-related expenses. But only one paycheck each month went toward my personal expenses; the second paycheck was for my parents.

Not long after I began working at the bank, I became romantically involved for the first time. Through one of my cousins I met Nery, a fourteen-year-old beauty. Soon Nery and I were spending every spare minute of our weekends together, and we dated no one else.

Often, Nery and I drove through Coral Gables, gazing longingly at the beautiful homes. "One day," I told Nery, "we're going to live in one of those houses. One day, I'm going to make it big." Nery believed in me. Maybe that's why, when my busy schedule of studies and work left us nothing but the weekends, she didn't mind. She knew I had my heart set on achieving success.

Nery's parents treated me as a son and constantly expressed pride in my accomplishments. After all, at age seventeen I was already taking college classes and had a steady job at the bank. By all indications, I had a tremendous future ahead of me.

Besides that, I was straight as an arrow, without shame or embarrassment. Nery and I would leave a party immediately if I saw someone doing any kind of drugs. I didn't want to be near the stuff. "I am a government employee," I told Nery, "and I don't want to get arrested."

If only that conviction had been based in something more solid than my own pride . . .

After finishing my semester of high-school and junior-college courses, I transferred to the University of Miami. Obsessed with being the best student in my classes, I refused to settle for second place in anything. One class in tax law was so difficult that nearly half the class dropped out the first week. Nevertheless, following the first test, the professor stood in front of the class and pointed to my paper. "This is the first *A* I have given on any exam in the last ten years," he said. More than ever, I was convinced I should pursue a career in tax law.

About this time I received a promotion at the bank, giving me full-time status, more responsibility, and more money. In addition to attending college and working at the bank, I was developing a part-time accounting business on the side and doing people's taxes. Many of my clients were fellow bank employees or bank customers. I ran my accounting practice out of my parents' garage, where I not only did the tax computations but met with clients as well. My twelve-year-old sister, Maria, worked as my office manager, secretary, and bookkeeper, a position she would maintain in many of my future businesses.

Dad had opened a small clothing store not far from our home. J.C. and I helped Dad pick out the clothes he wanted to stock. One day Dad had to run an errand, so he left me to mind the store by myself. A customer came in and purchased some beautiful outfits costing more than three hundred dollars. I was so proud of myself for making the sale, until we found out the customer had paid with a bogus check. I thought, *How can people be so corrupt and crooked?*

I was soon to find out.

Four

Big Shot

When my family still lived in Cuba, my father's closest friend and mentor was a successful businessman named Oscar Perez. Oscar had been a frequent customer at a café where my dad worked as a waiter. He took my dad under his wing and helped him get started in the furniture manufacturing business. He also became my godfather.

Oscar's family had been one of the three wealthiest in Cuba. Their lithographic company printed money for the government. He lived in a beautiful home and drove the finest cars. But they lost it all to Castro's regime and fled to America about a year after my family had emigrated.

In late 1975 I reestablished a relationship with Oscar, who was now living in Miami. A tall, proud, and handsome man, he wore clean, perfectly pressed clothing even while mopping floors at the grocery store where he worked. Oscar always tried to live an honest and upright life—in fact, I often teased him about his having never cheated on his wife. Like most of my peers, I viewed extramarital affairs as normal for a Hispanic man, something that showed how manly or powerful he was. But Oscar was the model of high morals. It hurt me to see a man of his distinction and integrity scrubbing floors. *If there is a God,* I wondered, *why would he allow this to happen to a man like Oscar?* Yet Oscar never complained about his lot in life.

Then he took a job that widened the horizons of both his world and mine. A company called Infocasa operated a sawmill in Nicaragua, and Oscar was hired as the general manager.

Infocasa was owned by Domingo del Valle, a jet-setting millionaire from Spain. Oscar told me that Domingo wanted to upgrade the Nicaraguan sawmill business and was looking for contacts in the United States who could offer expertise. I immediately connected Oscar with Jack Snay, my first accounting professor at the University of Miami. Jack was a former manager for Price-Waterhouse in Michigan and had opened an accounting firm in Miami. I had immense admiration for Jack and his business sense.

Oscar and Domingo invited Jack and me to tour the sawmill in Nicaragua and make recommendations for improving the business. I hadn't traveled outside the U.S. since arriving in Miami as a boy. Now, at age nineteen, I was traveling to a foreign country, all expenses paid, as a professional businessman. It was an exciting opportunity.

When we arrived in Managua, Domingo's representatives took us to our hotel, where I stared in awe at the beautiful fixtures in our room, amazed at the opulence. In reality it was just an ordinary hotel room, but to me it was magnificent.

In Managua I met Domingo's business associate, Aumary, an odd-looking fellow from the Dominican Republic with a striking resemblance to a monkey. But Aumary's wealth protected him from ridicule as he picked his teeth with a knife while driving his beautiful Mercedes-Benz.

Two things motivated my life at this time: success and money. I was drawn to Aumary and his obvious prestige, so we quickly became friends. One night in Managua we picked up two prostitutes at a nightclub. I'd never been with a prostitute, and my heart thumped in nervous excitement. Once I was alone with the woman, however, my conscience overcame my desire and I did not have relations with her. To keep up appearances with Aumary, I paid the woman to pretend that we had experienced unbridled ecstasy.

The following day, Aumary, Jack, and I traveled into the jungles of Nicaragua to observe the sawmill operation. Jack and I then developed a business plan and proposed a deal to Domingo.

The business never took off, but two good things came from the effort—my connection with Domingo del Valle and my friendship with Aumary. Both relationships would prove to be life changing.

Shortly afterward, Domingo came to Miami to work on some business deals, and I was glad to show him around town. He stayed at a prestigious hotel and exuded wealth. A good-looking, sharply dressed man in his early fifties, he was an astute businessman and bona fide millionaire. I couldn't help but notice that he carried a lot of money with him. *This is the kind of man I can learn from,* I thought.

Domingo invited me to travel with him as his guest to observe his business operations in the Dominican Republic, and I gladly consented. He called Aumary to let him know we were coming. I smiled knowingly, as I recalled our night out in Managua. With him in the picture, I counted on doing some hearty partying during this trip. Perhaps this time I would not have to pretend.

Domingo met me at the airport, and together we took a taxi to the Jaragua, an old hotel with a famous gambling casino. After getting settled in my room, I called Aumary and made plans to go out that night. He promised to arrange "dates" with several women.

A few minutes later, Domingo came to my room to ask a favor.

"I want to go out with this girl tonight," he said, "and her parents won't let her go by herself. She must be accompanied by her sister, so I need you to come with me and be her sister's escort." I wanted to protest, but it was an awkward situation since the point of my trip was to work with Domingo.

"But, Domingo, I've already made plans with Aumary for tonight."

"Don't worry," he replied with a wave of his hand. "We'll go out for dinner, and it will take only an hour or two."

Realizing I didn't have much choice, I reluctantly agreed.

As Domingo and I waited in the hotel lobby to meet the two sisters, I was still sulking, certain my night had been ruined. My mood didn't improve when the women arrived. Domingo introduced me first to Janet, his girlfriend. She looked to be in her late teens or early twenties.

Then Janet introduced her younger sister, Luchy. She was attractive, with skin the color of light chocolate. I guessed her to be about fifteen. She wore a slinky, white dress. Her black hair was tied up around her head and secured with a beige scarf, which highlighted her sparkling green eyes.

At the restaurant, Domingo and Janet were soon deep in their own discussion. I tried to make small talk with Luchy, but our conversation was rather stilted. Although I was cordial, I viewed her as an inconvenience keeping me from my night on the town.

After dinner, Luchy and Janet excused themselves to go to the rest room. When they returned, I did a double take. Besides putting on fresh makeup, Luchy had let down her hair—gorgeous dark locks cascaded to her waist. I couldn't believe how beautiful she was!

My attitude changed, and so did my conversation. I immediately started telling Luchy all sorts of lies, making myself out to be a powerful American businessman.

Later that night, I partied with Aumary and several attractive young women. But I kept thinking about Luchy.

I called her house the next day, but she was in school. Later that afternoon we met to go out for ice cream. When I saw her, I couldn't resist; I pulled her next to me and kissed her. Luchy kissed me back. We held hands and walked along the beach, looking at the ocean and talking. Meanwhile I continued lying to Luchy, making up all sorts of stories about what a big shot I was in the States.

When I returned to Miami, Luchy and I kept in contact by telephone. My phone bill for the first month was one thousand dollars. I had no idea how I would pay it, but to me it was worth it. I felt sure I was falling madly in love. Before long I was making plans to return to the Dominican Republic to see her again.

That summer I experienced many changes. Besides breaking up with Nery and meeting Luchy, I became a partner with Jack Snay. Jack had opened a new office complex in Miami, and he offered me rent-free space to run my own business. "In exchange," Jack said, "you can do the accounting for my Spanish clients. I don't speak the language, but I have a good base of clients who do. You'll be helping me, and I'll help you."

It sounded like a great deal. Although I still lacked two semesters to complete my degree, I thought I could take a break from school, leave my job at the bank, and give the business opportunity with Jack a try.

When I ran the idea past my parents, it received mixed reviews. Dad was firmly on the side of security, represented by the Federal Reserve Bank. But Mom told me, "You'll never be able to amount to anything merely working for someone else." If I thought I could make it working on my own, that's what she thought I should do. I moved my accounting business out of my parents' garage and into Jack's brand-new office.

One of the Spanish-speaking accounts I handled for Jack was a business called La Puerta del Sol ("Door to the Sun"). Despite its grandiose name, it was essentially a meat market, a little grocery store owned by two Colombians, Alvaro and Elizabeth. Twice a week, I'd camp out in their tiny office and organize their financial records.

The meat market was a wild, chaotic place. Alvaro and Elizabeth fought frequently. After they screamed for a while, Elizabeth would go behind the meat rack, grab a large ham, and throw it at her husband. Alvaro would pull a gun from his waist and shoot the ham in midair. Then he'd pick it up and put it back on the meat rack. It was the same scenario every time.

I soon was shocked to learn that Alvaro and Elizabeth had purchased two new Cadillac Seville automobiles. Since I handled their books, I knew their business wasn't making that much money. How could these people afford two brand-new luxury cars?

I was quite naive at this time, never suspecting Alvaro and Elizabeth of doing anything illegal. They paid me well, so I simply collected my fees and didn't ask many questions.

Meanwhile I saw a lot of unusual characters coming in and out of La Puerta del Sol. One man in particular, whom I'll call Luis Guiterrez, was a quiet, polite gentleman, not well educated yet apparently well off. Luis always took time to talk with me when he came in the market. Only later would I discover I had every reason to be suspicious of Luis's activities—and that this meat market was one of the original fronts for a group of drug dealers that came to be known as the Medellin Cartel.

Early in the summer of 1976 I went back to the Dominican Republic to see Luchy. When I met her in the hotel lobby, she looked even more beautiful than I remembered.

Each day during my visit, Luchy came to the hotel after school and we became intimate, stopping just short of going "all the way." Later I visited her at her mom's house, where we talked and made plans for our future together. I told her to get a visa, that I wanted her to come to the U.S. and meet my family.

I was ecstatic when Luchy got off a plane in Miami several months later. Mom was with me, and together we drove straight to my father's clothing store. I couldn't wait for Dad to meet my girlfriend.

"Dad, this is Luchy," I gushed as we burst through the doorway. "This is the girl I've been telling you about."

After one look at Luchy, the expression on my father's face dropped. I could tell immediately that he disliked her. He greeted Luchy politely but reservedly.

At my parents' house, I took Luchy's suitcase to my sister's room, where she was to sleep during her stay. In the middle of the night, Luchy would sneak over to my bedroom. One night, my father walked in and saw us there unclothed. He didn't say a word; he simply looked at me, then left. I was devastated.

For the next week and a half, my father refused to speak to me at the dining room table. He was disappointed that I had disrespected him in his house, that I would do such a thing where my mother and my sister slept.

The knowledge that I had hurt my father crushed and humiliated me. *What kind of person am I becoming?*

But Luchy and I were in love, or at least we thought we were. Because Luchy's visa was temporary and would soon expire, we decided to get legally married in August—which would allow her to remain in the U.S. with me—but have the formal wedding in December. During the interim, we took a trip with my mom and my sister to Orlando. While Mom and Maria enjoyed the sights at Walt Disney World, Luchy and I enjoyed each other, sneaking back into our hotel room every chance we could to be alone. It was there that we first consummated our physical relationship. After that, we couldn't stay away from each other.

Luchy and I wanted our public wedding to take place in a Catholic church, more in honor of our mothers than because of any personal faith in God. We went to several churches before finding a priest who would marry us. We had to pay the priest extra money because Luchy was so young and because we weren't members of that parish. While I was glad to pay the money, the fee reinforced my impression that the church was nothing more than a business.

By our wedding date, December 17, I was having second thoughts. I was so young, and Luchy was even younger. We barely knew each other; we had met only a few months earlier. Sure we had great sex, but what else did we have in common? These and a thousand other questions filled my mind. I was so confused, I showed up an hour late to the church on our wedding day. I thought I was in love with Luchy, but in truth, I didn't have any notion of what true love is. Nor would I for years to come.

After our wedding and a honeymoon in the Pocono Mountains of New York, we went home to our apartment for the first time as husband and wife. Almost immediately Luchy and I started having problems.

In pursuing my own business, I had learned from Domingo and Aumary that I needed to have call girls on standby to entertain clients. A friend directed me to a woman who ran a call-girl operation. I arranged a meeting and, to my delight, discovered that, like Luchy, she was Dominican and gorgeous. I went out with the woman ostensibly to talk business, but before the night was over I had sampled her wares for myself.

I felt horribly guilty and remorseful for cheating on my newlywed wife. When it was over, I was scared to death. I had crossed a line. I stood in the shower and scrubbed my body ferociously, trying to rid myself of the filth I felt. I thought sure I'd have a dozen diseases—and I would have deserved them.

But my interest in having normal husband-wife intimacies with Luchy diminished rapidly, partly because of my unfaithfulness and partly because there was nothing else in our relationship to hold us together. We conversed very little and shared few common interests.

My encounter with the call girl opened a Pandora's box for me and set in motion a perverse pattern. I started cheating on my wife regularly, often having casual sex with women I had just met. At age twenty I portrayed an image of success, driving a nice car, dressing to the nines, and working out of an attractive office. I rarely had to pursue illicit relationships; women were attracted to me like metal shavings to a magnet. I was propositioned frequently, and I seldom turned down an offer.

Luchy must have realized she was losing me, because she tried to lure me back into her arms with the one enticement that had worked in the past: her sexuality. Frequently, I came home from work and found her waiting for me by the stairs, naked and inviting. Despite her best efforts, I often feigned that I was too tired or that I had a headache—anything so I didn't have to have sex with her after coming home from holding another woman in my arms.

At times, of course, Luchy and I did have sex, so I wasn't surprised when she announced that she was pregnant. Perhaps Luchy thought that a baby would bring us together once again. If so, she was wrong. I told her that she couldn't have this baby, that we were too young to have children, and that we had to wait awhile. I forced Luchy to get an abortion.

Luchy desperately tried to please me and, even at sixteen, wanted to be the best wife ever. But I had entered a whole new world—the world of Sam Libbus.

FIVE

CON GAMES

My brother, J.C., had developed an import-export business, bringing Dominican produce into the United States. Through this connection I met Sam Libbus (not his real name) in early 1977. Of Jamaican descent, Sam also conducted business deals in the Dominican Republic and elsewhere. His immediate cash flow came from buying yams and ginger in the Dominican Republic and selling them to markets in London.

At the time we met, Sam needed a Spanish translator to travel with him in the Dominican Republic. The fact that I was an accountant and could help with his business transactions in Hispanic countries made me even more valuable to Sam.

I soon discovered that Sam was a con artist extraordinaire. He had developed an entire shtick, conning people into believing he was an Arabian sheik from Kuwait who was looking to invest his vast resources of petro-dollars. He could carry off the scam because he looked almost identical to Sheik Yamani of Saudi Arabia. Sam dressed the part too, sometimes in full Arab garb, including robes and a turban, sometimes in impeccable suit and tie—always flaunting an aura of obscene wealth. He was extremely intelligent and constantly read newspapers from around the world to keep up on global events and potential markets for his scams.

On our frequent visits to the Dominican Republic, Sam traveled as an Arabian sheik, and I traveled as "Dr. Valdés, chief of protocol for His Royal Highness Sheik Iwah ab Dalud Mamuud Zalani" or some other Arab-sounding name we made up as necessary.

In 1977, I traveled with Sam to the island of Tortola in the British Virgin Islands. There I met Cyril Rodney, the country's finance minister and a key contact for setting up foreign bank accounts. Although I was only twenty years old, it didn't take me long to develop a talent for forming foreign corporations and offshore bank accounts.

Long before I got involved in laundering money for what would come to be known as the Medellin Drug Cartel, Sam Libbus introduced me to bankers in both Tortola and Grand Cayman who were willing to work with me. A banker in Grand Cayman, for example, charged me $1,800 to create a foreign corporation. I then charged my clients $10,000 and pocketed the profit.

My clients had their own reasons for wanting offshore accounts, and although I could guess what was going on, I made it a point not to ask. Clearly, though, the main reasons my clients desired accounts outside the U.S. were to shelter money from the U.S. Internal Revenue Service and to "launder" money received illegally by placing it in a legally held account. Money in the offshore account could then be sent to partners throughout the world. Many of the bankers I met through Sam remained good contacts—the ones he hadn't bilked too badly—when I got into the drug business.

One day after Luchy and I had a big fight, I moved in with Sam at his house in Miami Beach. Soon afterward, Sam decided to go to the Philippines, and he invited me to go along. He was hoping to foist his petro-dollars scheme on the Martels, a fabulously wealthy family related to Imelda Marcos.

The trip was typical of many I experienced with Sam—a total sham. I called the airline ahead of time and identified myself as Dr. Valdés, chief of protocol for His Royal Highness. I requested first-class seats. His Royal Highness, Sam, traveled first-class only. I also instructed the airline that His Royal Highness was expecting his regular champagne, Dom Pérignon, to be stocked and that we would expect to be preboarded.

When we got to the airport, everyone at the airline seemed to know Sam. We were hastily escorted to the first-class lounge. Sam refused to speak in English to anyone. In actuality, English was the only language Sam *could* speak, but he spoke in what he thought was an Arab-sounding dialect, rapidly mumbling gibberish such as, "Mamutza hasidine ah ruhos!" Pretending to translate, I made up whatever interpretation I thought was appropriate for the circumstance.

Naturally, we boarded the airplane before anyone else, and of course Sam received service fit for royalty. After all, Sam *was* royalty. In amazement I watched—and learned—what the power of money could do.

I mulled over these events in my mind, convincing myself that there was nothing wrong or immoral with my part in what Sam was doing. In fact, I was developing an ethical framework that said, "Anything goes; nothing is immoral. Life is whatever you make it to be." Darwin was right after all, and I was determined—by all means and by any means—to survive as the fittest and the strongest.

On our way to Manila, we stopped for a few days in Hong Kong, where we were immediately whisked by cab from the airport to the Peninsula Hotel. In our reserved suite I watched as Sam made phone calls to his contacts in Hong Kong. I was sure he was once more trying to swindle someone. His favorite gimmick was to offer his investors a loan from his supposed fortune of petro-dollars, but then to require the investors to put up a significant amount of money to secure the loan. For example, if someone wanted to borrow $10 million, Sam demanded that a feasibility study be done—which I did and for which he charged his borrowers $10,000. Of course, he never really loaned anyone any money; he simply made off with their $10,000.

I never ceased to be amazed that intelligent, successful businesspeople could be so gullible as to fall for such a cheap gimmick. But fall they did, again and again, one after another. All the while, Sam got richer—and I didn't do too badly myself.

When we finally arrived in Manila, a military escort in full regalia received us at the airport. Then we were driven in a limousine to the Century Park Sheraton in Manila. Our suite included a huge ornate foyer, an enormous, elegant dining room, and a large living room, plus three bedrooms and maids' quarters. We had a full-time butler and full-time maids at our service.

Sam hosted numerous meetings in the suite, including visits from members of the Martel family. *Like sheep led to the slaughter,* I thought.

Shortly after breakfast our second day in Manila, we were picked up at the hotel and transported to the Presidential Palace. After being briefed by his staff on the proper protocol, we were escorted into the presidential office and introduced to Ferdinand Marcos.

The president sat behind a huge desk, and Sam talked to him as if they were old friends. I just sat there listening to Sam flattering Ferdinand Marcos, telling the president about what a wonderful country this was and describing all the tremendous business opportunities that he was offering to Manila. I couldn't believe Marcos was buying Sam's lines. But I went to school in that room, watching, listening, observing, and learning some fascinating lessons. For a twenty-year-old young man, I was moving in fast company.

Six

Moving Money, Making Money

To my surprise, Luchy was waiting for me at the airport when I returned to Miami from the Philippines. She hadn't seen me in nearly a month, though I had called her occasionally from Manila, and she seemed willing to reconcile with me. She was too innocent to figure out that my sexual repertoire was expanding at her expense, a result of my flagrant unfaithfulness to her. For my part, adultery was becoming almost second nature. I still struggled with my immorality, but after the first time I betrayed my marriage vows, each succeeding instance of unfaithfulness became easier. Eventually my conscience was so desensitized that it hardly bothered me anymore.

With the money I'd made in my accounting practice and by setting up foreign corporations, I saved enough to move out of Jack's office complex and open my own office. I gave my dad an office in my new headquarters, and together we decorated it. I was learning the value of having a front for business, so I formed a new company known as Traicorp, short for Transatlantic International Corporation, through which I handled many of my foreign business transactions.

I continued to work with Sam, helping him with his legitimate fruits-and-vegetables exporting business and traveling abroad with him extensively. That's what led us to Colombia in the late 1970s, to explore possibilities for banana exports.

In Medellin, Colombia, I talked with a wealthy woman named Julia Orozco, whom I met through other contacts—her niece was Maria Guiterrez, the wife of Luis Guiterrez, the quiet gentleman who was a frequent "customer" at the meat market in Miami. Julia agreed to facilitate our banana purchasing efforts. Although I didn't know it at the time, apparently she was the cocaine supplier for Alvaro and Elizabeth, the owners of La Puerta del Sol.

One night in our hotel room, Sam and I were drinking heavily. The call girls provided through Julia's associates were dancing and stripping for us. After a while, one of them asked if she could use the bathroom, which was off the bedroom. I thought nothing of it and said, "Sure, it's right inside there." While she stepped out, her friend continued to entertain Sam and me.

After the women left, for some reason I decided to check the pockets of my pants, which had been in the bedroom. To my dismay I discovered that $250 was missing—the only money I'd brought with me. Furious, I tried to find the women, but they were long gone. Years later on a business trip to Medellín, I was at a friend's office when one of the women walked in. She didn't recognize me, but I immediately recognized her. When I told her who I was, she was horrified. Although I'd become a big-time drug lord, making money faster than I could spend it, I made her repay the $250.

During this trip, Sam and I took a flight to Turbo on Colombia's northern coast to view the banana plantations. Julia met us there and introduced us to the owners of Colombia's largest banana company, Turbana Banana. We discussed business details regarding where the ships could dock and how we could best get the bananas to market. By the end of the day, we had a solid deal in place.

When we returned to Miami, we found that Sam's other schemes were beginning to catch up with him. Irate partners—people he had conned—were calling from all over the world, demanding to know where their money was. Although I liked Sam, I feared being trampled in the stampede for his scalp. When Sam decided to take refuge in Jamaica for a while, I told him I felt it was time for me to move back in with Luchy. Sam and I parted amicably. I had made many new contacts through my travels with him and had learned well the art of deception. It was perfect training for a life of crime.

I rejoined Luchy even though I knew that our marriage was irrevocably damaged. She became pregnant, and once again I pushed her for an abortion. Luchy reluctantly agreed but said she wanted to go home to the Dominican Republic for the procedure. I really didn't care and was glad to have her out of my hair.

Meanwhile I was extremely busy forming new foreign corporations for my Colombian friends. I was doing quite well financially, making seven to eight thousand dollars per corporation. I had a vague notion of what sort of businesses these Colombians were involved in, but it didn't bother me greatly. *After all,* I rationalized, *I don't have anything to do with their business; I'm merely their accountant.* I knew how to launder money, and in doing so I moved millions of dollars around the world for them. But I didn't lose a wink of sleep worrying about doing anything illegal. All I cared about was making a ton of money.

Seven

A New Venture

Late one afternoon my office telephone rang. It was Luis Guiterrez, sounding frazzled and upset. "Jorge, I need you to do me a favor."

"Sure, Luis, just name it." I'd become a sort of confidant to Luis and his friends at La Puerta del Sol, so I wasn't surprised when Luis confessed the personal nature of his favor.

"Jorge, Maria's son has been arrested."

"What did he do?"

"It has something to do with bringing some drugs into the country. I have an appointment to see an attorney right away."

"And?"

"And would you please go with me? You know how to talk to these people better than I do."

"Okay, Luis. I'll be right there."

The attorney, whom I'll call Monti Cohen, informed us that Maria's son had been arrested in Miami by U.S. customs officials while attempting to pick up thirteen kilos of cocaine from a banana boat at the river. After Monti's explanation, Luis handed him $50,000. I'd never before seen that much cash.

"Don't worry, Luis," Monti said, as he fondled the bills. "I'll get the kid out on probation."

The lawyer delivered on his promise. By the time the case was settled, Monti had convinced the judge to put Maria's son in a drug rehabilitation center rather than prison. The judge apparently bought the outlandish claim that the thirteen kilos had been intended for the boy's personal consumption rather than resale. It would be years before I found out the boy's release was the result of an intricate web of paying off corrupt judges—and that Monti Cohen was right in the center of the web.

I had no pressing need at the moment for Monti's professional services, but I knew I had found my lawyer. Anyone with his influence was someone I wanted on my side. We became close friends.

When Luchy returned from the Dominican Republic, I discovered that she had not gone through with the abortion. Instead she had given birth to a beautiful baby boy—Jorgito, she had named him. I was furious with her for defying my orders, but I couldn't discount the awe I felt at the sight of our son.

During this period in my life, what I sought most was to be recognized, admired, and praised. The most natural source of such adulation, I thought, came from my relationships with women. I especially sought admiration from the type of women who used to laugh at me as I was growing up as a poor, bespectacled kid in Miami. One such relationship was with Christine, a flight attendant I had met on a trip overseas. Christine called frequently, often from exotic locations around the world.

During one typical phone call, I was using my best seductive lines, promising Christine the time of her life—unaware that Luchy happened to be standing outside my office door, hearing every word. She listened long enough to figure out what was going on, then stormed into my office and came right across the desk, flailing at me.

When I got her calmed down enough to listen, I told Luchy it was time we put an end to our sham of a marriage. I promised her money to rent an apartment, and we went our separate ways.

One day in late January 1977, Luis Guiterrez brought two sharply dressed men to my office, having told me beforehand that they had an interesting business proposition. Felipe Arango (not his real name) was a clean-cut Colombian black man who exuded confidence in his demeanor and manner of speech. However, his partner obviously was the leader. Manuel Garces struck me as having a winsome, yet subtly persuasive, personality.

After a few minutes of small talk, the Colombians outlined the reason for their visit. They wanted me to begin a new company to import bananas from Colombia. They asked me to form the corporation and also to look for contacts from whom they could purchase a ship to transport refrigerated cargo. I did not know their real intention: to launch a new enterprise for bringing cocaine into the country.

Thinking only of a legitimate and lucrative banana business, I explained that I wouldn't work as a hired employee for anybody. If I was to do all the legwork, I wanted to be an equal partner in the venture. I openly admitted that I didn't have any capital to invest. All I could bring to the partnership was my talent and my office.

Manuel and Felipe seemed pleased with my offer. We sat in my conference room that day and decided that each of us—Manuel, Felipe, Luis, and I—would own twenty percent of the business. The additional twenty-percent share would belong to another partner, Jorge Ordoñez, whom they wanted in the business.

We formed the corporation, with me as president. We named the company Euro Hold, for European Holdings. And we decided to call our product Kiss Bananas. My new partners gave me $10,000 to produce a business plan and develop ideas for a product logo and packaging.

The plan called for Euro Hold to buy a ship, which would be licensed in Panama. The Colombians decided that I should travel to Europe as soon as possible to search for a suitable ship, somewhere in the $250,000 to $350,000 price range. "See what you can find, Jorge, and report back to us," Manuel instructed.

After making contacts with several shipbuilders through Monti Cohen and others, I traveled to France, Germany, En gland, and Spain. When I returned to Miami, I reported to Luis, explaining that there were plenty of ships to choose from and that many were in our price range, but the cost of bringing one to America and having it converted might be prohibitive.

Then one of our contacts in Miami mentioned another possibility, an old landing craft used during World War II. It had a large front-end loader and might serve our purposes well. The ship was in Stockton, California, not far from San Francisco. But the ship's owner, Sam McIntosh, lived in Miami, where he operated an electronics and ship supply business. I arranged a meeting with McIntosh, who informed me he wanted $300,000 for the ship. He assured me it wouldn't cost a lot more to convert the landing craft to a refrigerated cargo ship, and he could do the job in California if we were interested.

When I told Luis, he responded, "Let's do it!"

Luis then arranged for Manuel Garces and Felipe Arango, along with their wives, to meet us in Miami. They would accompany us to California to inspect the ship. Sam McIntosh would meet us in Stockton.

When I saw Manuel Garces on the morning of our departure, I was struck again by his aura of power. Manny exuded a rare combination of confidence and gentleness. He was a person genuinely concerned about others and a gentleman in the highest sense of the word. I thought, *With a man like this involved in our banana business, we can't miss. We're going to be extremely profitable.*

On the plane, I sat next to Manny. At first we engaged in typical small talk, but as we proceeded across the country, Manny pressed closer. In a businesslike yet fatherly manner, he asked about my past, about my work at the bank, and about my education. Then he asked, "What are your plans for your future? What would you like to do?"

I talked to Manny about my goal of "making it" in America, which to me meant acquiring power and money and providing a comfortable living for my family. I felt that this banana venture might be a great step for me. He agreed and assured me that the business could take off. Then Manny shifted gears. "You know, Jorge, I can see how you may be a key player in representing many of my businesses in Miami."

Intrigued but uncertain of his intentions, I kept my mouth shut and listened. Manny told me he was involved in an airline business as well as a large construction company. He added that he had a wonderful project he wanted me to be involved in. Manny lowered his voice and asked, "What is the possibility of you supplying some of the things I may need?"

I assured Manny that I was interested.

That night in San Francisco we walked around Union Square, taking in the sights and the shops. In one jewelry store, Manny's wife, Anna, fell in love with a gorgeous bracelet. Manny asked the salesclerk, "How much is it?"

"Eight thousand dollars," the clerk replied without batting an eyelash.

I watched in amazement as Manny pulled a stack of one-hundred-dollar bills from his pocket and proceeded to pay cash for his purchase. Anna wore the bracelet for the rest of the evening.

Later, Felipe and his wife stopped at another store where they, too, bought some jewelry. At Saks Fifth Avenue my partners and their wives each purchased a few thousand dollars worth of clothing. I couldn't help wondering how these people could throw so much money around. But in the back of my mind I was thinking, *I want to be able to afford this kind of luxury someday. But of course I won't make the mistake of wasting my money.*

I kept telling myself, *If only I could make $100,000, then I could put some money away and be set for the rest of my life.* In truth, within a short time, I would be throwing away more than $100,000 in a single day.

The bill for that night's dinner totaled nearly $800, but no one except me seemed to give it a second thought. I was trying to act like a big shot, but I knew I was out of my league.

My mind was churning. In one sense I felt superior to my partners, smarter and more capable, and I thought I'd paid a higher price to get ahead than they had. Except for Manny, most of the Colombians had no formal education, while I had sacrificed money, sleep, and my social life to attend school. Yet they reeked of money and were throwing it around left and right. I decided to view the situation as a challenge and embrace whatever my association with my new partners might lead to.

Eight

Turning Point

The morning after our high-rolling evening in San Francisco, we drove to Stockton, where Sam McIntosh was waiting for us. A man in his late fifties, McIntosh was an electronics wizard and a wise businessman. He welcomed us aboard the ship and answered all our questions without hesitation. He sounded as though he knew exactly what needed to be done to convert it to a refrigeration ship and how much the work would cost.

After a three-hour inspection, we concluded that the ship was a great deal. It would be a real asset to our business. We bid McIntosh good-bye and agreed to get together back in Miami where we could discuss further the matter of price. McIntosh was now asking close to $400,000, but we thought we could get him down to $300,000. The conversion, which would involve insulating the boat's compartments and installing air-conditioning and refrigeration units, would cost another $100,000.

I flew to Panama and met with some lawyers to create an offshore corporation under which the ship would be registered. By registering in Panama, the insurance was less expensive and we would avoid U.S. taxes on the ship. I completed all the paperwork and paid about $10,000 to arrange the registration.

Returning to Miami, I plunged into the new venture with a vengeance. We hired an agent from Honduras who in turn hired a ship's crew for us. For a captain, we hired a Cuban fellow who had worked for several other shipping companies.

At the office, I kept strict work habits and disciplined hours. I made it a point to be the first person at the office in the morning and the last person to leave at night. After work, however, I continued my carousing lifestyle.

I had stayed in touch with Christine, the flight attendant. By this time she had quit her job and wanted to come stay with me. In my obsession to garner another female conquest, I had led this woman to believe I loved her and wanted to be with her on a more permanent basis. I wasn't greatly attracted to her, but now that I had "conquered" her, what was I to do? I felt I had no choice but to bring her to Miami and get an apartment for her. I now had Luchy, my soon-to-be-ex-wife in one apartment, Christine the flight attendant in another, and a third apartment for myself.

Meanwhile I partied regularly, living the single life in Miami, keeping Christine happy, and even sleeping with Luchy occasionally. At the same time I dated a variety of other women, all the time acting the big shot in a Mercedes I'd purchased from Monti Cohen.

In California, complications arose in the work on the banana ship. I got word that the crew wanted to go back home to Honduras. They hadn't realized how much work was involved in converting the landing craft to a refrigeration ship, and now that they did, they felt betrayed. We had a rebellion on our hands.

My partners asked me to go to Stockton and take care of the problem in person. We had a lot of money invested in this project, and our deadlines were approaching. If the ship wasn't ready on time, we risked losing the banana harvest in Colombia.

I packed my bags and headed for California. After firing the captain, I set to work building relationships with the crew. I gave them time off when needed and paid them extra for working overtime. I made sure they received good meals on board the ship, and I took them to town to go shopping. I even stayed on board rather than in a motel so I could bond with the crew. Morale among our men slowly began to rise.

Every third week or so, I traveled back to Miami for a couple of days. I also made two trips to Colombia to report to Manny and Felipe Arango and to get more money for the ship conversion. Our costs were skyrocketing, far surpassing McIntosh's estimates of what it would take to transform the vessel.

On one of my trips back to Miami, Luis Guiterrez surprised me by joking that I could probably find a very good cocaine market in California. I could tell that he was only half kidding. For some time I'd suspected that Luis was involved in drug dealing, but never had he been so blatant about it with me. From then on, nearly every time Luis and I talked, he conjectured about how much cocaine I could sell in California.

"You can make a lot of money, Jorge."

"Luis, I am not interested," I told him. "I've never done any drugs. My life is about working, and I've worked too hard and sacrificed too much to risk everything, no matter what the price."

"Okay, Jorge, take it easy," Luis smoothed my ruffled feathers. "Just keep it in mind."

About the same time, I had an unusual conversation in California with a man I'll call Rick Sanders, a big, strong, jovial fellow we had hired to work on the ship. Rick and his wife often invited me over to their home.

One day he said, "Jorge, I know that this boat is a Colombian coke boat."

I furiously denied it. "How can you say that? I'm in a business partnership with the owners of this boat, and we're using it to transport bananas."

"Sure, Jorge," Rick said with raised eyebrows.

"I'm serious," I told him. "Besides, I've never used drugs in my life."

"Whatever you say," Rick responded with a broad smile, as if he knew something I didn't.

I was being bombarded with cocaine jokes on both sides of the country, by Luis in Miami and by Rick in California. Rick began saying, "Jorge, why don't you hook me up? I have some friends that are very interested in buying cocaine."

"No way, Rick. I won't have anything to do with drugs."

This hazing continued for months.

Meanwhile, my partners in Colombia were becoming much more specific about their plans for me, most of which had little to do with our banana ship. Whenever I traveled to Colombia, Manny and Felipe spoke plainly about wanting me to handle their "interests" in America—which incidentally, they said, included a fledgling but flourishing cocaine trade.

I was strangely honored that these rich and powerful drug lords would want me, a twenty-one-year-old, to handle all their cocaine business in America. On the other hand, I was scared to death. I told them repeatedly that such a relationship was against their best interests since I had set up many of their foreign corporations. I knew where all the money was, and if I got arrested, it would jeopardize their investments. "I'm not your man," I told them. "You need somebody unattached."

Despite my protests, the Colombians continued to show tremendous confidence in me. Manny, in particular, spoke frequently of a profitable future together and of the money I could make.

Meanwhile Luis kept up the pressure in Miami, and my friend Rick in California continued to assume I was a big-time drug dealer.

One day, almost on a whim, I thought of a way to end the pressure. From Luis I would find out the going price for cocaine, then I'd give Rick some ridiculously high price so he wouldn't bother me about it anymore. And I would tell my partners in Colombia, "Okay, I'll handle your cocaine business in the States. But if you want me involved, I have to be an equal partner." I knew there was no way that the Colombians would go for that. Bringing me in on the banana business was one thing, but drug smuggling was something else. Why would the Colombians share their money with me?

My brilliant two-pronged plan was certain to lay the cocaine issues to rest.

On my next trip to Miami, I said to Luis, "Just for curiosity's sake, how much is cocaine selling for here?"

Luis's eyes brightened and his eyebrows raised slightly, but he remained cool as he quoted me a price of $46,000 to $48,000 per kilo.

I nodded as if this made perfect sense, but inside I was thinking, *Forty-eight thousand dollars per kilo! That's outrageous!*

"Would you like me to get some for you?" asked Luis, smiling openly.

"Oh no. I was just interested. You know, just for curiosity's sake."

Luis smiled again, but said no more.

Back on the West Coast, Rick Sanders continued to prime the pump, telling me stories about the fast life in California. Apparently, some of his friends were selling cocaine to big-name personalities, including Hollywood movie stars. Rick continued dropping subtle hints as well as dangling overt drug-selling opportunities in front of me. Finally, in exasperation, I followed through with my plan.

"Yes, Rick," I said. "I admit that my partners and I are big cocaine distributors. But I'm going to tell you this right now: We only deal with the best coke, and it's expensive."

Rick smiled broadly, as if to say, "I knew it all along!" Finally, he wiped the smile off his face and quietly asked, "How much?"

Pulling a ludicrous figure out of thin air, I shot back at him, "It's $70,000 a kilo."

"Whew!" Rick said with a soft whistle. "Seventy grand. That's a bit high."

"That's the going price," I repeated and changed the subject. I felt sure I'd heard the last from Rick on the subject. But a week or so later, he asked me to meet his partner.

"Your partner?" I asked.

"Yeah, you know, one of those Hollywood connections I told you about."

"Well, tell him to come on over, but I really don't have anything to say to him."

A few days later, Rick brought a friend to meet me at the ship, a guy he introduced simply as Joey. We talked for a while, and against my better judgment, I found myself liking Joey. He was a good-looking guy who hung around with the fast crowd and drove a Porsche.

Over the next two to three weeks, Joey and I went out a couple of times and partied together. He often boasted that he had partied with movie stars as well as with people in the music business. Joey spent a great deal of time and money in San Francisco and Los Angeles. If he was putting on an act, he lived the part, and I enjoyed living it with him. Although I worked hard on the ship during the days, I quickly became acclimated to nightlife in the California fast lanes.

Meanwhile I was having nightmares in which I was on my way to prison and was imagining what it would do to my mother and father. I had flashbacks to the time I'd been caught stealing as a young boy.

On my next trip to Colombia, the subject of my partnership with Manny and his friends came up again. I took a deep breath, mustered every ounce of chutzpa in me, and said, "The only way I'll become involved in your cocaine operation is if I'm an equal partner, and you will have to spot me the capital."

There—I had said it! Now, at last I could have some peace. The Colombians would refuse my demand, and I could get on with my life.

But Manny and Felipe simply nodded. "Let us have some time to think about this," Manny said ever so graciously.

The next time I was with Luis in Miami, he steered the conversation toward cocaine. "How does it look out in California?" he asked. "From our last conversation, it sounded as though you had something going on."

"Oh no, Luis. I really don't. What's happening is . . . I was just wondering . . . I mean, I read a lot in the paper, and I was just intrigued as to how much money was involved in this cocaine business."

Luis smiled. "Well, Jorge, cocaine is the drug of the future. It's the next big thing in the high life."

I didn't doubt the truth of Luis's statements. At the West Coast parties I attended with Joey, I had seen with my own eyes that cocaine was the center of attention. It was the standard by which parties were measured. If you didn't offer cocaine, your party was a bust.

What really amazed me was that the cocaine business didn't seem to be about the usual junkies I'd imagined. At the parties I'd noticed that all the successful people—bankers, judges, politicians, movie stars, musicians—seemed to be snorting coke. They justified their drug use by saying that cocaine wasn't a narcotic and wasn't physically addictive. One day I would learn that those claims were all part of the big cocaine lie.

Luis broke in on my thoughts: "Jorge, you really need to think about getting involved."

He smiled somewhat deviously and draped his arm around my shoulder. "Look," he said, "we can get the coke for forty-two; if we pay someone a couple thousand bucks per kilo to take it out to California for us, that's forty-four, and if you sell if for seventy—like you said—that's twenty-six thousand we could split, thirteen apiece."

Luis paused to make sure he had my full attention, which he did. "Now, think about this: If you take six or seven kilos out there, or even five kilos, you're talking about making sixty to seventy thousand dollars profit."

"I need some time to think about this, Luis."

"Okay, but don't take too long. There's a tremendous opportunity right now."

That night, I couldn't sleep. I tossed and turned, mulling the matter over, trying to figure out if things could actually work . . . and what I would do if they did. I was beginning to feel that perhaps I wanted this cocaine thing to happen.

Besides, it wasn't a matter of *if* cocaine was going to flow into California; it was only a matter of *how*—and *who* would profit from it. If I didn't do it, somebody else would.

And I'd seen what sort of people were purchasing the coke. Although I had no intention of ever using drugs myself—I still believed drugs were for fools—I wanted to belong to this crowd. They seemed cool, attractive, upscale. Everyone was having a good time; nobody intended to harm anyone.

Maybe if I make two or three trips, I thought, *I can make a couple hundred thousand dollars and I'll be okay. I'll quit while I'm ahead, and I won't have to do anything else. I can buy a nice house, help my parents buy a better house, and still have money in reserve until my percentage of the banana business starts paying enough for me to live on.*

Before returning to California, I told Luis that I'd see how things developed with my West Coast contact. But when I stopped to think about it, I told myself, *This is never going to happen—$70,000 is ridiculous!* Even Luis had laughed when I told him the price I had quoted.

Back in California, the ship conversion was progressing smoothly. One night, Rick came to me after work and said, "Let's go have a couple of drinks." We went out to a club in Sacramento, and even before we had ordered our first drink, Rick said quietly, "My partners are very interested. They say that if you bring two or three kilos, and things are the way you say they are, they'll buy a lot more."

I could almost feel the adrenaline pumping in Rick's body. I knew it was flowing in mine. An overload of thoughts and emotions rushed through me. Rick's simple statement had suddenly brought my involvement in the cocaine business out of the realm of dreams, imaginations, and theories and had thrown it smack into the middle of reality. In one sense I was desperate, not knowing what to do. I kept flashing back to my mother and her godliness, and how she taught me the difference between good and evil. At the same time I was attracted by the sense of belonging, of being part of the crowd, of being part of this group of people who had it all together, who had no problems and certainly no financial need. They seemed to offer everything I had longed for since coming to America.

Not for a moment did I think that what I was about to do might destroy my family, robbing my parents of their health, their home, and their dignity, while driving my brother to death's door through alcoholism. I never saw my involvement with cocaine in realistic terms—until it was too late.

I told Rick I had to wait until I went back to Miami because I couldn't talk about this over the phone to my partner.

A week later in Miami, I explained the situation to Luis. "Some people are very interested. They want us to bring them three kilos so they can see if the coke is as good as it's supposed to be."

"No problem," Luis said. "Consider it a done deal." He said he could get the cocaine, but we needed to find someone to take it to California for us.

The person we found was Juan Puerto, a friend of my family. Juanito, as I called him, had lived with us for a while when he first emigrated from Cuba. A nice guy who liked to act much tougher than he was, Juanito was making about $3,000 per month selling small amounts of cocaine.

I met Juanito for lunch, got his attention by offering him an opportunity to make some big money in a cocaine delivery, and then explained the situation. He would fly to San Francisco, taking a suitcase with a false bottom in which would be stashed three kilos of coke.

"All you have to do is check it in at the gate in Miami, then check it out at the baggage claim in San Francisco. I'll be waiting for you at the airport. And I'll give you $10,000 for the trip."

It was a generous offer, and Juanito didn't hesitate one minute. He said it was no problem.

I was on my way to orchestrating my first drug deal.

Part Two

1978-1980

This was now a war, I decided: Harold and I were pitted against them all—the other prisoners, the guards, the DEA agents, the governments of Panama and the U.S., and anyone else.

And they will never defeat me.

NINE

THE NIGHTMARE BEGINS

Before leaving Miami on my first cocaine run, I stopped to visit my parents. While Mom prepared dinner, I slipped into my parents' bedroom. As memories of my mother praying so often in that room flooded my mind, I let down my guard and said in a hushed voice, "God, if you protect me in this deal that I'm about to do, I'm gonna buy a better house for my parents. God, please make sure that nothing happens to me. You know that I'm not hurting anyone, that the ones who buy this cocaine are rich people and movie stars, and that I'm not doing something immoral." I honestly thought that I was telling God the truth.

I went back to California and told Rick Sanders the deal was on. "Line up your people. We're bringing three kilos, and the price is $210,000. I want half the money up front, the minute the coke gets here. You can pay the other half in a day or so." Rick was ecstatic; his dream was coming true.

My nightmare was just beginning.

A few days later, Rick told me his people were ready. His partner, Joey, came over, showed me $75,000, and offered it up front as a token of confidence. We chose a Friday, around rush hour, for the delivery at the San Francisco airport. If all went as planned, I would never have to actually touch the cocaine; I would only pick up the money.

When the big day came I drove to San Francisco, checked in at a hotel, then picked up a rental car—a Chevy. *No use being too conspicuous.* As I drove to the airport, I kept worrying about what my mother would think of my new venture.

Juanito's flight was scheduled to arrive at five P.M. I pulled into the airport loading area a few minutes early and left the motor running as I waited in the car. Juanito was to pick up the suitcase in the baggage claim area and bring it to the car; then we would drive to the hotel.

At least, that was the plan.

I kept watching the clock. Well past five and still no sign of Juanito. Anxiously I left the car and walked inside the airport. The plane had arrived and passengers from his flight were already gathering at the baggage carousel, but Juanito was nowhere in sight.

I was really nervous now; ten minutes passed, fifteen minutes, and still no sign of my friend. Finally I saw Juanito, ashen-faced and sweating profusely, coming toward me. He told me he was afraid somebody was following him. He was so upset, I thought he was going to cry.

I tried to shock him back to his senses by growling quietly but intensely, "Juanito! We can't lose this cocaine!"

He was too frightened to care. "I'm not going to go pick up that suitcase, Jorge."

"What's the matter with you?" I responded. "We could get killed. How can I explain to these drug people that we abandoned their suitcase? I'd rather be arrested than have to face *them*."

"*You* go get it," Juanito said.

"All right, fine," I said. "Give me the claim ticket."

The suitcase, Juanito explained, was a black, hard-shell Samsonite. I hurried to the baggage claim area and crowded as close to the carousel as possible, scrutinizing each piece of luggage as it passed by on the conveyer belt. I tried to act nonchalant, though I felt as if every eye in the airport was trained on me.

I spotted the suitcase approaching on the conveyer belt. I looked around nervously, then froze. Somebody—airport security, FBI, DEA, CIA—might be watching and waiting to slap the cuffs on whoever picked up that suitcase. Motionless, I watched as the suitcase passed me by and continued on its way, back through the rubber flaps, behind the wall, then back outside again.

I stepped away, pretending I was going to use the phone, then returned to the carousel and waited again. The number of suitcases was quickly diminishing as passengers retrieved their luggage. When I saw the black Samsonite pop through the rubber flaps, making its way toward me again, I said quietly, "God, help me this one time."

The case was now only a few feet away. I reached down, snatched it off the belt, and headed toward the exit.

I tried to remain calm as I handed the claim check to the baggage attendant. He looked at the claim on the suitcase, compared it to the one I had given him, ripped them both in half, and waved me through.

I hurried to the car where Juanito was waiting. A furtive glance around revealed nothing unusual, so I put the suitcase in the trunk. As I carefully pulled into traffic, I kept glancing in my rearview mirror. No tails were in sight. Once we got into the flow of afternoon rush hour, I was sure we had made it.

Juanito was still perspiring when we arrived at the hotel. "Jorge, I think I had a heart attack in that airplane. I don't think I can do this anymore."

"Don't worry, Juanito. The worst is over. When the money comes, I'll pay you and you can get out of here. I'll take the rest of the money back to Miami myself."

Juanito breathed a sigh of relief.

When Rick came to our room, I told him Juanito and I were going for a walk; while we were out, he could take the cocaine. I didn't want to be there while he took it. If Rick got busted, I figured Juanito and I could at least claim that the cocaine had been planted on us.

Juanito and I went to the shops at Union Square. In Saks Fifth Avenue, I bought a sweater for $500—more money than I'd ever before paid for a sweater, but of course, I could afford it now. I thought, *This must be how Manny Garces felt when he and his wife browsed through these same shops.*

All remorse and any thoughts that I might be displeasing God disappeared the moment I returned to the hotel room and found the cocaine gone and $75,000 hidden in the closet. It would be a long time before I ever again concerned myself about God's attitude toward me.

Juanito and I expected Joey to bring the rest of our money at any moment. While we waited, we ordered room service—we didn't want to take a chance of missing Joey, and the less we were seen in the hotel, the better.

Hour after hour we waited, and Joey still didn't show up or call. I was getting nervous again. Rick came to our room to wait with us, and I terrorized him with stories of how the Colombian drug lords dealt with double-crossers by cutting them into tiny pieces with a chainsaw. I told Rick his whole family would disappear if Joey didn't come through.

Rick went out to look for his partner. He came back several hours later and told us Joey's customers were out of town, but by Monday we'd have all our money. To assuage our concerns, he brought with him another $50,000.

For four days we stayed in that hotel room, ordering room service three times a day and watching pornographic movies to pass the time.

On Monday, Joey finally showed up with our money. "Your coke is good stuff, Jorge," he said. "My people would like to put in a standing order. Do you think you could get me seven to ten kilos on a regular basis?"

My anger at his delinquency was quickly dispelled. "I'm sure it can be arranged," I replied, dollar signs dancing through my mind.

Juanito left San Francisco that afternoon. I waited for three more days, just to be safe, then returned to Miami. I paid Luis for the cocaine and tallied up the ledger. After expenses, I pocketed about $36,000. As Luis and I celebrated over a bottle of champagne, I felt certain I would soon be the king of cocaine in California.

Two weeks later, Joey and Rick brought me a down payment of $100,000 toward a purchase of seven kilos. We decided that, rather than transporting the cocaine by air, we should drive with it from Miami to California. I also thought it might look better if I had a woman with me, so I invited Christine along for a trip across America in a newly purchased van. Christine was ecstatic; she had no idea she would be traveling with seven kilos of coke.

At the end of the trip, we booked a hotel room in Oakland, where I doled out the cocaine to Rick one kilo at a time. Not until he had paid for one kilo would I give him another. Christine and I then returned to Miami where Luis and I split our profits. After covering the cocaine and transportation costs, we made more than $80,000 each—my biggest payday yet.

In Miami, I had purchased and furnished a townhouse for myself. Meanwhile Mom and Dad had their eyes on a property selling for $65,000, but they didn't have enough money for the down payment. I found out who owned the house, gave him $25,000, and instructed him to sell the house to my parents for only $40,000. I knew my dad couldn't pass up a deal like that. I gave my mother $10,000 to help furnish her new home and bought a Cadillac Seville for my dad, plus one for me.

With my newfound wealth, my parents suspected something was fishy. To reassure them, I explained that my new banana business was doing really well. I didn't like deceiving my parents, but I felt I was doing something good for them. Little did I know how much pain would result from my "innocent" venture.

In California, we cut Joey out of the picture when he got carried away, acting like a big shot and telling everyone in town what a big drug dealer he was. Rick found another contact, a fellow I'll refer to as Travis White. Travis was a more serious guy than Joey, with access to a lot more money.

Rick set up a meeting for me with Travis, who committed to buying up to one hundred kilos a month. In his friendly yet businesslike manner, Travis added, "If I'm going to move that amount of coke, Jorge, I need you to drop the price to $60,000."

I feigned a wince. It took only moments, however, for my accountant's brain to run the numbers. Even at the reduced price, I could take home a million dollars a month after splitting with Luis.

I turned twenty-two in February 1978. At my birthday party, Luis got drunk and started making crude passes at Luchy, who, despite our separation, was still my wife. I interceded on her behalf, and Luis responded by accusing me of sleeping with his wife, Maria, during my first trip to Colombia. That incensed me, especially because I *could* have had his wife in Colombia. She had crawled into my bed in the middle of the night, but out of loyalty to Luis I had pretended to be drunk and sick. I'd never mentioned the incident to Luis or to Maria. Now my partner was accusing me of crossing one of the few lines I had refused to violate.

"I'm finished with you," I told Luis. Pulling out my nine-millimeter Beretta, I roared, "I ought to kill you! Get out of my life or I'll blow your brains out!"

Looking back, I can see how God protected me at that moment. Luis was almost always armed and wasn't above pulling the trigger—he was rumored to have shot several people. In his inebriated state, it's a miracle he didn't pull out a pistol and blow me away.

When Luis later came by the office to clean out his desk, I told him to take over my interest in the banana business and the ship. The vessel at this time was nearly ready to sail to Colombia. Of course by now I realized that smuggling cocaine was the real purpose for the ship and the business. And I had completed all the paperwork concerning the ship, leaving a long, easily traceable paper trail—leading back to me. "It's a bigger hassle than I bargained for," I told Luis. "You keep it all."

Luis talked to the other partners, who agreed to his taking over my interest, and I signed over my portion of the business. After Luis walked out of my office, I never saw his face again. He was murdered several years later, and the killer was never found.

Two or three weeks after my birthday, Travis White called to tell me that Rick was bragging to people in California about the big coke deliveries he had done. That sort of advertising we didn't need.

I called Rick at his home in Stockton. He answered the phone congenially, "Hello, Jorge. What's up, dude?"

I maintained a somber tone. "I need to warn you, Rick. Some of my people got arrested, and they are now where the sun doesn't shine."

Whether Rick thought I meant these people were in prison or in graves, I never knew. Following our conversation, Rick disappeared, which was fine with me.

I was at home late one afternoon in late March when my telephone rang. A cold chill swept over me as I recognized Manny's businesslike voice on the other line. He wanted to see me that evening at his Miami apartment, and I quickly agreed.

As I replaced the telephone receiver in its cradle, my mind was racing, trying to anticipate what Manny might want. What had Luis told him about our blowup?

Although I had a good relationship with Manny, I still didn't know how to read him. Was he angry? Disappointed in me? Did he think my split with Luis was due to youthful arrogance? I couldn't tell by his voice. Manny weighed his words carefully and rarely betrayed his thoughts by emotional outbursts. He was always a gentleman, but he could be a dangerous enemy.

I worried that my meeting with him might be my last, that it might be an ambush, that I could be killed because I knew too much about the Colombians' business dealings. I still handled some of their bank accounts and knew where much of their money was. Now, since I had chosen to separate myself from one of their key players, perhaps I was seen as a problem to be dealt with.

I arrived on time at Manny's upscale Fountainebleau apartment. My host opened the door himself.

A good sign . . . he appears to be alone.

Even at home, Manny dressed impeccably. "Come in, Jorge." He opened the door widely and walked toward the bar. After pouring drinks for us, he said matter-of-factly, "I want you to tell me what happened between you and Luis."

My stomach tightened, but I forced myself to remain calm. My mind raced. *Maybe Luis hadn't informed Manny of our cocaine deals, and now the big boss is upset about it.*

"Look," I said to Manny, "I apologize if Luis didn't tell you I did those two deals with him. They turned out well, and we made some serious money. But Luis has no class. He's always drunk, and he accused me of an unforgivable sin. I simply don't want to work with him anymore."

Manny nodded understandingly, but his eyes remained riveted to mine. "Tell me about your clients in California." It wasn't a request.

I shuffled uneasily, still trying to guess where he was going with this. I told him I believed California could be a big market, since money was plentiful but pure cocaine was difficult to find.

"One of my partners used to work out of Los Angeles," Manny told me, "but he went to jail, so we have no venue out there right now." He paused, put down his drink, and leaned in my direction, "Jorge, would you be interested in distributing our cocaine, working directly under me?"

By "our cocaine" I knew he meant the coke belonging to himself and his fellow drug lords, the pioneers in the Medellin Cartel—the Colombians who eventually seized control of every aspect of the cocaine market.

"Yes," I answered Manny.

As we talked further, we decided that, for whatever cocaine his group acquired at Colombian prices, I could put up equal amounts of money and share the profits. I saw only one problem with this equation—I didn't have the kind of capital necessary to purchase the cocaine. Ten kilos could be bought in Colombia at this time for $180,000; my share of that expense would be a whopping $90,000.

"I will pay the up-front costs for the first load," Manny volunteered. I could hardly believe what I was hearing. "After that," he added, "we can split the costs."

Manny and I agreed to split the profits equally from the coke we purchased at Colombian prices and distributed for the other cartel members at $38,000 to $42,000 per kilo. I was to sell the cocaine to my California contacts at $60,000 per kilo, and Manny and I would split those profits also.

So we concluded our deal. There were no contracts, no legal documents—just the word of two men to deal honorably with each other in handling millions of dollars.

Manny and I embraced. Before I left he said, "An airline pilot will be bringing some cocaine through Tampa next week. I want you to go with me to pick it up. I'll call you when everything is ready."

I walked to my car, my head in a daze. Sitting in the driver's seat of my Mercedes, I thought, *I just agreed to go into business with the biggest drug lord in the world!*

TEN

GETTING AWAY WITH IT

"We're going tomorrow morning to Tampa. Four of us. You'll be driv ing the car. Be here at the apartment at six-thirty A.M." *Click.* Manny's call was abrupt and to the point.

That night I could barely sleep. In my previous deals, someone else had run the risks of getting the coke inside American borders and into our hands. Now I would help pick up a load of cocaine directly from the transporters. It was much more risky—but also much more thrilling.

I arrived at Manny's place promptly at six-thirty. Two other men were already there. I recognized Felipe Arango—Manny's partner in Colombia and now my partner as well—and embraced him with the customary kiss on the cheek. Manny introduced the other man simply as Mario.

We started across the state, with me behind the wheel of a rented white Chevrolet Caprice. During the four-and-a-half-hour drive I listened in fascination as the "elders" discussed the details of this run. They were paying only $5,000 per kilo for "freight," as they referred to the cost of transporting the coke across the border, and they were experimenting with a new route.

I just kept quiet and drove. The closer we got to Tampa, the more frequently I glanced in my rearview mirror to make sure we weren't being followed.

A few blocks from our destination, a Holiday Inn near the airport, we stopped for breakfast at a McDonald's. I had only orange juice; my knotted stomach revolted at the thought of food. *Is it a setup? Are we all going to be caught?* I drew comfort from the knowledge that a man of Manny's caliber did not make foolish mistakes.

We approached the hotel, then drove around the block several times. When Manny was satisfied that everything appeared safe, he said, "Pull off to a telephone." I eased the car over at the nearest phone booth, and Mario got out to make the call. Within seconds he returned wearing a broad smile. "Everything's ready," he said. "Let's go get it."

I drove to the Holiday Inn and pulled into the parking lot. Manny, Felipe, and I remained in the car. Mario was inside the hotel only about five minutes, but to me it seemed like hours. My eyes darted back and forth, trying to watch in every direction at once for anything unusual. Finally I saw Mario coming toward us, walking with a swift, even gait. Carrying a nondescript duffel bag, he looked as though he'd just checked out of the hotel. He put his duffel bag in the trunk, then climbed into the Caprice. I eased out of the lot as smoothly as if I was taking a driver's exam.

I would earn $15,000 for this trip—good money for a one-day drive—but those four and a half hours returning across Florida were some of the longest of my life. I noted every vehicle in front of us, beside us, behind us. I mentally noted any license plate I saw more than once. I tried to memorize the face of every driver around me. If someone was following, I wanted to know.

Arriving in Miami during rush-hour traffic, we made our way to Manny's apartment. Mario casually retrieved the duffel bag from the trunk and carried it inside. He opened it to reveal more than sixty kilos of cocaine.

Manny poured drinks for everyone. Everybody was happy, but the work was just beginning. Now that we had the coke, the challenge was to sell it. Manny kept about thirty kilos; Felipe and Mario split the rest.

After they left, Manny turned to me and asked, "How many kilos do you want for California?"

"I think I can sell twenty."

Manny smiled. "Take seventeen."

I called Travis White in California to tell him we were back in business. I bought a van, and Travis flew to Miami to help drive it across the country. I invited Christine to join us, and three days later we were on the road. We decided to operate from Lake Tahoe this time. Travis had rented a gorgeous house there—a palace overlooking the lake—at a cost of $1,000 a day.

After we settled in, Travis called one of his main contacts, and we threw a party. We were drinking champagne, laughing, and carrying on when Travis's contact opened a bag of cocaine so everyone could try it. My new friends encouraged me to join in.

I was feeling high already. "No, thanks," I told them. "I'm fine with my champagne." They couldn't believe it when I told them I'd never taken even a sniff of coke in my life.

But after everyone razzed me about it, I finally acquiesced. They laid out a line of cocaine on a table, gave me a tiny golden straw, and told me what to do. "Just put the straw at the end of the line and the other end up to your nose. That's it. Okay, now sniff real hard."

I sniffed into the straw as though I had a bad cold. The coke flew into my nose, and suddenly I felt a burning sensation blow through my head. Five minutes later I was nauseated and vomiting. I blamed it on the cocaine, not thinking that it could have been the combination of champagne and coke that hit me so hard. Or that maybe somebody was trying to tell me something.

Whatever the cause, I decided never to do cocaine again—and I kept that vow for a long time.

Christine and I stayed at Lake Tahoe while Travis serviced his clients, moving the coke rather quickly. Everything was going according to plan until we got word that three kilos of our coke were bad. Our customers said it tested only eighty to eighty-five percent pure, and it had a dull look and a funny smell. Pure cocaine, I had learned, has a bright white, almost shimmering, look and a pharmaceutical aroma.

At our prices, we couldn't afford to sell anything but the best. After we tested some of the cocaine in question and confirmed its impurity, I called Manny and told him the problem. Manny didn't question me. He simply said, "Bring it back." The thought of carting three kilos back across the nation, for nothing, did not appeal to me. But that was the order.

Travis came up with the idea of hollowing out some large books—dictionaries or encyclopedias—and hiding the cocaine inside. We used razor blades to cut brick-size holes in three books. Each book held a one-kilo cocaine brick, wrapped in paper and cellophane and encased in duct tape.

I talked Christine into flying back to Miami and taking the books with her, without telling her what was inside them. She was reluctant to leave me, but glad to help. As I drove Christine to the airport, I assured her everything was fine and she had nothing to worry about, which was partially true. Christine had no idea of my drug business; nor was she aware of what could happen if she was caught carrying cocaine. She was in love with me, happy to do anything I asked. And I was willing and able to take advantage of her vulnerability.

I dropped Christine off at the Tahoe airport, which at that time had metal detectors but no x-ray machines at the security checkpoints. She flew without incident to San Francisco, then on to Miami, where Manny picked up the three books.

Within a week I, too, headed back to Miami with all our money—more than $800,000, mostly in hundred-dollar bills. I kept nearly $500,000 with me in a carry-on bag, with the rest stashed in my suitcase with a false bottom.

At the Tahoe terminal, I stepped through the frame at the security check and was about to walk leisurely toward my flight when a security officer stopped me.

"Please open your bag, sir," he said courteously.

I quickly posed as a nervous, naive husband, embarrassed about carrying his wife's risqué belongings. "Oh, must I, officer? I have some rather intimate things in here that belong to my wife."

The officer scowled. "I'm sorry, sir. But I must ask you to open your bag."

Again I made up an excuse, but the officer wasn't buying it, and my reluctance seemed only to heighten his suspicions.

I was caught. How could I explain the money in the bag? And surely they would now retrieve my suitcase and find the rest. At that moment I knew I was going to jail. It was all over. My drug career—as well as the rest of my life—was finished.

Slowly, I started to open the bag.

Suddenly an alarm went off somewhere in the airport. Security officers with walkie-talkies to their ears raced through the corridor, away from the checkpoint. The officer who had stopped me looked around, saw all the commotion, then waved me on. "Go on through. Hurry up." As he joined the officers racing through the airport, I grabbed my carry-on and walked swiftly toward my gate, eyes straight ahead.

My heart was thumping like a racehorse as I took a seat on board my flight, the carry-on tucked safely beneath the seat in front of me. *A close call—but I got away with it.* I determined in the future to be smarter and better prepared.

Once safely back in Miami, I decided to buy my own jet to transport the cocaine. After all, with the kind of profit I was making, I could quickly pay for a plane. At a corporate jet dealership just outside Miami, I told the sales representatives that my partners and I were cattle breeders who traveled across the country, frequently on short notice. What could they do for me?

Within a few weeks, they found me a used Learjet 23. Our deal allowed them to rent out the airplane when I wasn't using it; meanwhile they would cover the plane's maintenance costs and keep pilots on call at all times. I was to pay the pilots for the hours they actually flew for me, plus the fuel charges.

Now that I had the jet, I figured there was no need to take large loads of cocaine to California only to sit around until we could sell it. We could store large quantities of coke in Florida, then take 25 kilos at a time to California. Before long, we were moving as much as 150 kilos per month this way.

The cocaine was kept at several warehouses I maintained in Miami as well as at a handful of "stash houses" in middle-class neighborhoods. I made sure these houses were in nice neighborhoods and had attached garages, easily accessible. I bought and furnished the homes and paid my people well to live there.

I also spent money freely on myself. I bought a boat, another new Mercedes, and a Corvette—a 1977 beauty, gray-silver with silver interior.

For our California operations, I rented—at $5,000 a month—a large house in Sausalito overlooking the ocean. I kept one Mercedes there and the other in Miami. I flew to the West Coast in my Learjet and was met by a limousine that took me to my house. I partied with movie stars, among whom cocaine was definitely the drug of choice.

I was living the high life I'd always dreamed about.

We had several ways of bringing cocaine into the United States. Some came aboard boats docking at the river in Miami. Much of it came through airports in various Florida cities, with the coke carried by diplomats or even by flight attendants. But my main connection was two elderly Cuban people who worked in U.S. Customs at Miami International Airport. They assisted in one shipment of cocaine per month hidden inside five to seven enormous, hollowed-out diesel engines built for large trucks, each engine packed in a crate. Within each engine was a fifty-five-gallon oil drum, which our people in Colombia had filled with up to 125 kilos of cocaine. The engines had been welded back together and sealed with oil and a thick layer of grease, which allowed the coke to slip by DEA dogs sniffing for drug shipments.

I hired smugglers to transfer the cocaine from the people who brought it in through customs. Once a month I provided the smugglers with a U-Haul truck for picking up the coke shipment. At a prearranged place and time, I would go to where they had parked the U-Haul and retrieve the keys, which were hidden under the truck inside a magnetic key-holder. Then I'd drive the truck and its cargo to one of my stash houses.

In addition to receiving and distributing the cocaine, I was respon sible for laundering the large amounts of money the cartel was making. I set up an intricate web of offshore corporations through which I could funnel money to Colombia. To get the money out of the country, I often paid bank managers in Florida as much as $10,000 per transfer. In the early days of my drug dealing, I often walked into a Miami bank carrying paper sacks filled with cash, depositing as much as $4 million at a time. The banker would transfer the amount to offshore accounts in the Caribbean, where it was then transferred to Medellin, to Switzerland, or to wherever the cartel members happened to want it.

Sometimes shady characters would drop off bags of money at my father's house. Dad seemed to buy my story that the money came from the banana business, but Mom became increasingly skeptical.

One time I was in my office at their house counting money—$4 million in bills of various denominations, all stacked up against the wall. My father was helping me when Mom came in. Certain I was doing something illegal, she flew off the handle—not just at me, but at my father as well. "Bebo," she chided him, "how could you allow this? After how hard we have worked in this country, how can you let this poison money in our house?"

Then she turned to me. "Get out, Jorge. Take your filthy money and go."

Dad tried to calm her down. "Teresa, this is America. You can make this kind of money here. How do you know it's bad money? Jorge says it's for his banana business. And he's your son; you can't kick him out of the house."

Unconvinced, Mom announced, "I'm leaving." And she did, staying with our relatives for two weeks. Finally, I admitted that perhaps the money was obtained illegally. But I told her I had nothing to do with it; I was only sending the money to Colombia. Taking money out of the country was not against the law.

Mom calmed down and moved back home. But in her prayers, she kept asking God to separate me from the new crowd surrounding me. Mom felt certain I was headed down the wrong path. She was right.

Eleven

Testing

Manny Garces constantly emphasized to me that we could not put a price on a human life and that we were never to take a person's life. So I was surprised one day, early in my relationship with Manny, when he asked me to go to someone's house to collect on a debt—in any way necessary.

A man named Miguel, who ran a bar in Miami's Little Havana, owed Manny $60,000. When Manny called me about it, I could tell he was irate.

I was playing in the big leagues now, handling millions of dollars for these Colombians. I knew that the first time I showed any sign of weakness would be my last. If anyone believed I was vulnerable, I was an easy mark. It would be a cinch to hire a killer for a few thousand dollars to finish me off. I realized early on that only if my colleagues feared me—only if they thought they could never get away with an attack on my character or my person—would they respect me.

Consequently, when Manny asked me to collect the money from Miguel, I called a couple of my bodyguards and we headed out to Miguel's house.

When Miguel saw us at his door, he ushered us inside with tremendous respect.

"Miguel," I said, "you know what I'm here for. Manny sent me. You owe him some money, and I came to collect."

Just then, Miguel's pregnant wife came into the room, crying. She knew what our presence meant. Normally the collectors would have asked this couple no questions; they would have robbed them, stripped and embarrassed them, and perhaps killed them both.

Miguel pleaded with me. "I know I owe Manuel; I am not trying to hide anything. But some people robbed me, and I just don't have the money." As Miguel spoke, I glanced around his home. He obviously hadn't spent the money on luxuries.

Miguel took me to the kitchen and opened the refrigerator to show me they didn't even have milk for his children.

Despite my callous heart, I started feeling sorry for Miguel and his family. I remembered what it was like to have so little.

"Please give me a chance!" Miguel begged. "Just allow my wife to give birth, and we will move into a little apartment and give Manny the deed to our house. We are eternally thankful to Manuel for all he has done for us. We have nothing but the utmost respect for him. Please understand, I didn't steal the money; we were robbed. But I know I'm responsible."

I sent my bodyguard to retrieve my briefcase from the car. When he returned, I said, "Miguel, don't worry about anything. I will pay your debt. And whenever you get back on your feet, you can pay me back. Don't worry about moving your wife and your newborn baby; here is ten thousand dollars so you can pay the doctor; and please, go out and buy milk and groceries for your family."

Miguel broke down crying. It took everything within me to keep from shedding tears as well, but I knew I dared not display any sign of weakness. After an abrupt good-bye, we left.

Later that afternoon, Manny phoned me. "Did you collect my money?" he asked.

"No, and not only did I not collect, but you owe me ten thousand dollars."

"What are you talking about?"

I told Manny the story. The other end of the line was quiet.

Finally, Manny broke the silence. "Son, that is what I expected you to do. I only sent you out there to test you. Always remember, no man has a price on his life. Money we can make and we can lose, but we can't bring back a human life."

From that moment on, I admired Manny immeasurably. I knew I would die for this man if necessary.

I thought to myself, *God is going to bless Manny mightily.* Then I caught myself. *What God?*

I loved Manny, but he was an enigma to me. His actions and character raised profound questions in my heart and mind. When we received cocaine shipments, Manny often would take out two kilos and announce that the profits from them would go to support a certain monastery, or to help nuns who were starting radio stations in the jungles, or to buy ambulances, or to build a school or hospital in Colombia. Manny was always doing things for his people.

Now, after coming into money myself, I made it a practice on two or three Fridays per month to open my office doors to people with some sort of need. Most wanted to borrow money. On any given Friday, I gave away $30,000 or more and never asked anyone to repay me.

We were the "bad" drug dealers, minions of the devil—yet I believed we were doing so much for the people.

I thought of all this whenever anyone mentioned God to me. "Where is God?" I responded. "And where is the church? What are they doing for all the people in need?"

It reaffirmed my belief that there was no God. If there was, then surely the church—his people—would be doing more good things. Instead I saw the church asking for money from poor people who could barely afford to buy food.

Despite their circumstances, I saw many believers within the Hispanic community, and in other ethnic groups as well, who resolutely believed that God is present. I marveled at their immense faith. I kept asking myself, "How can these people be so ignorant? How can they believe there is a God? If God existed, why would he allow their suffering?" I knew that in many of the Hispanic neighborhoods with which I was familiar, there was no law but the law of the gun. Why would God allow this? Why would he allow children to die because there was no money to send them to hospitals? Why would God allow such misery while these very people were seeking after him?

I concluded that the only way they reconciled their suffering with their belief in God was by admitting that this life means nothing. What matters is the hereafter.

Fairly or unfairly, when I saw Manny doing so many good things and the church doing so few, I wondered, *Who is the real God? If there is a God and a devil, then perhaps the one we need to serve is the devil, because he is the only one doing something to alleviate suffering in people's lives and putting food on their tables.*

Only in looking back much later would I see that my eyes were blinded. Although Manny and I and other drug lords like us were doing some recognizable good for many people, we acquired the means to do so at a cost we had no vision to foresee—wrecking our own lives, poisoning the world with drugs, and destroying thousands of lives and thousands of families.

■　　　■　　　■

Meanwhile, as my cocaine business grew, so did my acquisitions mood. I bought a 320-acre ranch for my parents and me in central Florida near Clewiston, about an hour and a half northwest of Miami. It gave us a place to relax away from city life, and it enabled me to pursue my long-held interest in owning horses and raising cattle. It also fulfilled my dad's dream to actually own a piece of land in America. When I called to tell him about it, he almost cried.

I was soon receiving about six hundred kilos of cocaine a month, distributing two hundred to three hundred kilos according to the cartel's instructions and taking the rest to California. Several times each month, my plane traveled to California carrying suitcases filled with cocaine and returned to Miami carrying suitcases filled with cash. I employed one person in the San Francisco area whose only job was to collect our money. I was making more than a million dollars every month. By now I was controlling most of the larger, bulk shipments of cocaine coming into the United States.

My clients had great confidence in me. When a customer paid for cocaine, I made it a practice never to count the money in front of him. I simply took the person's word for it, assuming that the correct amount of money was there. If I discovered later that someone had paid me too much, I credited his account and let him know. If ever there was less money than agreed upon, I simply charged the customer's account. I made it a rule not to deal with anyone I couldn't trust or who didn't trust me. Besides being good business practice, it also helped ensure that I'd never be arrested. Or so I thought.

One afternoon I took three suitcases loaded with cocaine to the Miami airport. Leonardo, an old friend of my family's and one of my first employees in the drug business, was with me. He was to travel with the coke on our jet while I remained in Miami. Just as I pulled my Mercedes up to the Lear, I noticed a police car parked nearby and two police officers looking inside the airplane.

Leonardo got panicky. "We're busted!" he shouted. "Let's run for it!"

"Calm down, Leonardo," I said. "If we're busted already, I'd rather they arrest us here than follow us to my house or to one of the stash houses. Just relax and let me talk." Leonardo looked at me as if I had ice water running through my veins.

I parked my car next to the airplane and got out. Dressed in a suit and tie, I looked like a businessman in a hurry, which I was. I stepped up to one of the policemen and said, "May I help you, officer?"

Startled, he asked, "Do you own this plane?"

"Yes, I do," I replied. "Can I help you?"

"Oh, we're just on a lunch break and we wanted to look inside."

"Help yourself," I said amiably. "Do you want a drink or anything to eat?" Prior to every trip, my plane was stocked with a case of champagne and platters of fruit, cheeses, cold shrimp, and an assortment of hors d'oeuvres. The officers said something about being on duty, but helped themselves to some snacks.

Opening the trunk of the Mercedes, I started to lift out the suitcases filled with cocaine. Out of the corner of my eye, I could see Leonardo watching me with a look of utter terror. I lifted one suitcase toward the airplane steps where one of the officers was standing. "Would you mind giving us a hand?" I asked.

"Sure, I'd be glad to." The officer reached over and hoisted the suitcase on board the jet, unaware that he was loading twenty-five kilos of cocaine worth more than a million dollars.

TWELVE

A NEW CONNECTION

The cocaine network in Miami at this time was minimal compared to our California sales. Most of the deals in Miami were limited to those done by my other partners, who were distributing through local dealers, and to those that involved smaller amounts of coke brought into the country on commercial airliners. But in the back of my mind, I thought, *Why not expand my operation to include a larger market share in Miami and on the East Coast?*

That opportunity came when I established a critical working relationship with Sal Magluta, an old friend of my family's. Sal and his partner were selling a kilo of coke here and there on the Miami scene, but he didn't like buying it through secondhand sources. "We have the potential to move a lot of coke," he told me, "but we need a hand in getting started." Sal introduced me to his partner, Willie Falcon, a young kid with self-confidence and an outgoing personality. I was impressed with him.

Nevertheless I was reluctant to help them, because they had almost no money to pay for getting started. Two months later, however, an opportunity came for me to provide them with thirty kilos of cocaine for distri bu tion in Miami, with little financial risk to myself. The thirty kilos came from an earlier shipment that had remained undelivered when the intended customer was unable to pay for it. To get rid of the product, we had planned to sell it ourselves at a reduced rate. I thought this might be the perfect opportunity for Sal and Willie.

I gave them one month to sell the thirty kilos. Sal worried aloud that this was too much coke to handle at one time—and too much responsibility. Willie jumped in: "I can sell it. That's no problem. We'll take it!" I laughed, but I liked the young man's enthusiasm.

It never crossed my mind that I'd just launched two of the biggest drug lords the world has ever known. According to the federal government, by the time Sal and Willie were imprisoned pending trial in 1991, they had reputedly smuggled into America more than seventy-two tons of cocaine, with an estimated value of more than $2 billion.

After a month-long vacation in Europe, I met again with Sal and was pleasantly surprised when he told me, "We have all your money, and we're ready to take more coke."

From then on, Sal and Willie moved a large quantity of cocaine for me in Miami every month. Sal and I became close friends, and much more than that. I loved him as my own brother. Meanwhile, Sal and Willie's arrangement gave me a source of income in addition to my California connections, plus a relatively risk-free opportunity to test the market in Miami in case something happened to reduce our market in California.

About this time we became painfully aware of a glaring problem in our operation: the erratic quality of the cocaine coming into the U.S. Some of our coke was pure; when a kilo was cut open, it shone like brilliant diamonds. Other coke, however, had a dull, off-white color with a flat, nonreflective quality like that of chalk. Some of the tainted coke also had a pungent or even foul aroma. I decided to find out what caused the aberrations and how we could consistently offer a high—quality product.

At Manny's suggestion I made arrangements to visit our Colombian sources. I wanted to trace the evolution of our product all the way from the raw coca leaves grown in the fields to the kilos we sold to our customers. I was in for a surprise.

I flew to Medellin, where I was met by one of the cartel's bodyguards. The next morning I boarded a small twin-engine airplane and flew to a remote airfield deep in the jungle, where I was met by a guide and some of our Colombian workers. We loaded our baggage on several donkeys, then mounted our horses. I noticed one decrepit-looking mule that looked nearly dead on his feet. I thought, *If he makes this trip, he definitely won't make it back.*

We trekked ever deeper and higher into the Colombian mountains, where our processing ranch was located. The thin, clear air was cool, despite the bright sun shining on the thick, emerald-green jungle. We scaled the steep path for about five hours, stopping only to water the animals and get an occasional drink ourselves.

When we finally reached our destination, I was shocked. This Colombian "ranch" was nothing but an open field next to a shed consisting of four poles supporting a roof of scrap tin. As we unloaded our supplies, the worker who would serve as our cook began setting up his "kitchen." That's when I realized the mule we had dragged through the mountains would be the primary source of our jungle cuisine.

The next day, as the workers built a roaring campfire, I got my first lessons in cocaine processing. The plan was to cook up about one hundred kilos at a time of cocaine "paste," which we had brought in with us on the animals.

I learned that our workers in Peru had already done the grueling work of producing the paste from coca leaves. They had placed a batch of crushed leaves in a large tub, then poured in kerosene and sodium bicarbonate. These workers used no formulas; they rarely measured any of the ingredients they added to the mixture. They simply estimated the amount needed and tossed it into the tub. The men took turns walking barefoot in the soupy mixture—trading places frequently to prevent their feet from burning—as they stomped the coca leaves as though they were crushing grapes into California wine. The chemicals slowly transformed the dark leaves into a mushy, mashed-potato-like paste. They kept it "cooking" until it reached a certain consistency, which, again, was determined arbitrarily by the workers.

Now I watched as the Colombian workers continued the process. The next step was to "shock" the paste. They put it in a large barrel, then tossed in buckets full of acetone and highly volatile ether. If they added too much acetone, I learned, the coke would come out looking more like chalk than snow; nevertheless, no precise measurements were used for the ether-acetone mixture.

The paste—now a milky solution—was poured through a bedsheet, which filtered out impurities while the liquid mixture flowed through into a large barrel. Hydrochloric acid was added to the solution, causing the coke to "snow," or crystallize, and sink to the bottom of the barrel. After the liquid was drained off, the remaining mixture was heated, then squeezed through a leather baker's funnel to extract more liquid. Afterward it was spread onto large metal "cookie sheets" to dry in the sun. When the cocaine was completely devoid of moisture, it was poured into one-kilo plastic bags, the closest thing to an accurate measuring tool in the entire process.

Everything in the procedure was done by taste or feel. No wonder our cocaine was so inconsistent! I didn't say anything at the time, but I determined in my mind to establish some precise formulas so we could guarantee our product's quality, even if it meant sending our own trained chemists to work alongside our Colombian suppliers to ensure the cocaine's purity.

Meanwhile my relationship with my lawyer, Monti Cohen, continued to flourish. We partied together frequently, as long as I could do so inconspicuously—looking back now, I realize that in the back of my mind I was ashamed of my behavior. Monti advised me that it might be wise to marry Christine, the woman who had accompanied me most often as I built my cocaine business. Although I never revealed to Christine the true nature of my business, Monti feared that she could testify against me if I were ever indicted.

I had given Luchy enough money to buy a townhouse in the Dominican Republic for her and baby Jorgito. On the day our divorce was final, I married Christine.

My marriage to Christine was a sham from the start. I liked her, but I did not truly love her. I was disgusted with myself for hiding behind a marriage license, but like so many other things, I justified it as "good business."

Ostensibly we lived together as husband and wife, but I came home only three or four times a month. I traveled a lot, and even when I was in Miami I frequented several other houses and apartments that I owned or rented as stash houses and living space for various women. At one point I had four houses fully furnished, with a mistress living in each. I was leading all of them on at the same time, telling each one that she and I would soon get engaged.

In late 1978, Sal and I met for the first time with Oscar Nuñez, a captain in the Bolivian Air Force. Sal believed we could get cocaine through this new Bolivian connection at a better price than what we were currently paying. The cartel had previously considered a possible link to Bolivia—where the cocaine trade was literally controlled by the government—but we had considered the situation too unstable and the savings not worth the trouble. Now, however, as we searched for a more consistent product at a better price, it seemed a worthwhile connection to pursue.

We never guessed just how much it would cost us.

At our meeting in a Miami restaurant, Nuñez made an offer we could hardly refuse: For every kilo of pure coke paid for in cash, he would provide another kilo on credit. Wanting to examine the product for ourselves, we sent one of Sal's workers to Bolivia with $300,000 to use as a goodwill deposit. When the worker returned, we were quite impressed with the quality of the Bolivian coke. Moreover, the price was better than through our other connections, and with our growing U.S. market, we thought we could move a much greater volume. We calculated that through the Bolivian connection we could net $7 million per run, with two runs per month.

In March 1979, I arranged for Sal and me to get a firsthand view of the operation in Bolivia. As we boarded the plane, he and I each carried about $300,000 on us—in stacks of bills strapped to our legs with rubber bands and held in place by pantyhose worn beneath our suit pants.

It was a long trip, made even longer when fog and turbulence prohibited us from landing in Bolivia. The pilot informed us that we were turning back to Lima, Peru. Sal and I exchanged concerned glances. If we stayed in Lima overnight, we might have to go through customs, which could be dangerous if we were discovered carrying such large sums of money. In Bolivia, a military escort was waiting for us, but in Lima, a more volatile place, we had no such protection.

This, too, was one of the few situations in my drug career when I cried out to God, perhaps in an instinctive reaction rooted in how my parents had raised me. I said, "Oh my God! Please don't allow us to get arrested."

At the airport in Lima, airline officials herded the passengers into buses to transport them to local hotels for the evening. I looked at Sal and shook my head. I told the airline officials we preferred to stay right there at the airport so we could catch the first flight available.

Hour after hour Sal and I paced around a lounge area in the terminal. Finally the rubber bands holding the money in place began cutting into our legs. It was almost a blessing when the airport security officers refused to allow us to stay in the airport any longer and forced us to go into town. We checked into a luxurious hotel but were unable to enjoy it because of our anxiety about how to get through customs without being discovered.

The following morning we discovered that our worries were in vain. We went through customs without a snag and boarded a flight to Bolivia.

When we finally arrived, our military escort took us to Oscar Nuñez, who ran a flight school at the airport. Oscar received us warmly at his office. After the initial greetings, he opened a safe to reveal a large stash of cocaine. Sal and I examined the coke and agreed that it looked especially good—very uniform, very shiny.

The next day, Oscar, Sal, and I boarded a Bolivian government airplane and toured a remote valley close to the Amazon River, an area that looked promising for developing airstrips and distri bu tion points. Sal and I discussed setting up laboratories, staffing them with our chemists, and processing our own cocaine right there. We decided to explore the possibilities further . . . and soon. We tentatively set a date of Easter 1979 to return to Bolivia and wrap up the deal with Oscar.

Meanwhile, I continued taking cocaine to California and bringing home huge caches of money. I had about $3 million put away for myself, but I was beginning to spend as recklessly as I had seen other members of the cartel do a few years earlier. My vows to be wise and frugal with my money had long since been abandoned.

One day Monti Cohen stopped by my office and we went out for lunch. "Let's take my car," Monti said, as he steered me toward his Mercedes. After a delightful lunch, Monti drove me back to the office. Nothing out of the ordinary. Or so I thought.

Two hours later, a man barged into my office. I knew him as El Loco—a hired killer from Colombia. We'd always gotten along well. In Colombia I had often taken him guns as gifts, and I knew I could always count on Loco if I had a problem with anyone. He always demonstrated a tremendous respect for me, but I knew that Loco had earned his nickname. He was feared by everyone in Colombia. Now here he was in Miami, standing in my office, obviously unhappy. What could he possibly want?

I greeted him enthusiastically, and he returned my greeting with a bear hug. I offered him coffee, and we sat down to talk. I could see in Loco's face that he seemed torn. As he sipped his coffee, he began telling me about his first few days in Miami.

I cut to the chase. "Loco, what brings you to my office?"

He looked at me squarely, then pulled from his pocket a picture of Monti Cohen. "Two hours ago," he told me, "when you got in the car with this man, we were getting ready to put a hit on him." Loco explained that Monti Cohen was supposed to have taken care of some immigration problems for the brother of Felipe Arango, one of our Colombian partners. But Monti failed. When the brother came to the United States, he was arrested. Moreover, Monti took $80,000 from him. Now Felipe had hired Loco to finish off the traitor.

I was shocked to hear Loco's accusations against my lawyer and friend. There had to be something wrong somewhere. I asked Loco to put the contract on hold, and I promised to talk with Felipe. Loco reluctantly consented to wait.

I called Felipe and told him the story. "There must be a misunderstanding. Monti Cohen has represented me for nearly two years now, and he's always been honest in his dealings with me."

Felipe stood by the story Loco had told me. Worse still, he was convinced that Monti's duplicity was intended to lead to the arrest of Felipe, rather than his brother.

I offered to pay Felipe the $80,000, but he wouldn't hear of it. He did, however, accept my offer not to charge him the transportation costs on his next shipment of cocaine—and that, I knew, would cost me far more than eighty grand.

I never mentioned the matter to Monti, feeling that the problem had arisen through some sort of miscommunication. Because of Monti's solid track record with me, I dismissed the incident, convinced he wouldn't sell out his friends or clients. It would be another five years before this event came to mind again—when I discovered that Monti Cohen had sold out someone else.

Thirteen

What Could Go Wrong?

Manny was intrigued with the possibilities offered by the Bolivian connection, but as we proceeded with our plans he warned me to be very careful. With traces of tears in his eyes, he told me about his nephew who had gone to Peru to make a cocaine deal and then had disappeared. Only after much pressure—and after Manny paid out a lot of money—was his nephew finally found. The young man was delivered in a box, his body chopped into four pieces.

Clearly, the Bolivian connection was not to be entered into casually.

Moreover, I was proposing a bold change in the rules of the game. Most of our cocaine came into the U.S. on commercial flights; the cartel's planes and pilots were used only to move drugs from one South American city to another and never entered U.S. airspace. Since our airline contacts on the route between Colombia and Miami were planning to retire soon, we were forced to find new ways to move our product. I suggested that we dare to bring cocaine all the way from Bolivia to Miami in our own plane.

This would significantly heighten our logistical problems. Because of the longer distance involved—it was 3,200 miles by air from Miami to Santa Cruz, Bolivia, compared to only 1,700 miles from Miami to Bogota—airstrips had to be identified in Colombia and in Central America where our transport planes could refuel. That would multiply our risks and challenges in security as well as in transportation. But the Bolivian connection boded well for us and looked to be enormously profitable.

In conjunction with our plans, Monti Cohen arranged a meeting for me with two topnotch American drug smugglers—"the best in the U.S.," he said. George Rawls was an expert in covert landing strips and landing crews, while Harold Rosenthal had a ready roster of drug-runner pilots. What Monti didn't tell me was that Harold was a fugitive, under indictment in the U.S. for drug smuggling.

At our meeting one evening in Miami, I liked both Harold and George immediately. Harold conversed easily in Spanish as he told me about his ties to the Mafia. He was a spark plug, obviously streetwise and hard-boiled by his years of drug running.

Before the night was over, I agreed to pay Harold and his pilots $5,000 a kilo for transporting 250 kilos from Bolivia to our people in the United States. This would take place on the run we had earlier scheduled for Easter 1979, during which we would also finalize our deal with Oscar Nuñez.

Manny and I would take a commercial flight from Miami to Bogota—not a direct flight, but one by way of Panama. In Bogota, we would meet up with Harold and two of his pilots, who would be flying into Colombia by another route. With Harold and the pilots, we would take a side trip to examine an airstrip near the town of Villa Vicencio, about two hours from Bogota. The airstrip, inaccessible by land, was located on a remote ranch in the jungle, and we wanted to assess its suitability as a refueling stop for future cocaine shipments.

After our return to Bogota, Harold and the pilots would make their way in one of our planes to Santa Cruz, Bolivia, where Sal would be waiting to oversee the cocaine pickup. After the 250 kilos were safely stored on our plane, Harold and the pilots would stop for refueling at the jungle airstrip near Villa Vicencio and again in Nicaragua, then fly to an airstrip in northern Florida, where our driver would transport the merchandise back to Miami. By that time Sal would be back in Miami to receive the cocaine. From there, it would be quickly transferred to our network of buyers, to be spread nationwide almost overnight.

While Harold and the pilots went to Bolivia for the pickup, Manny and I would fly from Bogota to Nicaragua to explore a potentially profitable opportunity. The cartel was considering the possibility of getting marijuana to the U.S. through Central America. From Nicaragua I would fly by private jet to the Dominican Republic to meet with Luchy. Despite my marriage to Christine, I was interested in reconciling my relationship with Luchy, primarily for the sake of my six-month-old son. From the Dominican Republic, Luchy and I planned to travel for a month in Europe, where our vacation would include picking up a new Mercedes I had ordered in Germany.

It was a detailed but relatively risk-free plan. What could go wrong?

On Easter Sunday, 1979, Manny and I met Harold Rosenthal for breakfast in a crowded Miami restaurant. With him were the two pilots: Verne Voll, an older, experienced pilot from Louisiana, and a man I'll call T.C. Michaels, a former deputy sheriff from Georgia who towered several inches above six feet. Together we pored over maps of the Villa Vicencio area in Colombia and concluded our plans.

The next morning Manny and I caught our flight to Panama. Aboard the plane, my conversation with Manny turned naturally to Panama's drug kingpin, Colonel Manuel Noriega. Manny told me that during his days of smuggling cigarettes and whiskey from Panama to Colombia, he had gone out with a girl who was one of Noriega's lovers. When the colonel found out, he arrested Manny and accused him of drug trafficking.

"It cost me seventeen thousand dollars to pay him off and get out of there," Manny said with a sly grin.

I chuckled along with my boss. We both knew that with enough money you could buy your way out of almost any trouble in Central America. The cartel had made a practice of dispersing huge amounts of cash to most of the key political figures in the Latin countries. One never knew who the next power broker might be or from whom we might need a special favor. Best to simply pay off the entire bunch.

When we landed in Panama, we were greeted by Manny's daughter, who was married to the son of Panama's minister of tourism. Although we hadn't called in any chips with the young man or his father, I had no doubt that we could.

While Manny and his daughter talked in the airport waiting area, I wandered over to the duty-free shop, where I purchased a new-model Polaroid Land camera.

"Why did you get that?" Manny asked when I showed it to him.

"Oh, I don't know. I'm going to take some pictures on this trip. Books always sell better with pictures," I joked. Manny laughed. Who ever heard of a drug lord chronicling his activities with snapshots? On the contrary, we had refined the concealment of evidence to a science.

Even on this trip, I carried a specially designed briefcase with a false bottom built to be undetectable by airport x-ray systems. In the secret compartment, I kept a ledger of all my current cocaine shipments and financial transactions—so I could go over them with our partners in Colombia—plus my address book and phone numbers of key people in our organization, including Manny's various addresses and private numbers. The hidden compartment would be a safe place to keep my Polaroid pictures, I decided.

When we landed in Colombia, a waiting car whisked us to the Bogota Hilton. There we discovered that Harold, Verne, and T.C. had been so bold as to check into our suite before Manny and I arrived. I was surprised and slightly irked. This was a violation of cartel protocol and security, especially since both Manny and I were traveling without our usual complement of bodyguards. Nevertheless, Manny and I remained calm, and we greeted Harold and the pilots with the obligatory hugs and small talk.

Our penthouse suite was gorgeous, with plenty of room for all five of us. But I told Harold to get separate rooms for the pilots. I felt that the airplane pilots were always the weakest link in any drug organization, and I never liked to talk business in front of them. Harold had highly recommended Verne and T. C., but I still didn't trust them.

We spent the night partying with call girls and champagne. Very late in the night, I walked out of my bedroom and made my way across the living room to get more champagne. The room was dimly lit, and I suddenly stumbled over something on the floor.

There was Harold, lying naked and asleep.

"What are you doing on the floor, Harold?" I said, waking him up.

Coming to, he answered, "You see, Jorge, that's the problem with you."

I stared back at him, bewildered. "What are you talking about?"

Despite his inebriated state, Harold waxed philosophical. "You're too used to this good life," he said. "Maybe one day you'll have to sleep on the floor, and you won't be able to stand it."

His comment grated against me. I looked straight at him. "Harold, let me tell you something," I said. "I slept on the floor when I came from Cuba, and I vowed I never would again!"

Harold laughed heartily. "Don't get all bent out of shape, Jorge."

I lightened up and laughed with him as I continued to the kitchen for more champagne.

Fourteen

A Problem
with Our Friends

The next day, Manny, Harold, the two pilots, and I all squeezed into a Range Rover and headed for Villa Vicencio. From there we took a short flight to the jungle airstrip.

On the way, our pilot carefully explained to Verne and T.C. how they should make their approach to the landing strip when they returned from Bolivia. At first I couldn't understand why the pilot was so meticulous about the landing procedure. But as the strip came into view in just a matter of minutes, I began to understand. The "airstrip" and "ranch" were nothing but an open field, a wide spot in the jungle. On the ground stood a tin-roofed shack made from scrap wood, where fuel was stored.

After landing safely, we explored the property's terrain and discussed its potential for our operations. That night we slept in hammocks we'd hung in the fuel shed. We returned the next day to Bogota.

Arriving at our hotel by midafternoon, I telephoned Sal in Santa Cruz. Across the 1,700 miles that separated us, I could feel his anger seething. Apparently we had a problem with our Bolivian "friends."

Sal was nearly screaming: "All they have is what we paid for!"

"Sal, calm down. What do you mean?"

He explained that the Bolivians had ready for us only the cocaine we had paid for and not the additional coke they had promised us on credit. They assured Sal that it was a mistake and that we could work it out, but he was irate.

I, too, was furious. What was going on with these new suppliers? All our arrangements for this trip were based on their promised two-for-one deal—an additional kilo of coke on credit for each one we paid for. Our plans were based on those quantities and on the corresponding profit from quickly selling the product back in the U.S.

Could this be another Bolivian double cross? Images of Manny's dissected nephew flitted across my mind. Was Sal even safe there?

"Jorge," Sal finally said in exasperation, "I think you'd better come down here and deal personally with these people."

Instinctively, I knew he was right. This was a new connection. We could not afford to start out by compromising on our arrangement. If we did, the Bolivian contacts would never respect us, and the problems would never end.

"Hang on tight, Sal," I told him. "I'm coming down."

I told Manny my plans. After flying to Santa Cruz, I would return on our airplane—the same plane in which Harold and the pilots would be transporting the cocaine. This would be the quickest way to get the rest of my travel back on schedule.

But Manny was irate. "There's no way I'm going to approve of you coming back on that transport plane. Anything can happen!" I knew exactly what he meant; plane crashes, ambushes by guerrillas or pirates, as well as interference from government authorities were all possible in this volatile region.

"Okay," I said, but in the back of my mind I knew I would come back in the airplane. I hated to deceive Manny, but this was business. Once the run was over and we were enjoying its profits, Manny would be more than satisfied and would forget that I'd risked my life.

Sal was waiting for me when I arrived in Santa Cruz. He took me directly to Oscar Nuñez's office. We walked in calmly, but with menacing voices we immediately began accusing him of breaking their agreement with us. Oscar was totally unprepared for my virulent demeanor. As Sal and I continued our tirade, Oscar called in his partners. I roared at them, "If you ever mess with us again, I will kill you!"

The military officers laughed. "Ha!" one of them said. "We have your money and we have your coke. Don't you realize if we wanted to cheat you, you'd be dead right now?"

I stepped right up to the man's face, so close I could smell his foul breath. "Listen, you," I hissed. "I dare you to cross us. We have the power to come in here and wipe your little country off the map!"

Sal backed me up. In a matter of minutes, the Bolivians were apologizing profusely. Oscar explained that there had been a raid on their supplies and that they couldn't get the cocaine out.

Sal and I finally agreed to take the 130 kilos the Bolivians already had ready, and Oscar agreed to provide us another 200 kilos on credit within a week.

The next day Harold, Verne, and T.C. arrived in Santa Cruz, landing in a Beechcraft Queen Air twin-engine workhorse. Not a large plane—about thirty-five feet from nose to tail, with a wingspan of forty-five feet—the Queen

Air was designed to carry roughly three thousand pounds of cargo and could be configured with five passenger seats, plus the two cockpit seats. It was used frequently by business travelers, easily accommodating five full-size men plus their golf clubs and luggage. Ours was configured to seat two passengers plus a lot of cocaine.

Harold explained their delay: "We lost one of our alternators."

Sal and I took Harold and the pilots to our hotel, where I informed Harold of our problem with the suppliers. In light of that, I told him we wanted to renegotiate our payment to him. "If you'll take half the loss along with me," I said, "you can come back in ten days for two hundred more kilos and do another run. We'll allow you to buy some of that coke for yourself to make up for your losses." I promised him twenty-five kilos at $10,000 each, which he could sell back in the States for $50,000 per kilo. "You can make an extra million dollars," I told him. The prospect turned Harold into an amicable partner.

While we were in Santa Cruz, we had planned to pick up an additional fifteen kilos that belonged to the cartel through another connection. The Bolivian contact came to our hotel room that night, and we watched with amusement as he began taking off his clothes, revealing kilos of coke strapped to his chest and legs.

I had agreed earlier to pay $10,000 for each kilo. Without thinking, I opened my briefcase—right in front of Harold and the pilots—and proceeded to pull out $150,000 from the false bottom to pay the Bolivian. The men all laughed about it. "Well, looky there," one of the pilots gushed, wide-eyed in amazement. "Who would have thought you could hide that much money in there?" We laughed some more, I paid the Bolivian, and he made a hasty departure.

Later that night, I told Sal of my plan to leave Santa Cruz on the plane along with the coke in order to meet with our Nicaraguan connection on time. Like Manny, Sal was upset at the thought of my traveling with a shipment.

"Don't worry, Sal," I assured him. "Nothing's going to happen."

The next day the Queen Air took off from Santa Cruz, headed for Colombia, with Verne as pilot and T.C. as copilot and Harold and me aboard as well. The cocaine—worth $4.5 million to us—was inside the Queen Air's luggage compartments in hard-shell suitcases.

We planned to spend the night at our refueling stop at the jungle airstrip outside Villa Vicencio. When we landed, I was surprised to find Manny there to meet us. He didn't seem upset to see me aboard the aircraft—no doubt Sal had alerted him that I was coming. Now that we had safely negotiated the most unfamiliar segment of the trip, perhaps he was more at ease about my being on board.

I planned to stay with the plane until it reached Nicaragua. I could meet with our contact there, then catch a commercial flight and head off on vacation.

"Manny, there's nothing to fear," I told him. "We're having a little problem with the alternator, but we have two of them on board the plane, so don't worry."

Almost flippantly, I added, "The real danger won't be until the plane enters U.S. airspace, and I won't even be on that leg of the trip."

At the airstrip we picked up another ten kilos of coke from the two brothers who owned the property. They were beginning to acquire large volumes of cocaine themselves, and we agreed to take their ten kilos to the U.S. as a sample of what they could provide. They had placed the coke in a duffel bag, which we would carry on board.

We slept in the open-air shack and were up early the next morning, ready to go. Manny seemed more at peace with my plans, though not totally convinced.

Just before I boarded the Queen Air, he kissed and hugged me and said, "Vaya con Dios."

His words struck me strangely. *Go with God?*

Fifteen

Caught!

On a gorgeous blue-sky morning, we crossed the northwestern corner of Colombia and were soon soaring five thousand feet above the pristine waters of the Pacific. We planned to fly just far enough west, over the ocean, to pass by Costa Rica and Panama without notice, then veer eastward to land in Managua, Nicaragua.

We stayed in radio contact with Manny back at Villa Vicencio. While I was talking with him, about thirty-five minutes into the flight, we suddenly lost contact.

"Hey! What's going on?" I shouted.

From the cockpit, Verne yelled back, "The alternator! We've lost the second alternator!"

"So what does that mean?" I wanted to know.

"We can keep flying, but we won't have any power except the juice that's already in the battery."

Verne and T.C. were turning off anything they could to conserve energy—lights, gauges, and passenger compartment amenities.

I glanced quickly toward the wings and drew small comfort from the fact that both propellers were still turning.

Like most drug planes on long-distance runs, our aircraft was equipped with a 200-gallon balloonlike bladder resting inside the cabin. This extra-fuel bladder was full, but there was no way now to get power to the bladder's pumps. The extra fuel had become a curse. With more than 200 gallons of fuel, more than 150 kilos of highly flammable cocaine, and a large tank of ether, we were a flying bomb.

I watched helplessly as Harold and the pilots screamed back and forth to each other, trying to come up with a solution. Harold's face creased with worry.

Verne banked the plane sharply eastward, not exactly sure where we were since our radar was out, but hoping we might be able to make landfall and find a place to bring the plane down before losing power.

Too late. The left engine sputtered and stalled. In the distance, we could see an outline of land. Verne headed for it, but we knew that at any moment the second engine could shut down.

Just as we flew over a beach, the second engine went out. With no radio and no lights, there was no way of warning anyone we were coming. We were about five thousand feet in the air, traveling at about two hundred miles per hour, and losing altitude rapidly.

Verne maneuvered the plane's rudder, desperately trying to keep us from tipping one way or the other. Meanwhile T.C., Harold, and I fiercely scanned the thick jungle below, searching for any clearing that looked wide and long enough to land a thirty-five-foot airplane.

Finally we spotted a small open field lined by thick banana trees. We were five hundred feet above it—and dropping.

"What's going on, Harold?" I yelled.

"Buckle up tight. We're gonna crash."

My pounding heart drowned out every sound except Harold's caustic warning to stick our head between our legs and kiss our rear ends good-bye.

■　　　■　　　■

It could have been only seconds while the plane streaked toward the ground, but it seemed like hours as my life passed before my eyes. I wasn't thinking about all the money, the cars, the houses. Instead, I thought about my toddler, Jorgito, who would never again see his father. I thought of my own father, whose heart I was sure would fail when he learned I had perished in a plane crash in some Central American jungle. I thought of my brother and sister whom I loved so much, and my mother who loved me unconditionally and prayed for me daily.

Suddenly I heard a loud screech as the plane's belly slammed into the ground. We skidded a short distance, bounced a few feet upward, then dove nose-first into the ground with a crunching thud. I felt my seat belt ripping into my waist, suspending me in midair.

I opened my eyes and looked up. *Is this life or is this death?*

I heard Verne and T.C. scream. They weren't screaming from pain, but from joy—sheer joy and amazement that we were still alive. The plane had plunged nose-first into mud up to the pilots' knees, with our tail up in the air.

"We gotta get out of this plane!" I heard Harold yell. "It could blow at any second!"

My brain was reeling and the adrenaline was pumping at a furious pace as I extricated my self from the seat. I grabbed my briefcase, Harold grabbed the duffel bag with the coke we'd picked up at Villa Vicencio, and the five of us scrambled out the rear door of the aircraft. We stumbled away from the fuselage as quickly as possible.

I composed myself and tried to act tough as usual. *Nothing can hurt me. I am Jorge Valdés.*

From a safe distance, I took my first long look at the damaged plane. The front end was totally destroyed, the nose buried deeply in the mud, the propellers sheared off. The underbelly and sides of the aircraft looked as though they had been strafed by enemy gunfire.

As I gazed at the crumpled plane, my mind filled with accounts of other drug planes that had merely scraped a tree or a hillside before bursting into fireballs. Yet here we were, alive and well except for a few bruises and cuts.

I brushed aside any thoughts that I should thank God for this. It was just another instance of beating the odds.

Harold took the duffel bag filled with coke, ran into the thicket, and pitched the bag as far into the brush as he could. Wherever we were, it was only a matter of time before someone discovered us. Our main cocaine shipment was relatively secure in the Queen Air's luggage compartment, but we didn't want to be found with any compromising evidence on us. Better to toss the ten kilos than to take a chance, at least until we found out what—or who—we were dealing with.

The thought crossed my mind that I should get the flare gun from inside our plane, step about fifty feet away, shoot the plane, and watch it explode in fire and smoke, thus destroying any drug-smuggling evidence. But the thought quickly vanished. I had 4.5 million reasons to take a chance. Unbridled greed easily overcame logic.

As we had anticipated, in less than an hour the woods were crawling with people. The local police lieutenant arrived and asked us what was going on.

I told him we were cattle ranchers from Nicaragua who had been scanning the area for potential land to buy when we lost control of our plane and crashed.

The officer nodded.

"Can you help us, sir?" I asked. "We need to find a telephone and call somebody to help us fix our airplane." *Fix the airplane!* There would be no fixing that baby, but I didn't care. I just needed to contact someone who could help us get our cocaine out of there.

While I spoke with the lieutenant, out of the corner of my eye I saw a small boy running toward Harold. "Sir, sir!" he called out. "Your bag!" To my horror, I saw that the boy had discovered the duffel bag in the brush. Harold was trying to put the boy off, telling him he had no idea where the bag came from.

I turned my body so the lieutenant would have to look away from the bizarre scene behind us. "Sir, can you take us to a nearby hotel?" I asked more loudly than necessary.

"Of course, let's go," the obliging officer answered. Harold quickly joined us after locking up the duffel bag in the plane.

On the way to a hotel, the officer informed us that we had crashed in western Panama. We were in the rural province of Chiriqui in the heart of the country's banana region, about twenty-five miles from the nearest major town.

The hotel to which he took us was a dump, but it had a telephone. That was all that mattered. We weren't far from the Costa Rican border, and my plan was to hire a cab or anyone who could drive us there. I had plenty of contacts in Costa Rica who could help us. I was confident that if I could just get word to them, they could clear us through customs and immigration at the border.

Meanwhile I gave our passports to the lieutenant and asked him to have them stamped for us. Then I called Manny's son-in-law who lived in Panama City and informed him that we had a "problem" in Chiriqui. I asked him to make the necessary calls to Costa Rica so we could cross with no hassles when we arrived at the border.

With my plan in motion, I relaxed and breathed a little easier, feeling confident.

Two hours later, the driver I had hired to take us to Costa Rica arrived to pick us up. He took us first to the police station so we could retrieve our passports. After that, we would go back to the airplane and pick up our "luggage" before heading to the border.

The lieutenant was waiting for us at the police station, his expression quite serious.

"Did you get our passports stamped?" I asked, reaching for my wallet.

The lieutenant ignored my question and replied brusquely, "Come with me, Dr. Valdés." He ordered his subordinates to take my companions to separate rooms.

We were in big trouble.

The lieutenant locked me in a cell. When he left, I took four hundred-dollar bills from my wallet, rolled them into the thinnest cylinders possible, and lined them around the gums of my mouth. *Perhaps this money will come in handy.*

Half an hour later, the lieutenant returned. "Some people have come from Panama City to talk with you," he said as he led me out of the cell and into an office where three men were waiting.

One of them, I was informed, was Agent Art Sedillo, head of the U.S. Drug Enforcement Agency in Panama. With him was Lieutenant Jorge Latinez, whom I later learned was the head of G-2, Panama's national guard—the police force that enforces the country's martial law. Known simply as Lino, he was one of the most feared men in Panama.

The third man identified himself as a representative from the U.S. consulate in Panama City, Consul Joseph McLean.

All three wore grim expressions. Clearly they were here on serious business.

McLean spoke first. "Your airplane has been searched, and drugs have been found."

I tried to act calm and cool. "I'd like to speak with my attorney."

Latinez broke out in cruel laughter. He positioned himself in front of me and belched a litany of curses. "You're in Panama," he roared. "We operate under Napoleonic law here. That means you're guilty until you prove yourself innocent. You have no rights to an attorney; you have no rights at all!"

I struggled to maintain a calm demeanor. "I have nothing to say," I told them.

I was returned to my cell. Two hours later, the lieutenant came to check on me. "If you had only told me what was in the airplane," he said, "I could have protected you, and I wouldn't have had to call Panama City to clear your passports."

I was soon reunited with Harold and the pilots, but it was not a happy occasion. The officers put us in a common cell, then stripped us of our clothing while they searched every cavity of our bodies.

A half-hour later we were herded into another room. To my surprise, there on a large conference table was our cocaine.

"Stand behind the table," we were ordered.

Harold, Verne, T.C., and I lined up behind the cocaine-laden table while the officers began taking our pictures.

I refused to look at the camera. I just stared blankly at the cocaine on the table. My mind was running wild. I knew that if I was going to survive this ordeal, I had to keep a clear head, staying one step ahead of everyone else. I wasn't overly worried about escaping; I had been dealing with Latin American politicians, police, and other government leaders for some time, and I knew that money could buy anything in those countries. My biggest concern was the loss of our cocaine.

I should have shot the airplane with that flare gun, I told myself.

As the officers continued taking pictures, a worrisome thought crossed my mind. *My briefcase.* The main compartment was loaded only with typical business papers and a few livestock and cattle-ranching magazines I carried with me—not only because of my involvement in ranching, but also to substantiate our ruse that we were ranchers looking for property. In the briefcase's secret compartment, however, were plenty of incriminating documents concerning my latest cocaine deals—as well as the Polaroid pictures I'd been taking throughout this trip, including some that showed us standing with the stack of cocaine in Bolivia.

After being transferred to another jail, where all four of us were locked in one small cell, we had our first chance to talk without someone hearing us.

I asked the other three what they had told our interrogators. Harold and Verne had maintained their cool, but one comment from T.C. disturbed me. "They told me if we ever wanted to go home and see our family members again," T.C. said, "we better cooperate with the government."

A rage suddenly boiled within me. I knew there was no such thing as cooperation with the government in a case like this. I could tell by Harold's expression that if he thought for a moment Verne or T.C. might squeal on us, he'd kill them right there in the cell.

"Don't worry," I assured the men. "Everything will be okay. We have the money to buy our way out of anything, and I can negotiate with these people. Just be patient."

The following morning we were transferred to yet another facility. We were fingerprinted and photographed again, then separated once more. I was taken to an office where the well-dressed man behind the desk was thumbing through some papers and magazines.

A cold chill swept through my body. They were the items I'd been carrying in my briefcase.

He introduced himself simply as Miranda, the attorney general of Panama. As he idly thumbed through a cattle magazine, he said, "I'm sure you know this case will be investigated."

He paused as he flipped to another page. "It will probably take a few years," he added.

He paused again, his attention captured by a photo of a bull in the magazine. "You know," he said, "I'm a cattle breeder myself." As if I cared.

"Mr. Miranda," I said, "my name is Jorge Valdés."

Miranda's expression changed abruptly. "I know who you are," he answered icily. "I also know that the U.S. government says you're one of the biggest drug lords in the world."

"I don't know what you're talking about."

"I'm not going to get into that game."

"Neither am I. Sir, I only want to ask you two questions. One, how much will it cost to buy back my cargo and my belongings, and two, how much will it cost for my friends and me to leave the country?"

Miranda stared at me. His forehead wrinkled, and his eyes squinted narrowly as though he was trying to bore a hole right through me. He continued to watch me intently, wordlessly, for a full two minutes.

I returned his stare.

Finally, Miranda broke the spell and spoke calmly. "Young man, first of all, your drugs have already been sold. Noriega took care of that. Number two, it will cost your workers $50,000 each to get out of here. But for you—the boss—the cost is $100,000."

A slight smile crossed my lips as I replied, "I'll pay you the $250,000 and give you one of those bulls you're looking at in that magazine."

Miranda smiled broadly as he stood to his feet. "I'll send an attorney in a couple of days to see you, and he'll make all the arrangements. As soon as the money has been paid, you'll be taken to Panama City to be interrogated by the G-2. Make up some story, as you did here. The investigators will establish that you hadn't intended to land in Panama but were forced to crash because of mechanical failure. When the state is satisfied with your story, you'll be released immediately."

I was taken behind bars again, this time into a large room surrounded by open cells. Harold, Verne, and T.C. were there, along with a number of other prisoners.

I gathered my friends and described the deal I had cut.

"Jorge," Harold said, "we don't have that kind of money. Get yourself out first, then do something about us. We'll repay you."

"No, Harold," I told him. "Either we all leave or nobody leaves. But don't worry, I'll make arrangements to have enough money sent for all of us."

We were soon informed that the few beds in the cells around us belonged to the leaders of various prison gangs. The filthy place was rat infested, and the putrid stench of uncleaned toilets filled the air. Nevertheless, by now I was so exhausted that I lay down, took off my glasses, and fell fast asleep on the floor—too weary to remember my conversation with Harold only a few nights earlier when I had stumbled over him in the Bogota Hilton.

When I awakened some hours later, I reached for my glasses. They were gone, and I could barely function without them. I shook Harold, who was sleeping next to me.

"Harold, someone stole my glasses."

"Come on," Harold said, as he got to his feet. We went into the bathroom area, where several drug addicts were sniffing handkerchiefs doused in kerosene. Harold grabbed one man and I grabbed another. We threw the two Panamanians up against the walls as I bellowed, "Which one of you has my eyeglasses?"

The Panamanian prisoners fought back. Before we knew it, Harold and I found ourselves surrounded by a half-dozen other attackers and embroiled in a full-scale fistfight. Despite the odds, Harold and I were easily stronger and in better physical condition than the emaciated, sickly druggies, and we started beating the daylights out of three or four of them.

Verne jumped in to help. T.C., however, refused to get involved, though at six-foot-plus he was a giant compared to the little Panamanians. He was scared to death. As the altercation settled down, Harold walked over to T.C. He slapped and cursed the pilot for not helping us.

Meanwhile, I had grabbed one of the Panamanians and shoved his face into a toilet filled with excrement. "Where are my glasses?" I screamed at him.

I let him up slightly, and the man started crying.

"Where are my glasses?" I screamed again.

This time he handed them over.

Harold and I knew we'd have to watch our backs from now on, but we didn't care. We had made it clear that, no matter what happened, we'd go down fighting.

Rather than branding us as targets, the brawl actually served to gain us respect. One of the Panamanians, a man named Pedro, offered me his bed.

I told him I appreciated his offer and that I would repay his kindness someday. Pedro told me he had been incarcerated for three months because he couldn't afford to pay a $200 fine. His wife was working and trying to care for their young children, but she hadn't been able to earn enough money yet to get him out.

"When is your wife coming to visit you?" I asked him.

"Tomorrow morning."

Pedro watched in amazement as I pulled two $100 bills from my gums. I handed the moist but intact bills to Pedro. "Only one thing I ask," I told him. "When you get out of here, I want you to call a phone number in Miami, which I'll give you, and tell my family I'm alive. Tell them to stand strong, because someone else will be calling them soon."

Pedro took the money, tears streaming down his face. "Thank you, Jorge. Thank you, Jorge," he kept saying.

That night I slept peacefully, confident that I was back in control.

The following morning, Pedro smuggled the money to his wife during her visit. An hour and a half later, the guards came to announce his release.

As Pedro hugged and thanked me, he said, "God has answered my prayer."

"No," I answered. "God didn't answer your prayer. Jorge Valdés did."

Sixteen

Doomed

The following morning an attorney came to see me. True to Miranda's word, the attorney promised to make the necessary arrangements to facilitate our release from Panama. I gave him several phone numbers to call, including that of my brother, J.C., who I knew would contact Sal. Then Sal could make arrangements to get us out.

By this time, Pedro, the grateful Panamanian prisoner, had already telephoned my parents. Though I had been missing for a number of days, my mother wasn't surprised to hear I was alive and well. In a dream she had seen me being involved in a plane crash but escaping alive.

My father hadn't been so certain and was greatly relieved to learn I was okay. So was Manny, who had virtually camped out at my parents' home upon his return to Miami. The last Manny knew of my whereabouts was when our radio had gone dead. For all he knew, we had crashed somewhere and all been killed. He had sent search teams to Central America trying to locate our plane, but they had turned up nothing.

Two days later, the attorney showed up again to tell me that everything was in order and that plane tickets to Costa Rica had been obtained for us. First, however, as Miranda had explained, we would be taken to Panama City for interrogation. "No matter what they say or do," the attorney said, "stick to your story."

I assumed that the $250,000 ransom had been met; otherwise, the attorney wouldn't be there. But I didn't know where the money had come from, nor did I ask.

Unknown to me—and against the advice of many of our associates—J.C. and Sal had flown from Florida to Panama to secure my release. Sal was smart enough not to bring the money with him. He had dispatched the payment with two of our bodyguards on a separate flight, which was a good thing: The moment Sal and J.C. landed in Panama, they were arrested and taken to the G-2 office and brought before Lino, one of the three men who had first questioned me after the crash. Lino allowed Sal to leave but kept J.C. in custody, perhaps assuming that the brother of Jorge Valdés must possess valuable information.

Meanwhile I had carefully rehearsed our "story" with Harold and the pilots: They thought I was a fugitive they were transporting, and they had been paid $25,000 for their efforts. "Just stick to that," I told them. "You don't know anything else."

The four of us were handcuffed and taken to an airport. Filthy, disheveled, and still handcuffed, we boarded a commercial plane along with the guards. The other passengers on board stared at us as if we were dangerous wild animals. I didn't care what they thought; I was headed for freedom.

When we landed in Panama City, armed members of the G-2 herded us into a military transport car and hustled us to a downtown office. Inside, I recognized Lino immediately. He began to interrogate me about our trip and the suitcases filled with cocaine.

"I don't know anything about any cocaine," I lied with an earnest face. "I was given the suitcases in Colombia by some Cuban revolutionaries. I was told that they were arms and that I was to deliver them to the Sandinistas in Nicaragua."

"What about the pilots?" Lino asked coldly. He was writing notes on a legal pad as I spoke.

"They don't know anything," I answered. "I take full responsibility. The pilots are just hired help." Wanting to reduce the probability of the pilots being harshly interrogated, I continued spinning my yarn: "I'm only making fifty thousand dollars on this deal. Now that I see what the cases contain, I'm furious. I hope those people who are involved will be arrested!"

Lino stopped his note taking and raised his eyebrows. I knew he wasn't buying anything I said, but I didn't really care. I was certain he had been well paid and had already been told what he must do.

Across the room, Harold, Verne, and T.C. sat with worried expressions. When Lino left the room, I tried to reassure them. "This is just the way these things have to be done so the Panamanians can save face with the DEA." I knew the DEA and G-2 were in collusion. I had no idea how deep their alliance went.

Lino returned and launched once more into his interrogation. The longer he questioned me, the more agitated T.C. became. He grew pale—actually, I had seen little color in his face for two days now—and perspiration glistened on his forehead. He kept looking nervously at Verne. T.C. was panic-stricken, and for all his size and strength, I knew he was the weak link that could destroy us. I only hoped he could keep his mouth shut a little longer.

Suddenly the door to Lino's office burst open and Panamanian officers rushed in, dragging a short, dark-skinned young man. One of the officers shouted that this was a man Lino had been looking for. In a matter of seconds, the officers had stripped the man and pushed him facedown on the floor.

Lino hovered over the frail, wretched fellow, slapping the man's head as he shouted questions at him. Had the man tried to answer, it would have been impossible.

The officers bludgeoned their defenseless victim again and again. Harold appeared unmoved by the awful scene; Verne turned away. But T.C. looked as though he might collapse at any moment. Sweat was dripping from his face.

Lino grabbed a sawed-off broomstick from behind his desk. "Hold him down!" he ordered the officers. Lino sauntered around behind the prisoner. With unimaginable viciousness, he thrust the broomstick into the man's rectum. The man screamed in pain.

"Talk!" Lino roared. With that, he shoved the broomstick even farther inside the victim. Blood spurted in every direction, spattering the floor and walls. The battered man on the floor could endure no more. He urinated on the floor and passed out.

"Get that piece of crap out of this room!" Lino ordered the officers. "And clean up this mess."

Lino glowered at me. This torture was obviously his way of letting us know what he was capable of—and what we would receive if we failed to cooperate.

Through the doorway, I caught sight of Agent Sedillo, the DEA head for Panama who had also been one of my initial interrogators. Given the close cooperation between the DEA and the Panamanians, if Sedillo had not orchestrated the despicable event, he must have at least condoned it.

T.C. leaped to his feet and began shouting, "They're gonna kill us! They're gonna kill us!" Harold slapped him across the face. "Shut up!" he yelled. "This has nothing to do with us!"

But T.C. broke down, bawling. He shrieked at Lino, "I'll tell the truth! I'll tell the truth!"

A smirk crossed Lino's face. He knew he'd won a major battle. He ordered his men to take Harold and me to a separate room while he questioned T.C. and Verne.

An hour passed. Two hours.

While I tried to coolly consider my options, Harold paced the room, cursing T.C. with every step. "I'm gonna kill that punk the minute I get my hands on him!"

Three hours passed. Then four. *To save his own skin, what was T.C. telling them?*

We soon found out. After four and a half hours of interrogating T.C., Lino took great pleasure in letting Harold and me know what he had learned. Apparently, the pilot had given detailed information describing our Bolivian trip, including where I kept my ledgers and the names of people in the snapshots I had taken. He told them I was the head of the operation and that Harold was a fugitive in the U.S. Worst of all, T.C. revealed that I had bribed the attorney general of Panama.

The DEA had assured T.C. and Verne that if they would talk, they could be on a plane back home within an hour. T.C. and Verne talked, and the DEA stuck to their bargain. The two pilots were soon boarding a plane to Miami. At the same time, Harold and I were being shoved down a dark, steep, tunnel-like staircase, descending into the bowels of the Modelo, the largest, most secure, and most vile prison in Panama.

When I paused momentarily to get my bearings on the dimly lit steps, a guard slugged me in the back with a stick. I winced in pain, certain my ribs were broken, but stumbled on.

Everything was cold and damp, and the deeper we descended the more foul the smell became. The only light came through a tiny window high above the stairs.

We came to a cellblock consisting of eight small cells with a narrow hallway running in front. Harold and I were forced to strip to our underwear, then we were thrown together into a cell of our own. In the cell next to us—a cubicle that might hold two or three men in an American prison—more than thirty men were crammed. They looked like wild animals, mostly naked and filthy. Many were hollering at the top of their lungs, "Who are you? Why are you here?"

The smell of human excrement and vomit saturated the air. I could barely walk. My brain was numb, and I was physically exhausted.

"Don't let them defeat you, Jorge," Harold kept saying. "Don't let them kill you. The harder you fight back, the easier this will be."

I knew I would fight—it was part of my nature—but I wasn't sure anymore what I was fighting for. Since T.C. had spilled the beans, even the people who could have aided us would be hunkering down—or running for their lives. Nobody could help us now. We were doomed.

In our underwear, Harold and I lay motionless on a concrete floor stained with a sticky mosaic of blood, excrement, and vomit. I wondered how many tears had been included in the mixture.

Harold suddenly began to laugh uproariously. I feared he'd lost his mind.

"Are you crazy? What are you laughing about?"

Gulping in another guffaw, Harold reminded me of our conversation in the Bogota Hilton about sleeping on the floor. In spite of myself, I started laughing too, while the other prisoners gawked at us as though we were deranged animals.

"They won't be laughing for long," I heard one of the men say. "Wait till the G-2 comes."

That comment sobered us somewhat. Harold confirmed the likelihood that the G-2 would soon come to torture us. "I've been in situations like this before," he told me. "The only way I survived was by fighting back. The more they tortured me, the more I'd fight. By fighting back, you release energy. It makes the pain more tolerable.

"Jorge," he told me again, "if we're going to survive in here, we have to fight back."

This was now a war, I decided: Harold and I were pitted against them all—the other prisoners, the guards, the DEA agents, the governments of Panama and the U.S., and anyone else.

And they will never defeat me.

SEVENTEEN

TORTURED

The sheer cacophony in the dimly lit prison made it difficult to think clearly. The other prisoners bellowed a constant litany of obscenities.

Is this hell? I wondered.

Sometime later—we didn't know if it was day or night since it was always so dark inside this hellhole—a squadron of eight Panamanian soldiers rushed into the cellblock. The other prisoners screamed in terror.

The soldiers opened our cell, grabbed Harold and me, and threw us to the ground. To defend ourselves, we tried biting and kicking the soldiers, but they quickly overpowered us. Pulling our arms behind our backs, they clasped our wrists in handcuffs and our ankles in leg irons. Then they picked us up and threw us facedown on the cement floor.

The sergeant, a small but burly man reeking with body odor, barked orders in Spanish. "Kick them! Beat them! Make them talk!" he roared. "These men are trying to poison our country. They're trying to bribe our politicians. Who do these filthy gringos think they are, to come into our country and do these things?"

A soldier's jackboot crunched into my face, bouncing my head off the concrete floor. Blow after blow followed. After about ten or fifteen minutes of continuous beatings, I ceased to feel anything. But my thoughts were still cogent: *Somehow, I'm going to beat them! I will not give in.*

Suddenly I found the strength to fight back, lunging and kicking karate-style with my shackled legs. Harold, too, was fighting back, both physically and verbally, loudly cursing the Panamanians.

I quickly realized our tongues were our only real defensive weapons. "Is that the best you can do?" I taunted. "Can't you punch any harder? No matter what you do to me, you can't break me!"

Four soldiers picked me up in the air and slammed me against the wall. They pushed my head against the bars while they continued kicking and beating me.

95

Bent forward, with my face scrunched to one side, I could see DEA Agent Sedillo outside the cell, laughing with Lino and two other Panamanian officers. Immeasurable, raw hatred toward Sedillo exploded within me.

With my head still stuck between the bars, I screamed at him, calling him every insulting epithet I could think of. "Why don't you take off our handcuffs and come into the cell with us and be a man about it? No, that's how you government boys are, all chickens hiding behind a badge. You pig. That's why I buy and sell your kind every day. That's why I'm gonna poison your kids!" I fired one volley after another.

The louder and more obnoxiously I screamed, the more the soldiers beat me, until I was totally numb. Finally, they slammed my head against the bars, and I passed out.

I awakened lying on the cement in a fetal position. I slowly opened my blood-caked eyelids. The handcuffs were gone. I tried to move, but my body would not cooperate, so I just lay there focusing my brain. Harold was lying on the floor across from me, his face covered with blood. We had won the first battle, but would we win the war?

Grimacing in pain with every move, Harold and I slowly inched ourselves up against a cell wall. We sat and talked quietly in the darkness, not knowing when the next attack might come.

We tried to sleep, lying on the concrete, turning one way then the next, trying to adjust our bodies to the searing pain and the cold of the concrete against our bare skin. Insects and rats crawled over our bodies in the darkness. Fresh blood must have been a treat for them. After a while, I removed what remained of my underwear and wrapped it around my face to keep the vermin from getting in my mouth.

The pain enveloped me. I felt like a piece of meat that had been beaten by a butcher. I finally escaped into sleep.

I awoke to the sensation of hard rubber and leather crushing into my rib cage. What looked to be about ten guards were in the cell again, kicking and beating Harold and me. They didn't handcuff us; they had enough guards this time to restrain us.

Our defensive tactic was the same—kicking and screaming insults at them.

"I suggest you talk to the DEA," the smelly sergeant screamed back at us. "I suggest you tell the truth. Who are your partners? Who is this Manuel Garces? You were taking the drugs to Miami, weren't you?"

Again, the soldiers beat us until we passed out on the floor. With my last gasp of consciousness, I screamed an obscenity at the sergeant and lapsed into darkness.

When I awakened, I was too sore to move. Apparently, Harold was in similar shape. We acknowledged that we were alive, but didn't talk much. With no energy to roll over, we lay where we were.

We heard an inmate coming by with a pile of slop, which he was feeding to the other prisoners through the bars. He stopped in front of our cell. "They're going to kill you guys," he said. "You better talk."

But talking was not an option for me, since I had given my word to stay loyal to my friends.

■   ■   ■

We had lost all sense of time, but it seemed that about a day went by without the soldiers coming to beat us again. Harold and I sat on the floor, staring through the bars, anticipating the next attack.

None of this was shaking Harold. When our circumstances seemed hopeless he laughed, and his laughter became my source of strength, the fuel that empowered me to go on. How bad could this be when the naked guy next to me was laughing?

Then we heard the other prisoners yelling, "Here they come!"

Harold and I mustered our strength and moved closer to the cell's bars. We didn't want to give our attackers space to barge in and pin us against the wall. To slow them down further, we had wrapped our underwear around the cell-door bars. We were willing to try anything that might give us even an extra second to fight back before the bludgeoning began.

The soldiers—too many to count this time—gathered at our cell door, broke through the tied underwear, and barged in, slamming us to the floor. As several soldiers began pummeling me, I heard Harold shout, "You're going to kill him! He's just a kid. Come fight me, you bunch of cowards!"

We knew our best efforts were futile; by now we were too weak to punch or even throw a kick. The sheer force and number of the soldiers would overcome us, and we would be at their mercy. Still, we struggled.

We were handcuffed again, and our feet secured with chains. Then they dragged Harold out of the cellblock. For the first time since being incarcerated, stark fear overcame me. *Where are they taking Harold? What are they doing to my partner?*

The soldiers returned to the cell, carrying gasoline cans. As I lay on the floor with my hands shackled behind my back, I saw the sergeant motion to the men holding the gasoline. They approached cautiously, then doused me. My body shrieked in pain as the gasoline poured into my open wounds.

I was certain I was about to die. It would be my ultimate victory over my captors. They wouldn't be able to hurt me anymore, and they wouldn't have the information they sought.

I had no plans of going to heaven, but hell couldn't be any worse than where I was.

I took one last opportunity to tell my torturers what I thought of them. I cursed the soldiers. I cursed Lino and Sedillo, who I knew was responsible for these atrocities. I cursed the officer in charge of my torture. "I'm going to rape your daughters," I roared. And to the smelly sergeant I sneered, "And I'm going to rape your wife right in front of you!"

"You'll never get the chance," the sergeant laughed. "I'm going to see what you look like on fire!"

He reached for a pack of matches. "I'll give you one more chance. Tell me you're ready to talk to the DEA."

I filled the air again with another litany of expletives.

The sergeant made the motion of striking a match and throwing it on me, but the match wasn't lit. He reached for another.

Suddenly my mind filled with thoughts similar to those I had experienced as our plane dropped from the sky. It was almost as though I was watching the entire scene on a theater screen in my mind. *Am I on fire right now? How long will it take my skin to burn? How long before I die? Is this death?* I decided not to struggle, not to make death a drawn-out process, but to go quickly, with dignity. *Soon it will all be over.*

The sergeant glared at me as he fingered the pack of matches. But rather than strike one, he motioned to another guard who was holding something that looked like a baton. To my horror, I realized that the stick was an electric cattle prod.

The soldiers moved closer to me and spread my legs apart. The one holding the prod hovered over me. "Let me see what kind of a man you really are," he said.

He rammed the prod against my testicles and jolted me with electricity. My body recoiled and jerked in the air. I screamed a loud, guttural wail. Again and again they rammed the prod between my legs, sending electric current surging through my private parts. I felt myself going into convulsions. As I faded into semiconsciousness, I urinated all over myself, while my torturers laughed uproariously.

I snapped back to reality for a moment, then disappeared into a deep, dark hole. I didn't know if I was alive or dead, in this world or another.

I regained consciousness long enough to hear Harold cursing our captors, calling them unspeakable names. Then I heard him groan as they kicked him repeatedly and turned the prods on him.

Finally, my mind and body could take no more. I went totally blank.

I drifted in and out of consciousness numerous times before I fully awakened. When my eyes opened, my vision was blurred, but I saw Harold's bloody form lying next to me.

I couldn't move any part of my body, and my lips were too swollen to speak. All I could do was slowly open and close my eyes, rousing slightly, then dropping off to sleep again. It was far too painful to stay awake. Sleep became my best friend.

EIGHTEEN

SMELLING FREEDOM

Our torturers made a crucial mistake in allowing Harold and me to remain in the same cell. Had they separated us, one or both of us might have given up. But together, our power increased exponentially. When one of us was near the mental breaking point, or when the intense pain seemed too much to bear, the other would joke about our circumstances. What little laughter we were able to summon served as an anesthetic, keeping our spirits up and helping heal our bodies.

During a lull in the beatings, I noticed a small mouse scurrying in and out of our cell. He approached us brazenly, as though he knew we were helpless and couldn't hurt him. We had no food to give him, but he continued showing up. He became almost like a friend. I named him Mickey and began looking forward to his appearances.

Mickey became our Paul Revere, warning us of impending danger. He'd come to visit us for a while, then suddenly race into the shadows. Whenever he disappeared, a "visit" from the guards followed soon after.

What seemed like two full days passed uneventfully, and Harold and I began to recuperate. We were still sore from the beatings and weak from not eating. Our bodies were swollen and bruised, but our spirits were up. We were still alive, and we had given no information to the guards.

Then the cellblock door burst open, and soldiers swarmed toward us again. Harold and I couldn't move too quickly now, and we were still crawling along the floor when the soldiers entered our cell.

"Stand up!" one of them ordered.

We struggled to our feet. I counted only five soldiers inside the cell with us. As they shoved us out of the cell, a bit of hope shot through me. Perhaps we were being transported elsewhere.

We were forced along the corridor and up a staircase to the roof, which was covered with cells full of prisoners. Though we welcomed the fresh air, we shivered uncontrollably as the chill struck our naked bodies.

"Walk," the leader ordered. "This is your exercise time." Harold and I started walking the roof, shuffling past the cells. The other prisoners jeered at us, calling out, "Hey, Gringo!" as they exposed their genitals and announced how they planned to sexually violate us. It seemed senseless to answer back, since we needed every bit of our energy for the next battle with the soldiers. Besides, we had to keep moving just to keep from freezing.

We walked for hours before the guards finally prodded us back down to our cell. For the rest of the night I couldn't stop shivering.

More beatings followed. Sometimes the soldiers cuffed us to the cell bars while pummeling us with billy clubs. At other times they simply used their fists and feet. With every beating, the message was reiterated: "Eventually you'll talk to the DEA; you might as well make it easy on yourself and talk now."

Sometimes they reminded us that T.C. and Verne had already squealed. "Your associates told us everything. We know you were taking drugs from Colombia to the United States." And they repeatedly asked me, "Who is this man, Manuel Garces?"

As Harold and I refused to talk, one day bled into another. My nerves frayed. *When will the soldiers come next? What new atrocity will they subject us to? How can I endure?*

One of the guards who checked on us from time to time was friendlier than the others and didn't get involved in any of the tortures. Occasionally, he stopped to talk to Harold and me. He came by one day after a particularly brutal beating.

"Are you okay?" he asked quietly.

I dragged myself over to the bars and growled, "I want you to go tell Noriega that unless he kills me, I'm going to rape his wife and children, then I'm going to kill him and his whole family. I'll destroy his whole exis tence! He knows I have the power, so he better do away with us while he has the chance."

The guard shook his head. "You're crazy!" he whispered hoarsely. "I'm not going to say that to Colonel Noriega. They'll kill you for certain."

That's exactly what I want, I thought. But the guard needed some incentive. "Bring me some paper," I told him

He brought a scrap of paper, and I wrote a note to my brother instructing him to give the guard $10,000. I added that this guard had helped me and had not participated in my torture. I signed the scrap of paper, then handed it through the bars. "Now, go tell Noriega what I said."

The following day, someone swaggered to our cell and stood outside the door. From where Harold and I were lying on the concrete, I looked up. Even with my eyes swollen and my vision impaired, I recognized Noriega. I almost laughed in his pockmarked, cratered face, as I instantly realized why people had nicknamed him Pineapple Face. Nevertheless, in his military uniform he cut an imposing figure, emitting an aura that said he owned everything and could do as he pleased.

He looked directly at me. "Are you the man who threatened my life? Are you the man who is going to rape my children and my wife?"

Instinctively I knew this was our last chance. It was an all-or-nothing gamble. In a calm but forceful manner I hurled obscenities back at Noriega.

The colonel looked surprised at my audacity. Here was a naked, beaten prisoner hurling abuse at the most powerful man in the country. His eyes seared into me as he came closer, squatting right next to me. "Just calm down," he said quietly. "Don't blame me; blame those two workers of yours."

I knew he meant Verne and T.C., but I said nothing.

"By the way," Noriega continued sardonically, "you paid the wrong man."

I took this as a sign of hope. I thought, *Maybe we can negotiate.* My mind raced a thousand miles an hour, trying to devise a plan.

I looked at him icily. "I'm not going to speak to the DEA, so you might as well kill me."

Noriega shrugged his shoulders. "I don't care if you talk or not. This is not our case. But we get money from the DEA, and we have to do certain things for them in return."

"I have money," I responded coolly. "And I have the power to pay you whatever you want, no strings attached, if you will just give the order to release us."

For a long moment, Noriega stared at me. Then ever so slowly, a smile creased his pineapple face. "Your attorney will come and visit you," he said simply.

With that, he whirled on his heel and strode out.

A day or so later, several soldiers came to our cell. "You have a visitor," one of them announced matter-of-factly, as though it was an everyday occurrence.

Harold and I stumbled to the cell door, but the soldiers pushed Harold back. "No, only him," the leader said, nodding at me.

I was taken to a nearby open area with a makeshift shower. "Wash," the leader ordered.

He didn't have to tell me twice. The water was freezing, but I relished every drop pouring over me. I slowly scraped the blood and filth from my body.

"Come on," the guards were already shouting. "Get out. It's time to talk to your attorney."

They took me to an office where I saw the same lawyer who was to have facilitated our release after I talked with Miranda, the attorney general. At first I wanted to choke the man for not securing our freedom. Then I realized it wasn't his fault.

The attorney informed me that someone had found out about the money being paid to obtain our release, which amounted to attempted bribery of the attorney general of Panama. He also explained that my brother, J.C., had been put in jail, but had now been released and ordered to leave the country.

"He's waiting outside to see you before he must go," the attorney added.

"My brother?" I shook with emotion. "He's here?" Tears filled my eyes.

An avalanche of emotions rushed over me when the attorney escorted my brother into the room. Suddenly I felt alive again. J.C. and I ran to each other and embraced. Tears flowed freely down our faces.

Finally he released me, stepped back, and cried out, "Look at you, Jorge! Have they hurt you? You're all bruised up. Did they beat you?"

"No," I said, "those marks are from the cell where I've been sleeping on the floor. They haven't touched me."

I struggled to maintain my composure as we talked of how Mom and Dad were doing. It took every bit of my remaining willpower to keep from breaking down and crying. I wanted J.C. to go back home and tell them, "Jorge is fine; he's lost some weight, but he's okay." I thought, *They must never know what the torturers did to me.*

With my brother there, the attorney informed me that Noriega was willing to let Harold and me go, but it would cost another $250,000.

I looked at J.C.

"Don't worry, Jorge," he said. "I've already informed the right people. You'll be out of here shortly."

"Make sure that they send us to Costa Rica," I said.

"Yes," J.C. replied. "You don't want to go back to Miami. Monti Cohen said he needs time to figure out what's going on. Some grand juries have been convened, but he doesn't know whether there have been any indictments concerning you." At the moment I was unconcerned about any legal proceedings I might be facing in Miami. All that mattered was the chance to leave Panama alive.

J.C. had purchased a big hamburger for me. I was grateful, but as soon as I tried to eat, I began to throw up.

Then he and I talked for another twenty minutes. "Wait for me in Costa Rica," I told him. "Everything's going to be fine."

J.C. and I embraced and kissed, then the guard returned me to my cell.

Harold was ecstatic when he heard the news. We were going to be free! He patted me on the back and said, "I told you so!"

Within hours of learning we were to be released, Harold and I began planning our next cocaine run. We wanted to make up for the money and cocaine we had lost in Panama.

My desire to smuggle drugs into the U.S. was now driven by something even more powerful than greed: the desire to get even. An uncontrollable desire for vengeance would soon drive me to passionate heights and horrendous depths.

From now on, my attitude toward the government was, "You know who I am, you know what I do; now catch me if you can."

Harold and I talked all through the night. Occasionally, I'd glance over at him and just shake my head, amazed at his stamina. He was filthy and his body reeked with a horrible stench, but his spirit was that of a warrior. He had the heart of a giant.

Another day passed. Then the guards came for us and ordered, "Go take a shower." On the way to the shower, I passed the guard who had conveyed my message to Noriega. "Don't worry," I whispered. "You'll get your money—I assure you."

After our cold but welcome showers, the guards gave us back the clothing we had worn the day our plane crashed. They returned my glasses and shoes, which they had taken from us when we were first taken to the Modelo, but they kept my jewelry, including a diamond ring and an expensive, blue-dialed Rolex Submariner watch, a birthday gift from Manny Garces. When I asked the guards about them, the officer in charge answered brusquely, "We have no jewelry."

The guards hustled Harold and me into the backseat of a car. We weren't handcuffed, but a guard sat between us and two more guards sat in the front. The car roared away from the Modelo, and with every mile closer to the airport I could smell freedom in the air.

When the guards dropped us off at the terminal, they told us to get out of the country—an order we were only too happy to comply with. Harold and I walked to the gate from which our flight to Costa Rica was to depart in about two hours.

We sat down and were just starting to relax when a platoon of soldiers streamed onto the concourse. They surrounded us, and one of them looked at me.

"Jorge Valdés?"

"Yes?"

"Harold Rosenthal?"

Harold nodded.

"Come with us, your flight is ready," the officer said sternly.

I thought perhaps the airline had changed gates and Noriega's people were just making certain we left the country. But as we approached the new gate, I realized they were putting us on a flight to Miami.

I told the officers, "We aren't going to Miami; we're going to Costa Rica."

One of them put a gun behind my back and said, "Shut up."

The soldiers crowded around us and pushed us through the doorway and inside the aircraft. They literally threw Harold and me into the plane like two sacks of potatoes.

The passengers on board stared at us in horror, but nobody dared lift a finger against the military police. The passengers quickly went back to their magazines and their conversations. Eventually Harold and I were seated, and the flight took off to America.

Again the fear of the unknown crept in, but I wasn't about to let it control me. I leaned back and closed my eyes. *The worst is over,* I told myself. I had not been caught running drugs in America, so U.S. authorities had nothing against me. Besides, even if they tried pressing charges in Miami, my people owned the legal arena in that city. We had prosecutors and judges on our dole, as well as an array of city, state, and federal officials. *There's no way I'll ever be convicted of even a parking violation in Miami.*

When the plane landed, we remained on the runway for a long while before the pilots pulled the aircraft up to the gate. Soon several DEA agents appeared in the plane's doorway and rushed to where Harold and I were sitting.

The man in front announced, "I'm Agent Adam Degaglia, U.S. Drug Enforcement Administration. You're under arrest. You have been charged with conspiracy to bring narcotics into the United States." The agent looked down at me and said quietly, "Welcome to the big leagues, son."

As the officers led us from the plane, I saw a legion of reporters, police, and other security officers waiting. I thought, *Why all that fuss just for us?*

We were led to a police transport, then driven to a DEA office near the Miami airport. On the way, Agent Degaglia informed me that the DEA had incriminating videotapes clearly showing me doing cocaine deals in Miami's Mutiny Hotel, where Sal and I kept several rented rooms for meetings and for out-of-town clients. I was confident he was bluffing.

Harold and I were herded into an interrogation room and asked to make a statement.

"No," I said. "I want to speak to my attorney."

"Fine," Agent Degaglia replied. "You're to be taken to Dade County Jail. When you get there, you can make a phone call to your attorney."

He then spoke in an almost fatherly voice, "You know, young man, I've heard you're a smart guy. And when I look at you, I think of my own son who's about your age." He shook his head sadly, then continued, "I want to give you something to think about."

I stared back at him blankly, unwilling to betray any feelings.

"Think about these odds, Jorge. We can afford to let you get away with your smuggling a million times. You can bring in a million loads, and we lose nothing." He paused, looking me directly in the eyes. "But you can't afford to get caught once."

My eyes focused on the floor, and my heart stung at his words. I had no answer for him.

Nineteen

Surprises in Court

After the DEA agents fingerprinted Harold and me and took our mug shots, we were taken to Miami's overcrowded Dade County Jail to await arraignment. All the bunks and cots were taken, so Harold and I would again be sleeping on the floor.

That evening we had our first meal back in the U.S., a bland prison sandwich that tasted to me like filet mignon.

Later that night, Monti Cohen came to see us. After we embraced and chatted briefly, Monti informed me in a businesslike manner that he couldn't represent me in this case; he had a conflict of interest due to representing our pilot-turned-informant T.C. Michaels in two other cases, one in the past and one pending. In light of this, I agreed to Monti's suggestion that I allow his partner, Art Tifford, to represent me.

We were scheduled to appear in court the following day, and Monti predicted that my bail would be set at about $200,000. "I don't think we have anything to worry about," he added, "since the government doesn't have an indictment against you." Monti added that an indictment had been issued against my partner, Sal Magluta, in another drug case.

"Do they have anything on me?" I asked.

"Well, they haven't indicted you," Monti replied, "but they do have you in a couple of their wiretaps."

"But no indictments, right?"

"No, none."

I wasn't too concerned about Sal's plight. With his connections, he could easily raise the bail bond to get out of jail. Besides, in the Florida legal system we could pay off whomever we needed to.

I was just as confident about my own case; I naively reminded myself that the government hadn't caught me doing anything illegal in the United States.

As Monti and I talked longer, he filled in the blanks on how the DEA had snared us so quickly in Panama. It never occurred to me to ask Monti how he'd gathered so much information so quickly. Instead, I listened with rapt attention as he explained how a wide-ranging DEA investigation, centering on Harold Rosenthal and his plane, had been launched a number of weeks before our crash in Panama. Apparently the plane had been tracked as we traveled to South America for our Bolivian run and had quickly been identified after the crash in Panama. The DEA suspected that the plane was headed back to the United States loaded with drugs.

As I listened to Monti review the background of our arrest, it seemed obvious that the forces working against us—the police, soldiers, and Noriega in Panama, as well as the U.S. DEA—were all on one payroll from the beginning.

I hugged Monti as he prepared to leave. "I'll see you in court tomorrow," he said.

The next morning—May 10, 1979—federal marshals handcuffed Harold and me, then marched us toward the courtroom. As they ushered us down the corridor, I thought, *We'll be out of here in a matter of hours.*

"Harold, what do you want for dinner tonight?" I asked lightheartedly. We hadn't had a full meal since our party in Bogota several weeks earlier. I was dying to have some Cuban food, and I invited Harold to my mom's house that night for a feast.

Stepping inside the courtroom, I saw my parents sitting on a bench. Next to Mom was Luchy—my ex-wife and mistress—and next to her was my wife, Christine. I couldn't believe it.

"All rise," I heard the bailiff say, as Magistrate Herbert Shapiro entered the room. I leaned over and whispered to my attorney, Art Tifford, "Tell my family you'll take me home in a few hours. Don't let me go out now; I don't want to have to decide which woman I leave with." The last thing I wanted was to get Christine angry with me. As my wife she couldn't be forced to testify against me, but if she became upset enough over Luchy, she might do so anyway, though she had little idea of my drug dealings.

Art laughed and promised to drive me home once the court proceedings concluded.

After making certain Harold and I understood the charges against us—conspiracy to smuggle cocaine into the United States—Judge Shapiro moved directly into a bond hearing to determine if we could get out on bail and, if so, at what price.

At this point I learned that Monti Cohen had failed to reveal a key piece of information when he first recommended our working with Harold Rosenthal. Peter Koste, the federal prosecutor, announced to the judge, "I wish to advise the court that there is a two-bench warrant against Mr. Rosenthal for bond-jumping in the middle district of Georgia, the Macon division."

I looked in amazement at Harold, who allowed the glint of a smile as he shrugged slightly.

Monti Cohen, meanwhile, was nowhere in sight.

Koste continued by requesting a one-million-dollar bond on Harold; then he added, "Mr. Valdés is a five-million-dollar recommended surety bond."

Five million dollars! I could hardly believe my ears. How could they set a $1 million bond on Harold, a fugitive facing charges in another state as a bond-jumper, and sock $5 million on me, a twenty-three-year-old with no criminal record or previous charges?

I turned to see my mother dabbing tears from her eyes. I tried my best to give the impression I was unconcerned about the bail, but my heart was pounding.

I was sworn in as a witness and the interrogations began, the first of my hundreds of hours of testimony in court. Magistrate Shapiro did much of the initial questioning, trying to establish my income. Then Peter Koste grilled me on the same information. Although he was only doing his job, I felt disdain for his arrogant attitude and all that he represented. *I can buy your kind any day of the week,* I thought, as I glowered at him. I answered curtly, giving up a bare minimum of information. This was war, and I wasn't about to give the enemy any more ammunition than they already had.

The proceedings focused mainly on my financial assets, my ability to support myself outside the country, and the resulting risk of my fleeing the country if I were released on bail. Because of the intricate system I had developed to launder money, my salary from my banana-shipping company was listed at only $50,000 and my net worth at about $150,000—which was less than I spent on champagne in a given year.

The magistrate and the prosecutor weren't buying our contention that I was simply a frugal businessman. They wanted to know all about my travels outside the country, the people I met with, my customers in the banana-shipping business, and all sorts of details as they tried to show I had other assets on which I could comfortably survive in Europe or South America.

The lawyers spent a considerable amount of time pegging a value to the cocaine found in our crashed plane, eventually arriving at a figure of $5.8 million for the retail market value in Miami. The discussion also turned to the money paid to the Panamanian authorities for our attempted release. Art Tifford was masterful in derailing the government's efforts to pin me down, and he worked diligently to get my bail reduced so I could go home. I liked Art; he was bright and a straight shooter, a no-nonsense sort of lawyer, a former marine and a former U.S. attorney. I felt I was in good hands.

The court battle raged back and forth throughout the day—and this was only the bail hearing! At first I enjoyed verbally sparring with the judge and prosecutor, matching wits with them point for point. But after a while the questions became repetitive and tedious.

Finally Judge Shapiro announced, "The court has determined that the defendant has considerable assets outside the United States, has access to such assets, and would be able to flee the country and exist outside the United States . . . . Unless this court sets a substantial bond, this court has no assurance that this man is going to appear at all stages of these proceedings. Accordingly, the court therefore sets bond at two million dollars."

Art Tifford immediately announced that we would appeal; the judge set another court date for May 18, 1979.

Although $2 million was far better than $5 million, it was still a huge amount of money. I could easily raise it, but that wasn't the point. Why should I? How could I justify coughing up that much to the government when the likelihood of my being convicted on the available evidence was highly debatable? After all, the chief evidence was gone; Noriega had already sold the cocaine. Besides, I knew that if I paid the $2 million, the government would seek relentlessly to determine where it came from.

I was bewildered, angry, and discouraged as the marshals began escorting me back to jail. I tried putting on a tranquil face as I walked past my parents, yet I couldn't help noticing the tears streaming down my mother's face. *How many bullets have I shot into her heart?* Overwhelmed by emotion, I quickly looked away. The prosecution that day had made a point of emphasizing the millions of lives destroyed because of my purported drug activities, but as I walked out of that courtroom, the person whose pain I felt most was my mom's.

Harold and I were taken by bus to the Miami Correctional Center (MCC). Inside we went through the routine receiving procedures, filling out forms, enduring a body search and a brief medical exam, and getting our prison clothes. Harold and I were housed in the same cell, with two beds, a toilet, a sink, and a desk—almost like a college dorm room. The air-conditioned prison featured a large carpeted common area, a television room, and recreation and exercise facilities. Harold and I quickly learned the prison routine, the inmates' code of ethics, and the illegal but flourishing system of acquiring better food, pressed clothing, and even cleaner bedsheets.

I struck up a friendship with an inmate named Celestino, who became my eyes, ears, and hands within the prison. Whatever I wanted or needed, Celestino made it happen.

Because of my status as a drug lord, I soon had a squadron of inmates wanting to be around me. Some hoped to get money, some wanted drugs, and others were simply enamored by my reputation and power. Regardless of their motives, they took care of me, so I took care of them financially.

My partners from the outside managed to smuggle me $1,000 plus a bag of cocaine to use in bartering. Cocaine was the premium currency among inmates, possessing more purchasing power than cash. I gave the coke and the cash to Celestino to stash for me, and we doled it out to our "workers" as needed.

One day I received a visit from a contact linked to the legal system, who casually mentioned that he'd heard the judge presiding over my case could perhaps be "reached," meaning he might be open to a bribe through another lawyer who could "exert some influence." The lawyer's price was $30,000.

"Let's see what can be done," I responded.

We mapped out a best-case scenario to pass along to our go-between lawyer—a $500,000 surety bail backed up by my ranch and my parents' home. If the judge set the bail at this figure, I would assume that the judge had been reached and that I hadn't been scammed.

"If this works out," I promised the contact, "I'll pay you $50,000."

At the next hearing on May 18, Art seemed incredibly confident, and Judge Shapiro seemed more relaxed and less overbearing. At the beginning of the day's proceedings, Peter Koste threw us a curve by insisting that my bail be increased from $2 million to $5 million. He and Art Tifford squared off again as all the details of the case were reviewed. Art spoke convincingly and articulately; he knew the law and could quote relevant cases from memory.

At one point Magistrate Shapiro interrupted their debate to mention the court's concern about all the "money floating around" in the evidence of my business dealings, money that could help me leave America to escape extradition.

Judge Shapiro and Art Tifford continued their verbal tussle. When the judge turned to Peter Koste and asked if he had anything further to say, the prosecutor answered succinctly, "It is the government's opinion that if the court sets Mr. Valdés's bail at $2 million, he will flee. If the court sets bail at $5 million, he will flee."

At that, the prosecutor and the judge engaged in more prolonged discussion. "It's a bad risk, your honor," Koste concluded. "He's facing fifteen years. He's got every reason to flee, and he has the money to do so."

The judge seemed anxious to return to the discussion of my assets and those of my parents and my brother that might be used as collateral for bail. At that point I felt certain the judge was in the bag.

Art turned to me. "Mr. Valdés, if the court were to reduce the financial portion of your bail, do you promise to abide by each and every order of the court?"

I looked straight at the judge. "Yes, I would, Your Honor."

To make our closing points, Tifford called to the stand William Bailey, an elderly attorney and a close friend of Judge Shapiro. Bailey pointed out that the crime of which I was accused was not a capital offense and emphasized that the purpose of bail was to guarantee my appearance in court, not to set it so high that it would keep me in prison until my trial.

I felt sure we had won the day.

Bailey continued, "One other criteria that the court is to use in setting the bail is the weight of the evidence against him . . . . The court has stated that the evidence is not that great. They are not going to have an easy time convicting this man. Mr. Valdés sat and listened to that as well as I did. He is not going to muff his chances by running."

I'm walking out of here today, I thought.

Finally Judge Shapiro made his decision. "The court has taken into consideration the evidence against the accused, the accused's family, his employment, his background, and his financial resources . . . . The court is going to reduce the bond to five hundred thousand dollars . . . ."

I will always wonder whether my contact actually approached the judge—or whether he had simply scammed me. Regardless, Koste wasn't content to let the judge's decision stand without a fight. "The government would ask Your Honor to stay the effect of the reduction until twelve noon, Tuesday," he said. "The government intends to appeal this matter."

Judge Shapiro looked irritated but replied calmly, "Let the government appeal it today."

"Judge, it is twenty till three, on Friday," Koste protested.

"Let us stay it until five o'clock," Judge Shapiro answered.

Koste appeared exasperated. "Your Honor, there is not enough time . . . . I would ask that Your Honor stay the matter until Monday at least to give the government an opportunity to appeal." He bandied about the issue with my lawyer and the judge, but it was clear that Shapiro was bent on releasing me.

"Your Honor denies my request?" Koste asked cynically.

"I will grant it till five o'clock this afternoon," Shapiro answered. He suggested other judges who might be able to immediately hear the government's appeal.

It had been a long, contentious court session, and everyone seemed a bit edgy—everybody but me, that is. Victory rushed through me like a lightning bolt.

As I again walked past my family on my way out of the courtroom, I said, "Mom, make me a good dinner. I'm coming home."

TWENTY

"MENACE TO THE COMMUNITY"

The moment I walked back in the courtroom late that afternoon, I knew the game had changed. Koste had arranged for a district court judge, Sidney Aronovits, to examine the case, and we trudged again through the same motions and material.

After a brief recess to evaluate the case, Judge Aronovits returned to render his ruling. With phrase after phrase of his pronouncement, my heart began to sink: "The court feels that there does exist a likelihood of flight on the part of the defendant . . . . The street value of the cocaine involved can reach as much as forty million dollars . . . . One thing I am absolutely certain of is that I feel the magistrate has set the bond too low . . . . This court hereby orders that the bond be set in the sum of two million dollars . . . . The defendant is remanded to the custody of the United States Marshal."

I'm going back to jail!

I couldn't put all the pieces together. Why was the government so insistent on keeping me in jail? What had they heard about me?

I was taken back to MCC to await my next court appearance. I still had absolute confidence that I'd be getting out soon, that I'd be back to business as usual, only better.

Art Tifford informed me that we would appeal again. Furthermore, he had filed for a speedy trial rule. The grand jury had not returned an indictment in my case; if it didn't formally charge me within ninety days of my being brought from Panama to Miami, the authorities would have to set me free.

The weeks went by. Although I was in prison, I continued to run my cocaine operations. Through partners who visited me I sent orders concerning what needed to be done to keep my contacts supplied in California. All in all my stay at MCC wasn't that bad. I was still making a lot of money, while spending far less than usual. And I was still acting the big shot. In prison I established relationships with some powerful individuals, contacts that I knew could come in handy once we were released.

Celestino made sure I had tailored, neatly pressed prison clothes, plus plenty of food. My "people" were paying the prison guards to bring in for us everything from barbecued ribs and pizza to lobster and wine.

I paid attorneys to visit me every day, never the same one two days in a row, and through them I sent messages to people I needed to contact on the outside. Many of these attorneys knew next to nothing about my case; all they knew was that they were being well paid to visit me in prison.

In July 1979 I was scheduled to appear in court. Certain I would at last be going home, I had instructed my brother to buy me new clothes from Miami's finest clothing store, and I went to court that day in a sharp-looking suit, ready to resume business.

Monti Cohen continued to be conspicuously absent from all my court proceedings, and I couldn't understand why he hadn't come to visit me in prison. But I passed it off—he was busy, perhaps, or he didn't want to get too close to my case because of his having recommended Harold and the pilots to me. Still, it wasn't like Monti to be out of touch.

We gathered in the courtroom presided over by a Judge Palermo. Right away the judge asked the government prosecutors, "Has the grand jury returned an indictment?"

The prosecutor replied dejectedly, "No, Your Honor, no indictment has been returned."

Judge Palermo scowled as he announced, "I dismiss the complaint. Mr. Valdés, you are a free man."

My rush of happiness was quickly checked. As I was about to leave, another U.S. marshal rushed up to me and said, "We have just received a fax from Macon, Georgia. Mr. Valdés, you are under arrest on an indictment from the middle district of Georgia."

Macon, Georgia! I had never been there in my life, not even on my way to somewhere else. *What kind of cruel joke is this?*

Art Tifford rushed to my side. "Art, what's going on?" I asked. He promised to find out.

Apparently the government prosecutors had shopped my case to various grand juries, and the only one that would indict me at this time was in Macon. Their indictment was based upon my relationship with Harold Rosenthal and my alleged involvement with him in his previous case in that court. It was highly unlikely that a charge against me could be proven, especially since none of my business dealings took place anywhere near Macon. Nevertheless, it was the best case the government could muster against me.

I remained hopeful of getting a reasonable bond in Georgia that would set me free until the time of my trial.

My cell at Bibb County Jail in Macon consisted of four metal walls with a metal sink and a toilet in the corner. A large metal plate covered with a thin, nylon pad served for a bed. The only clothing I was permitted to keep was my underwear, which was just as well, since my body was soaked with sweat in the sweltering summer heat of Georgia. The jail wasn't air-conditioned.

I soon befriended a guard named Mike, who tried to talk with me about Jesus. I listened patiently, not because I was interested but because I enjoyed his company. Mike seemed to regard me differently from many of the other authorities around me. One day he explained why some of the guards refused to pay attention when I called to them. They were afraid to come near, Mike said, because they'd heard I was a friend of Castro and that one day he would send a goon squad to bust me out of jail.

I laughed so hard I almost cried. The Georgians couldn't imagine how far I was from being friends with Fidel.

Day after day Mike visited me, and inevitably our conversations gravitated toward spiritual things. He spoke as if he and Jesus were really friends, and his faith seemed the most important thing in the world to him. I told him of the pain I had gone through as a child, how I had felt so abandoned that I became convinced God didn't exist. "If good and evil powers are real," I told my friend, "the devil is the one to be allied with because he's the only one who's ever done anything about my welfare."

I told him how I felt about the church not helping anyone, how we in the drug culture had built houses for people in the slums and given vast sums of money to orphanages and for radio stations in the jungles.

"If there is good and evil," I concluded, "evil rules."

Mike didn't attempt to argue with me; he just continued doing everything he could to make my stay in Macon as comfortable as possible.

My preliminary appearance in Macon was before Judge Wilber D. Owens, a tough but fair man who had a reputation for being a stickler for the law. After reviewing my case, Judge Owens issued a benchmark ruling that changed the course of drug trials in the United States. He denied me bail on the basis that my alleged involvement in drug dealing made me a "menace to the community"—with the "community" being the entire United States. Previously, drug trafficking had not been generally viewed as a violent crime, but now anyone indicted on a major drug offense would find it extremely difficult to receive bail.

Because of the court's delay in holding my trial, my attorneys petitioned to allow my return to MCC until the trial. Since my lawyers and family members were in Miami, the judge granted our request.

In the weeks before my transfer, I was kept in solitary confinement. Life in the Bibb County Jail seemed only a few cuts above that in the Panamanian prison, minus the tortures. I refused to allow my family to visit me in Macon, not wanting them to see me in that environment. I used the excuse that it was too far for them to travel and tried to reassure them that I'd be home soon anyway.

I asked Art Tifford to hire a local attorney simply to visit me every day, getting me out of that dark, sweltering cell for a few hours into a conference room with light and air-conditioning. The lawyer we hired was Brayton Dasher, who often brought me books and sandwiches. We'd talk and tell stories for hours at a time.

To celebrate my return when I was finally transferred back to MCC, my inmate friends there wanted to throw a party—not exactly the easiest thing to pull off in prison. Nevertheless, my associates gave the guards $400 to bring in a bottle of champagne and some lobster.

I focused my attention on getting the best legal defense team I could hire—and I could afford to hire anyone. Now that I had been formally indicted in Macon, Art Tifford could no longer serve as my attorney. He had a professional conflict of interest because of his involvement with Monti in representing Harold Rosenthal and T.C. Michaels in a previous Macon case. Art passed along Monti Cohen's suggestion for my next attorney: Marty Weinberg of Boston. He had graduated from Harvard Law School at the top of his class and was considered one of the best—and most expensive—lawyers in the country.

After meeting Marty, I hired him on the spot. Eventually he represented Sal Magluta as well, and Sal and I enjoyed teasing Marty about his toupee. "As much as we're paying you," we told him, "surely you could afford a nicer wig." But beneath Marty's fake hair was the brain of a brilliant lawyer. He could recite the law backward and forward.

Art Tifford also advised me to hire a respected attorney, someone the jury of a small southern town would be more likely to identify with than a Harvard-trained drug lawyer from Boston. He recommended Shelby Highsmith, a former state judge from Miami. A polite Southern gentleman in his early fifties, Shelby was shrewd, intelligent, and smooth—perfect for the Macon jury.

There was only one problem, Art told me: If Shelby knew I was actually involved in narcotics, he would not represent me. When Shelby came to meet me in prison, he made it clear that he never represented any drug criminals. "I believe in the legal system," he added. "I have worked in it all my life, and I want justice to prevail."

We talked for several hours, and I convinced Shelby that I hadn't committed the offense with which I had been charged—I told him I'd been involved in military arms trafficking. Shelby decided to take my case and work alongside Marty Weinberg.

Not long after I returned to MCC, I was surprised to discover that Oscar Nuñez, the military officer who had been our cocaine source in Bolivia, was also incarcerated there. I could hardly believe he had been arrested. More disturbing, however, was what Oscar told me. He said the DEA had lied to him, telling him I had already testified against him.

One day I learned—through my system of paid informants among the guards—that Oscar had just met with a DEA agent for nearly three hours. *Now what could Oscar be telling them?*

Moreover, Oscar's cellmate let me know that Oscar blamed me for his being in jail, claiming that I had testified against him.

I put together a quick and easy plan to find out more.

Oscar's cellmate was a violent guy named Jack, a reputed Mafia hit man. I instructed Jack to hide in the bathroom while I called in Oscar to talk.

When he came into the bathroom, I said, "Oscar, who have you been to see?"

"Oh, my lawyer," he replied nonchalantly.

"There are rumors," I continued, "that you've said I testified against you."

"No, Jorge, that's a lie."

Suddenly Jack jumped out from the stall where he'd been hiding. He slugged Oscar in the face, and the Bolivian slumped to the floor, out cold. I could easily have paid Jack $5,000 to kill Oscar—but something held me back.

When he came to, I confronted him again. "You are a liar!" I said. "Your lawyer didn't come to see you; it was a DEA agent."

Flustered, Oscar blurted out, "I thought my lawyer was coming, but when I got there, this man said my lawyer sent him. I didn't know who he was, so I didn't speak to him."

I shot back, "You were there for two and a half hours!"

Oscar started to cry. He knew he was trapped. Despite my fury, I suddenly felt pity for this military officer crying like a baby.

"From now on, Oscar, you'll go with the lawyer I tell you to."

The next time I saw Shelby Highsmith, I asked him to recommend an attorney for Oscar. Shelby arranged a meeting with Alan Ross, a young Miami lawyer just beginning to make a name for himself.

Upon meeting Alan, I was surprised to see a man in his late twenties, only a few years older than I was. Although somewhat flamboyant, Alan had a keen mind. I could sense that he was "hungry" and a fighter. He agreed to take Oscar's case.

Together with Alan, I soon discovered more about Oscar's situation. He had been caught in Panama only two months after our plane crash. He had foolishly taken a flight there while attempting to set up a lucrative deal smuggling videocassette recorders. Oscar should have known better; he knew about my arrest in Panama. Like so many others, he couldn't pass by another chance to make big money.

Oscar was taken to the office of Lieutenant Jorge Latinez—the dreaded Lino. The cruel lieutenant subjected him to a grueling interrogation concerning his knowledge of me and the cocaine found on the plane. Oscar was repeatedly punched in the stomach, then stripped and threatened by Lino while DEA Agent Sedillo looked on. Oscar, too, was beaten and abused by Lino's infamous broomstick, after which the poor man confessed.

He remained in solitary confinement, where he was made to sleep on the floor and fed only bread and water. Eventually he was taken to Florida, where he was immediately arrested and charged in a companion case to mine.

When Alan Ross told me what had happened to Oscar, I couldn't remain angry with the Bolivian for having squealed on me. I forgave Oscar, but I made sure that from now on I was in control of his case.

■   ■   ■

My trial was delayed yet again in October. That was too much for Shelby. He had filed numerous motions complaining that I was the only person—other than Harold Rosenthal, against whom there had been preexisting charges—who had been indicted in this case and who was still in prison; everyone else had made bail. One day Shelby called me and said he had struck a deal with the judge permitting me to be out on bail if we would consent to a further delay in the trial. I agreed immediately, and my family went to work to secure the $500,000 bail with their property and mortgages.

Finally, on Thanksgiving morning, 1979, I walked outside MCC into the fresh air and my family's waiting arms. After one of the best Thanksgiving meals I'd ever eaten at my parents' house, I went to a hotel suite with Sal, his partner Willie Falcon, and others. We partied all night long.

Art Tifford brought me the new Mercedes convertible that I'd intended to pick up in Europe before the plane crash derailed my plans. The car was more gorgeous than I expected.

Finally, I was back in control of my life.

Later that week I met with Monti Cohen, the first I had seen him since arriving in Miami after the tortures of Panama. Naively, I told Monti I thought the government was up to something and was trying to set me up. Monti couldn't have agreed more, and we discussed my need for a bodyguard. Monti said he knew the ideal person.

William "Bubba" Leary was a former U.S. marshal who had served as a bodyguard for the shah of Iran. Bubba was six foot five, over two hundred pounds, and a great shot. I paid him $1,000 a week to be around me at all times. The only problem with Bubba was that he was too big to fit in my Mercedes.

While I was awaiting trial, my cocaine business perked along smoothly. I sold my jet because I felt certain the government could easily track its travels. Instead of shipping larger loads of cocaine to California by jet, we packed smaller loads of about fifteen to twenty kilos inside a Lincoln Continental driven by one of my trusted workers.

Assuming that the government would be tailing me, I kept my distance and let Sal and others become more directly involved with the coke distri bu tion. I spent a lot of time with my father and mother, who seemed to have aged years during the few months I had been in prison. Clearly, my drug activities had taken more of a toll on them than I had realized.

TWENTY-ONE

"I AM WHAT I AM"

My tremendous legal team put together our strategy for the trial, now scheduled to begin early in January 1980. We would not argue that I was innocent of trafficking drugs. Without admitting anything, we would contend that *if* I had been involved in drug trafficking, I certainly had never committed an offense in Macon. Therefore the court in Macon, Georgia, had no jurisdiction over me.

I felt confident I would walk away from the charges unscathed.

Shelby Highsmith and I forged a strong relationship as we worked together, and I began to confide in him. I let him know that many judges and other government officials were on our payroll—without directly telling Shelby *why* they were. Shelby, the epitome of a man above reproach, was devastated to think public servants could be so easily corrupted. He and his wife, Mary Jane, were devout Christians, and Mary Jane had often written to me in prison, filling her letters and cards with encouragement to stand strong and have faith.

I awaited the trial by settling into the life of a cartel godfather in Miami. Upon my release from prison I had notified Christine that I needed some time away from her to think things over. In reality, she knew our relationship was finished as well as I did, but I didn't want to take any definite action until the trial had concluded.

In the meantime, I renewed my relationship with Luchy. She and I partied like there was no tomorrow, often staying up all night drinking and watching porno films. My influence on her was horrendous. She was a young girl who knew no better, and she was in love with me. I'd left her once, so now she was willing to do whatever it took to keep me—and I continually raised the ante. Luchy's devotion, however, did not engender faithfulness on my part. Every chance I had, I cheated on her.

As usual, I spent Christmas with Mom and Dad, this time at the ranch. With the impending trial, our celebration was subdued but nevertheless heartwarming. It was the calm before the storm.

Shortly before the trial, my attorneys informed me the government was willing to make a deal: If I pleaded guilty, they would give me two years in prison plus probation. Harold, Oscar, and I were being tried together, and the government's case apparently had been weakened when two of the key witnesses against Harold had been caught smuggling cocaine in Colombia. The DEA paid $60,000 to get the dummies out of South America, but their credibility as witnesses was seriously tainted. Although the judge was sure to disallow this information in our case, my lawyers felt confident that it might come in handy if we needed to appeal.

I listened carefully as the lawyers explained the deal, then looked resolutely at Marty. "Don't you ever again offer me any deals with the government," I said. "I don't deal with the enemy. This is war, and I am ready to fight. If we beat them, we beat them; but if they beat me, they beat me."

I talked further with Shelby about it. "Son," Shelby responded, "there's no way I can tell you what to do. I've seen these cases go both ways. You always have the chance of losing."

"I want to take my chances," I told Shelby. "I've fought all my life, and this is just one more obstacle."

Shortly after New Year's, I returned to Macon to stand trial. To prevent the DEA from eavesdropping on my conversations, I rented the whole top floor of the Macon Hilton, including a large suite where I could meet with my lawyers, plus rooms for all the lawyers, their assistants, and our family and friends. Luchy came with Jorgito, and Mom was there as well, but the ordeal of my being on trial for drug smuggling was more than my dear father could take. My brother, J.C., stayed home in Florida to help steady him.

I unpacked an entire wardrobe of expensive new suits that I planned to wear to trial. Luchy, too, had brought along an exquisite array of designer dresses, all slinky and exotic. When Alan Ross saw our clothing, he cringed. "Jorge, you really shouldn't dress like that in front of the jurors. You're playing right into their images of what a big-time drug lord might look like."

"Alan, let me tell you something," I said. "I am Jorge Valdés. I am what I am, and those that don't like it—too bad for them."

Luchy and I arrived at the courthouse in a Lincoln Continental. When we stepped out of the car, dressed as though we'd come straight from a cover shoot for *GQ* magazine and surrounded by my bodyguards, the local media went wild. I could hear them talking into their microphones, "The twenty-three-year-old multimillionaire drug lord and his ex-wife arrived at court today . . . ."

During the pretrial hearings, I spotted Jorge Latinez, who had come from Panama to testify against me. Utter revulsion flooded my being to see Lino, the madman who had ordered my torture and that of Harold and Oscar. Now Latinez played the part of the consummate foreign military officer, decked out impeccably in his Panamanian dress uniform. As I looked at him, I nudged my lawyer and whispered tersely, "Look! He's wearing the Rolex watch he stole from me!" Latinez must have heard me; when he reappeared in the courtroom after the first recess, he was no longer wearing a watch.

As the trial got underway, I observed the expert way Alan Ross, the lawyer I'd hired to handle Oscar's case, manipulated the jury's emotions. Alan had bought the most humble-looking clothes he could find for Oscar and his wife to wear. They looked so poor that many times I almost felt sorry for them.

Throughout the six-week trial, Marty Weinberg put on an incredible display of legal skill, often quoting case law from memory when an objection came up. At one point Judge Owens complimented the Harvard lawyer, saying it was an honor to have him practice in his courtroom.

Judge Owens seemed to recognize that the prosecution was incapable of competing with the legal team I had put together; whenever the prosecutor missed a point, the judge took it upon himself to cross-examine the witnesses, making sure he plugged the gaps in the questioning. My sentiments toward Judge Owens ran the gamut from hatred, anger, and disgust to deep admiration.

Things seemed to be going our way in the trial's early weeks. Shelby Highsmith was masterful, his down-home charm scoring many points with the jury. Alan Ross did a fabulous job representing Oscar, and Marty Weinberg seemed extremely successful at destroying the government's witnesses against me.

Then, without warning, we suffered a setback. The government offered Harold Rosenthal a deal: If he pleaded guilty to cocaine conspiracy, he would be sentenced to only fifteen years, and the charges against him of smuggling marijuana and Quaaludes would be dropped. Without consulting our legal team, Harold accepted the government's offer. My main codefendant had declared himself guilty. Harold's admission was bound to have a powerful effect on the jury.

When the testimony and the lawyers' arguments finally concluded, we returned to our hotel rooms to await the jury's decision. A day passed without word from the courtroom. A second day went by, and the jury remained out.

Mom spent those agonizing days praying continuously, it seemed. I appreciated her concern, but I didn't feel the same need. I'd spent more than $500,000 in legal fees to make sure nothing went wrong. All the angles were covered. *I'll let my mom deal with her superstitions. As for me, my money is on the lawyers.*

At last, on the third day, I got a call from Marty informing me that the jury had reached a verdict.

"Get ready," I told Luchy and my mom. "We're going to the courthouse." Before we left the hotel room, Mom prayed fervently again.

We met Marty and our team in the hotel lobby. Then we were whisked off to the courthouse.

When the jury entered, the judge asked the foreman if the jury had reached a verdict.

"Yes, Your Honor, we have."

"Is the verdict unanimous?" Judge Owens asked.

"Yes, Your Honor, it is."

Oscar's verdict was read first: "Oscar Nuñez," the foreman read, "not guilty on all counts."

A wave of excitement washed over me, and I breathed a sigh of relief. If Oscar wasn't guilty of selling me the cocaine, I was assured of victory. *I've beaten them,* I thought. *I've won again.*

The judge instructed me to stand for the reading of my verdict. I rose confidently, as though I was about to receive an award.

"Jorge Valdés," the foreman read, "guilty as charged on all counts."

I could not believe my ears. *Impossible!*

My spine turned to jelly. I wanted to fall down. I felt as though my heart had stopped beating, or worse, that someone had ripped it from my chest.

I could hear the surreal sound of my mother sobbing, but I didn't know what to do, what to think. Shelby put his arm around my shoulder and squeezed my shoulder, but I was numb.

And I was angry, but I refused to show any emotions. I turned to look at my mom. "It's okay, Mom. We knew it all along. We're going to beat them in the appeal."

Mom looked back at me, her eyes puffy and red, her cheeks stained by tears. Mom still believed in me, but I was making it tougher and tougher.

Shelby informed the judge that we planned to appeal and argued that I should be allowed to remain free on bond while I awaited sentencing. Judge Owens granted the request and even removed all conditions of my bail.

I took a plane back to Miami. Within a few days my lawyers gathered to discuss how we could win our appeal. Shelby was particularly distraught. "Son," he said, "I was thoroughly convinced that we would win this one." He said he felt cheated out of the decision. I could feel the pain in his heart.

But I had committed a crime—and I was about to pay for it.

PART THREE

1980-1987

I tried to talk, but all the words caught in my throat. It didn't matter . . . .

I hung up the phone and suddenly realized that for the first time in my life, I felt a peace in my heart. I had no idea what was going to happen, but I knew I had to make a clean cut with my Colombian business partners. I couldn't go halfway. Intuitively, I knew that if this change stood a chance, it would require drastic action—all or nothing.

Twenty-Two

New Kid on the Block

Two weeks after my conviction, I invited several friends to attend the Houston Livestock Show, the biggest horse show in the country. It would make for a grand party prior to my sentencing.

Manny, Sal, Willie, and several others joined Luchy and me for the trip. Each of us took about $50,000 in spending money to blow at various exhibits. I bought numerous expensive gifts and trinkets for family and friends, as well as fancy saddles for our horses. We were an exhibitor's dream as we walked through the show, buying everything in sight without even asking the price.

I called a popular Mexican restaurant and arranged to pay them $10,000 to close for the evening and offer us a private party. That night, after we had eaten our fill of Mexican food and had drunk more than our share of margaritas, I sat in a corner of the restaurant with Manny to discuss future cocaine shipments. Regardless of my sentence, the business would go on.

From Houston I returned to Macon for my sentencing. Before leaving I told Sal, "Wait for me here. I'll be gone only a day."

Back once more in the Macon courtroom, Shelby Highsmith presented my case for a light sentencing. He argued eloquently that I was a young man and, as such, was entitled to consideration under the Youth Offender Act, making me eligible for parole after one year in prison regardless of my sentence.

As Shelby sat down, Judge Owens stared coldly at our legal team and at me. "Mr. Highsmith," he said flatly, "not only does this court believe that Mr. Valdés will not benefit from the Youth Offender Act, this court believes that Mr. Valdés will not benefit from the fifteen years in prison I am about to give him."

Owens proceeded to formally sentence me to fifteen years in prison, a $25,000 fine, and an assessed percentage of the prosecution cost. I was to be remanded without bail, to begin serving my time immediately. I was not going back to Houston, I was not going home to Miami; I was going to prison—for fifteen years.

And I hadn't even brought a change of clothing.

I looked around and saw tears in Luchy's eyes. My mom wept uncontrollably as the marshal took me by the arm and led me toward the door. "Don't worry, Mom," I said as I passed her, "I'll be out in no time." The words sounded as hollow as I felt.

I was taken back to jail in Macon to await transfer to a federal prison. As the cell door slammed shut behind me, I crawled onto the bunk in a daze. I didn't want to get up ever again. Closing my eyes, I tried to shut out the world. I slept all afternoon and into the following day.

Reality began to settle in a day and a half later. It was February 28, 1980—the morning of my twenty-fourth birthday—and I sat in jail, convicted, sentenced to fifteen years of this monotonous life.

Two weeks later, the U.S. marshals took me to the Federal Corrections Center in Tallahassee. Except for the razor-wire fence surrounding it, the facility resembled a drab college campus, with a courtyard bordered by four large, brick buildings containing cellblocks. When I arrived, I learned that I had the longest sentence of anyone there.

During orientation on my first day, while waiting for my name to be called, I went to the TV room at the end of the cellblock. The room was vacant. I turned on the television, pulled out a metal folding chair, and sat down. I was idly watching a program when another inmate came in, pulled up a chair in front of me, and switched the channel. Without a word, I simply stood, walked up to the TV, and changed the channel back to the one I'd been watching. The other man cursed me and said, "What do you think you're doing?" He got up, changed the channel again, and sat down.

My prison mentality was forming rapidly. I would do my time, and I would respect others, but I was not going to be disrespected. I stood, folded my metal chair, and used it to smash the other man over the head as hard as I could. He tumbled off his chair onto the floor, blood gushing from his wound. I dropped the chair and left the room.

The man had to go to the hospital for stitches. I later found out he was the orderly in charge of keeping the TV room clean; that room was his domain, and until four P.M. each day it was his acknowledged right to watch whatever he wanted.

When he returned from the hospital, I apologized. We became friends, but he never again sat in front of me in the TV room.

Even before my transfer to Tallahassee, I had been in contact with my friend Celestino, who had been moved there some months earlier. By the time I arrived, Celestino had everything arranged: Not only had he assembled my entourage and researched the best work detail, but he had provided fresh prison clothes for me and new sheets for my bed. With Celestino's pledge to be my assistant and bodyguard in prison, my arrival at Tallahassee seemed like a welcome home party.

Marijuana was the currency of choice for the Tallahassee inmates, and I soon had Celestino rolling out joints. To make sure my "currency" was top quality, I had Celestino roll out only eighty joints from the standard ball of marijuana that made a hundred joints of normal size. I wanted everyone to know that when they did business with Jorge Valdés, they would be treated better than by anyone else.

Ten other inmates served as my associates, staying close to me at all times. In return for their service I arranged to have money deposited in their commissary accounts. Since inmates weren't permitted to carry cash, each prisoner had a commissary account into which his prison pay, as well as any money sent from friends or relatives, was deposited. The commissary was like a small general store from which inmates could purchase food, cigarettes, and other luxuries.

I also provided my associates with numerous other privileges. For some I paid motel expenses so their families could afford to come visit. And at Christmas my associates and their families received special gift packages. In many ways, I bought the loyalty of the men around me, and I considered it money well spent.

Our cellblock was one large, open square room, similar to a military barracks, with rows of bunk beds and lockers against the wall, enough for two hundred inmates. During one of my first nights there, I was awakened from sleep by sounds coming from the bunk below mine. Peering over the edge of my bunk, I saw two inmates engaged in homosexual activity. I jumped off my bed and started screaming at them, cursing them in the strongest terms I knew.

They stared back as if there were something wrong with me. "You better get used to it," one of them said. "This is the way of life in prison."

Maybe so, but it wasn't my way of life! And there was no way that I was going to get used to it.

Once I had established a power base, I decided to do something about the homosexual rapes in the prison, which for various reasons often went unreported. One night, a big bully raped a young twenty-year-old who hadn't been able to defend himself. I gathered my associates together and told them, "We're going to stop this!"

Soon afterward I stopped by the guard station and told the guard on duty, "Just overlook any noise you hear tonight." By this time, the guards knew who I was, and they were more than happy to allow me the opportunity to bring some order to the place.

After the midnight count, my associates and I removed padlocks from our lockers, then stuffed and tied the locks inside a couple of gym socks. Then we filled pitchers with near-boiling water from the spigot used for making coffee.

Having previously identified the sexual predator, four men and I crept toward the bully's bunk. Moving as quickly and quietly as a military commando team, we swept down on him, grabbed the man's arms and legs, and doused his eyes with the boiling water so he couldn't identify his attackers. He screamed in pain and began yelling for someone to help him, but no one dared. One of our guys pulled down the man's underwear, and I stepped closer. Using the padlock weapon like a heavy slingshot, I hit him as hard as I could in his private parts. On the third blast, the rapist passed out and we left him lying there.

As we walked past the guard station, we knocked on the window. The guards came running, the lights were turned on, and they found the predator still unconscious in his bunk. The guards took him to the infirmary, and we never saw him again.

I was soon able to move to a special dormitory at Tallahassee. Much nicer than the regular facilities, this dormitory housed inmates who were participating in an experimental program known as the Community. The inmates were housed two men to a room—in actual rooms rather than barracks—and the guards paid little attention to them unless there was an emergency. The dorm ran itself, with inmates dealing with aberrant behavior by coming together for discussion in a circle setting and recommending discipline or other self-improvement procedures.

I joined the Community simply to improve my external environment, but before long it began to change my attitudes as well. The program's emphasis on introspection caused me to examine my life, to see myself for the person I had become, a man far removed from the values my mom and dad had instilled in me. I didn't like the person I saw in the mirror. For the first time, I began admitting to myself that perhaps some of my ways were wrong. But my confession was only a tiny crack in the diamond-hard shell around my heart. My conscience had been so seared by sin that it was easier to patch up my harsh exterior than to acknowledge the broken boy within me who was crying out for acceptance, forgiveness, and love.

Part of the Community's work included a ten-week program of court-ordered meetings with kids who had committed minor but serious crimes. The idea was to show them a realistic picture of their future in prison if they didn't change their direction. Hopefully, our warnings would scare them into going straight, inspiring them toward rehabilitation before it was too late.

For the first four of the ten weeks, one Community team of inmates would meet with the kids while another team met with their parents. Then we'd switch and meet for another four weeks. During the last two weeks, we brought parents and kids together in one room.

As I learned more about myself, a desire began to build within me to help kids avoid the mistakes I had made. One fourteen-year-old girl we worked with had a heroin addiction and had been living as a prostitute for two years. She was assigned to the program after using a knife to rob a man. She was the hardest, most callous girl I had ever seen—mean, rebellious, and obnoxious. Nothing we did in our sessions made a dent in her defenses. We cursed her, trying to be appropriately harsh with her, and she cursed right back at us.

Then in one group session, while we were talking to someone else, she started to cry. I stopped the group and directed our focus toward her. I began to speak with her in a soft, nurturing tone. All our threats and warnings had failed to touch her, but now, just a hint of unconditional love began peeling the layers off her heart. Having been molested by her stepfather when she was young, she admitted that all she ever wanted was for somebody to love her, to tell her that she mattered, that she was needed, that she was loved.

I began to realize that so many of the kids in gangs and in prison must be hurting from unmet needs deep inside. Within the Community, my desire and burden to help kids find the right path was born.

My Community activities also inspired me to do more reading, and I was impressed enough with the program to arrange to buy more than a thousand dollars' worth of books to create a library for the Community. I wrote a paper—"Therapeutic Communities in Prison: A Transactional Analysis Approach"—that was published in a magazine, and I was invited to attend a conference in Tallahassee on corrections, where I presented the paper.

Soon afterward, however, a new warden was installed at the prison, and the Community program was discontinued.

My heart was especially softened during the first Christmas season I spent in prison. My family came to visit me on Christmas Eve and Christmas Day, then returned to Miami. On New Year's Eve, I called home just before midnight. My father answered the phone. After talking to me only briefly, he started to cry. He put my mother on the line, and before long, she was crying too. Mom gave the phone to J.C.

"Are there a lot of people there?" I asked my brother. I remembered how even when we were poor, our house was always bustling with friends and family members during the holidays, eating, drinking, and celebrating together.

I expected J.C. to give me a long list of people who were visiting, but he surprised me.

"No, Jorge," he said softly. "There's nobody here but us."

Suddenly, the fickleness and the shallowness of my "success" hit me. With pain I realized that the many people who once clamored to be around me because of my money and power had abandoned my parents.

Trying my best to sound upbeat, I wished my family a happy New Year and promised that we would be together again in the coming year.

Then I went back to my cell, climbed into my bunk, and cried for hours.

Twenty-Three

Eyes Opened

Christine and I had divorced shortly after I was convicted. I appreciated her staying with me that long, especially since she knew I had been seeing Luchy again. I felt badly about the way I had treated Christine, and in my own way I tried to compensate by purchasing a house for her and giving her one of my Corvettes and enough money to start a fresh life.

I called Luchy repeatedly one night, and she didn't answer the phone. When I finally reached her, she said she'd been out helping a friend. In my mind that could mean only one thing: She was cheating on me. After all the many times I had cheated on her, I had no right to be so judgmental, but that didn't keep me from being furious. I called my dad and told him to kick her out of the house and get back my Mercedes. I wasn't going to let her cheat on me in my house and my car.

Luchy denied that she was being unfaithful, but what little trust we had between us was gone. She came to visit me less and less, and we both knew our relationship was over. I bought her a house and a car, and I gave her enough money to take care of herself and Jorgito until I was released from prison.

The devastating breakup with Luchy sent me into a depression, and I didn't know how to bounce back. For a while I decided I didn't want any more visits while in prison. Then my emotional pendulum swung the other direction, and I put everybody on my visitor's list—especially pretty women from my past carousing days. Week after week, gorgeous fashion models and other attractive women showed up at the prison to visit me, and my status among my fellow inmates soared to new heights.

As a result of my activities in the Community, I had established favorable relationships with many of the top people in the prison administration. When the Community program was shut down, my caseworker asked how I felt about transferring to a facility where inmates were afforded a higher degree of personal freedom than the "big house" in Tallahassee.

"That would be ideal," I told my caseworker, "but I've always been denied a transfer when I requested it."

"Well," he responded, "I'll put your paperwork through one more time." To grease the system, I paid a large fee to an official at the prison bureau regional office, but I was still surprised soon after to receive notice that I'd been approved for transfer to the federal prison camp at Eglin Air Force Base near Pensacola, Florida. Even more encouraging was the news that the parole board had determined that, with continued good behavior, I could be paroled after serving only five years.

The prison camp at Eglin was a much more relaxed atmosphere. Instead of razor-wire fences, painted white lines on the pavement marked the boundaries for inmates. Most inmates worked on job details at the Air Force base adjacent to the prison camp, so inmates, military personnel, and civilians mingled freely.

Perhaps the best thing about Eglin was that families and friends were permitted to bring food to the visiting room. Mom could bring some of her Cuban specialties, and I usually devoured them before she left the room. On the downside, Eglin was two hundred miles farther from Miami than Tallahassee was, so it was more difficult for my family to visit. But Mom, Dad, and J.C. made the twelve-hour drive each week. I later learned that Dad cried on every trip.

Besides the long drive, they frequently parked in front of the prison gates and slept overnight in the car so they could be first in the crowded line of visitors waiting to be processed for admittance the following morning. They made great sacrifices so we could spend more time together.

My reputation as a multimillionaire drug lord had preceded my arrival at Eglin. During my orientation, the warden said I would not be permitted to work at the Air Force base. He assigned me to the maintenance crew working inside the prison camp's perimeters, which meant for the next few years I'd be cutting grass all day long, every day.

I soon learned, however, that one of the best places to work at Eglin was in the hospital, especially in the dentist's office. When I heard that the inmate assigned to the prison dentist was scheduled to leave in two weeks, I made a point to meet the dentist. He was a young fellow from California, and we hit it off well. Within a few weeks, I was working in the prison dentist's office, wearing a white uniform and all. My work for the dentist ended, however, when I was caught pursuing an affair in his office with a civilian hospital employee. As punishment, I was reassigned to a work detail at the Air Force base—exactly where the warden had told me I would never work.

The guards at Eglin were not nearly as susceptible to bribery as those at other prisons. The guards knew that to be housed at Eglin was considered a privilege within the prison system, so the officers had more leverage over the inmates. Most inmates refused to risk getting on the bad side of the guards.

Most, but not me.

It didn't take long for me to get my "people" together. I soon had my cadre of associates helping me smuggle contraband through the checkpoints and obtaining other prison perks for me.

At Eglin, inmates were allowed to attend chapel services with their visitors. Although I was still a long way from believing in God, I attended mass regularly. The chapel was a good place for visitors to smuggle me money, watches, and other contraband. It was also a great place for the guys to show off their wives and girlfriends.

A former big-name attorney happened to be incarcerated at Eglin, and for a hundred bucks he offered to do all the necessary paperwork to obtain inmates' case records, which were now available through the Freedom of Information Act. For many inmates, this was the first time they ever saw the documentation concerning the government's case against them. I figured, for $100, why not? I gave the attorney the money, and he prepared the requests to get all the information available about my case.

When the large official-looking envelope arrived in the mail, I didn't even open it. I shoved it in a drawer and forgot all about it for a time. Then one day I was cleaning the drawer and noticed the envelope. I opened it up and began to read.

Suddenly, electricity flowed through my veins. The pieces to the puzzle of my imprisonment in Panama and Noriega's selling me out to the DEA began to fit together. For the first time I understood why the government had become so obsessed with nailing me. Now I understood why my lawyer and friend, Monti Cohen, had stayed away from me after my arrest.

In the Freedom of Information material, I read about a meeting Sal and I had with another person, whose name on the document had been blacked out by the government. Throughout the report, the government investigation described information obtained from this individual who was referred to as a "criminal attorney who also represents high-level drug dealers." The traitor could be only one person: Monti Cohen.

I sat down in a daze. Monti Cohen had betrayed me. Monti—one of the guys who had been with me from the beginning—had turned me in.

I called Marty Weinberg immediately. "Marty, I know who it is! I know who did it to me!" I practically shouted into the phone.

"What are you talking about, Jorge?"

"I know who was cooperating with the government."

"Slow down, Jorge," Marty said in his Boston brogue. "What do you mean?"

"Now I know why the government was always a step ahead of us in everything we did. I know who did it!"

"Who?"

"Monti Cohen."

I could hear the shock in Marty's voice as he replied, "No, it can't be."

"Marty, it is! I see it right here in black and white."

After I described the material I had obtained, Marty remained silent for a time, then responded, "Jorge, I'm sorry. I hope you're wrong."

Shortly after that, Monti Cohen came to visit me at Eglin. We met in one of the lawyer-client rooms at the prison, and I wasted no time in confronting him. "Monti, you turned me in. You betrayed me!"

Monti denied it, but I refused to listen to his lies. I moved closer and looked him in the eye. "For the rest of your life," I told him, "look behind you, because one day I'm going to put a bullet in the back of your head." Although I knew in my heart I could never harm Monti, I wanted him to believe it could happen; I wanted him to pay in some way.

Turning my back on him, I returned to my room. As furious as I was, anger wasn't the overwhelming emotion I felt. Hurt, disappointment, frustration, and disillusionment surged through me. I simply couldn't believe the pain I felt from being betrayed by someone I had loved so much.

But what did I expect? After all, this was the survival-of-the-fittest world I had both chosen and created. When it came to protecting someone else, who would ever sacrifice himself? Who would lay down his life to save and set free another? Who would do such a thing?

Nobody in my world.

Twenty-Four

Invitations

One Saturday, as I met with my brother in the visiting room at Eglin, two women sat down at a table close to us. The younger of the two, who looked to be a few years younger than I, had long, wavy hair and bright hazel eyes. The woman with her, also attractive, appeared to be her mother.

As I talked with J.C., my eyes kept wandering over to them. The mother was quite friendly, so we struck up a conversation. She told me that she and her husband owned an optical business. Their accountant had stolen money from them and set up her husband, a devout Christian, to take the fall—six months in prison for tax evasion. Now she was left to run the business herself and to take care of her daughter.

Glad the subject had finally turned in the direction I wanted, I asked the daughter her name. She replied coyly, "Sherry."

"I'm very glad to meet you, Sherry. My name is Jorge Valdés." I turned and began speaking to my brother in Spanish.

"What are you saying to him?" Sherry asked.

I answered with a twinkle in my eye. "I told him you were going to be my wife."

She laughed, and we talked further.

Sherry came every weekend to visit her father, and I developed a friendship with her and her family. One day I said to Sherry, "I would like to date you."

"How can you?"

"Don't worry," I said. "Just say yes, and I'll find a way."

"Okay, sure," she answered.

Finding a way to date Sherry while in prison was no easy task, but I figured the best possibilities would center on my work detail, which was cleaning the landscaped areas surrounding the officers' housing at the air base. Eventually Sherry obtained a pass onto the base because her father had been in the military, and we began meeting in a wooded area next to where I worked. It was simple to elude my supervisor—he met us at seven in the morning and checked us back in around three-fifteen P.M. each day, leaving plenty of time for a rendezvous with Sherry.

Eventually I was running the work detail myself. Over time, I placed men in the crew whom I could trust, so I could leave whenever necessary and the work would still get done. I paid the men by funding their commissary accounts as well as covering their families' visiting expenses. The guys were extremely loyal and would do anything I asked. Plus it was prestigious for them to be known in prison as part of my entourage.

Later I secured a base pass from a colonel's wife in exchange for some favors I'd done for her; I told her I wanted the sticker for my family to have in their car, to help them get in earlier when visiting me. Instead, I placed the sticker in the window of a new Chevrolet van I had bought for Sherry. Several days each week, when Sherry came to visit, I left the work detail, changed into civilian clothes I'd hidden in the brush, then joined Sherry in the van. We drove out through the checkpoints as if I was a civilian leaving the base. We went to a townhouse I'd purchased not far from the prison camp, and eventually I even went shopping with Sherry in town. She would return me to the base in time to rejoin my work detail at the end of the workday. We carried on this routine for nearly a year.

Because of my interest in Sherry, I forged a solid friendship with her stepfather, Joe, a quiet man with a gentle spirit. I promised Sherry and her mom that I would watch out for Joe and make sure nothing bad happened to him while he was serving his time.

Joe often talked to me about the Bible. Since I respected him and was interested in his daughter, I listened. Eventually I even accepted his invitation to attend a Bible study group with other inmates.

Joe intrigued me. I marveled at the quiet strength he exuded, and I could feel a peace emanating from within him, though he was in the most desperate situation of his life. I could only imagine how difficult the prison environment must be for someone like Joe. Yet he was content. He felt no compulsion to keep getting new pairs of shoes or boots, as I did, or to taunt the officers, as I was prone to do. And yet, amazingly, all the other inmates seemed to respect Joe.

One day Joe invited me to attend a special seminar at Eglin. The speaker was Chuck Colson, known as President Nixon's hatchet man, who had gone to prison for his part in the Watergate cover-up. Now he was involved in a ministry known as Prison Fellowship.

"I'd be happy to attend," I heard myself telling Joe, almost to my surprise.

Chuck Colson was a powerful, brilliant spokesman for Christianity. Because of his prison experience, he seemed to have a genuine concern and compassion for the men in the audience, and I was deeply stirred by what he said. At the same time, another force sounded within me: "These Christians are nothing but weaklings who need religion to be able to handle their situations. And some of these guys are just telling people they're Christians, when they're really no different than I am."

I told myself I was okay, yet I knew I was deeply involved in many things that were wrong. I couldn't deny the tugging at my heart as I listened to Colson speak. When he invited any man to come forward who wanted to ask Jesus into his life and be forgiven of his sins, many inmates responded. Suddenly I felt myself moving forward along with them. I walked boldly to the front, talked with some of the counselors, accepted their literature, and even repeated the words they encouraged me to pray—a "sinner's prayer," as they called it.

But nothing happened. I told everyone at the seminar that I was "giving my life to Jesus," but my heart had not been changed. I was still the same sinful person I'd been when I walked into that meeting—maybe a little worse, because now, in addition to conning everyone else, I was attempting to con God . . . if God existed.

Despite my spiritual duplicity, I couldn't deny that something was happening to me. I was feeling convicted, not about my drug crimes, but about the type of person I was at my core. Not understanding this spiritual conviction, I fought hard against it. I continued telling myself that I hadn't hurt anyone through my drug business, that I was a good guy, and that with the money I made I helped a lot of people by paying for houses and schools and sometimes even churches. All those good things cancelled out the bad. So why was I feeling guilty?

Perhaps in an attempt to smother my sense of spiritual guilt, I decided to resume my drug business. For a number of reasons, I had recently reduced my level of involvement in the cartel. Though it was possible to continue running the business from prison, working cocaine deals through my visitors was inefficient and sometimes cumbersome. Also, I'd heard that Manny Garces had been forced to flee the country. His return to Colombia—and his subsequent indictment in the U.S. on charges of money laundering—had led to the "retirement" of most of our people who had worked together from the beginning.

It made sense for me to retire as well, since I'd certainly accumulated enough money to live comfortably for the rest of my life. After my release from prison, I could simply focus on making my cattle business more prosperous.

Nevertheless, I stayed on the alert, looking for the right opportunity to begin building another drug network. I was in contact with Travis White in California, and I knew that with one phone call, I could deliver cocaine there again.

The opportunity came unexpectedly. One day in the visiting room, a young man called out my name: "Jorge, it's me, Carlos." It had been more than four years since I'd last seen Carlos, who was one of the guys working for Sal back when we'd first started in the cocaine trade.

After I hugged him, Carlos explained that he was visiting his father-in-law, a truck driver who had been imprisoned for bringing in a load of cocaine for another organization.

"So what are you doing these days?" I asked.

"The same thing," he said with a smile, "but I'm on my own now. So I'm looking for work."

A plan was already forming in my mind.

"I have a strong connection in California," I told Carlos. I outlined an arrangement for our working together and promised him a percentage of the take.

Carlos was thrilled. I called Travis White, and he came to visit me at Eglin. I introduced Carlos to Travis, made some phone calls—and we were back in business.

Carlos began regular deliveries to California, and we were making money. My main interest, however, was in getting more people in place. I was determined to develop my cocaine business into something even bigger and better than before.

This time it wasn't about money; it was about getting even with the government.

During my final year at Eglin, I proposed to Sherry and we decided to get married while I was still in prison. I applied for a weekend furlough—a privilege routinely granted to inmates nearing release—so we could have a "normal" wedding and reception. I told Sherry to rent a nearby resort and to invite all our friends from near and far.

Four days before the wedding, I was called in to the associate warden's office. He had discovered that I planned to spend over $30,000 on our wedding. "There is no way I'm going to let you flaunt all that drug money in my face," he declared. "Your furlough has been cancelled." They couldn't prevent me from getting married, but they planned to have me taken into town for the ceremony, then escorted back to prison by the chaplain.

I maintained a calm demeanor, but my stomach was churning with frustration.

Later I called Sherry and informed her of the disappointing news. She was extremely upset, but I told her I had a plan.

At that time Eglin's rules for visitors placed no restriction on how much food or what kind of food they could bring to the prisoners. The only conditions were that drinks had to be in clear plastic bottles—no cans—and the guards had to be able to inspect the food.

With this in mind, I asked Sherry to call the catering company we had already hired. I wanted twenty waiters—dressed in tuxedoes and carrying silver platters—to deliver a huge feast to the prison's visiting room at twelve o'clock sharp on our wedding day.

Sherry must have thought I'd flipped out, but she did as I asked.

I also had one of my workers order a six-foot ice-cream cake. And I ordered an entire pig, roasted Hawaiian luau style.

Meanwhile I spread the word to the other inmates that on my wedding day, no one's family needed to bring any food to them—there would be more than enough for everybody, compliments of me.

On the morning of our wedding, I had $12,000 worth of clothes delivered to the prison so I could choose what to wear. Just as the associate warden had planned, Sherry and I were married in town that morning, then we returned to the prison. At noon, just as *I* had planned, an army of tuxedo-clad waiters paraded into the visiting area carrying silver platters stacked high with lobster, steak, and all manner of delicacies. The roasted pig was laid out on a table, complete with an apple in its mouth.

The guard in charge of the visiting room called the warden and said, "You have to come see what's going on. In all my years of working here, this is the biggest spectacle I've ever seen." When the warden and the associate warden arrived, they stood, mouths gaping, as the waiters served the inmates and their families as though they were guests at the finest restaurant in the country. They also watched as I allowed the tantalizing ice-cream cake to simply melt in front of their salivating mouths.

Unlike most federal prisoners, I wasn't permitted a transfer to a halfway house as my sentence drew to an end. I remained at Eglin until July 25, 1984, when Sherry picked me up at six o'clock in the morning. I was once again a free man. And it was time to go back to work.

Twenty-Five

Life and Death

To celebrate my release from prison, Sherry and I threw a small party at my ranch in Clewiston. Strangely, many of my closest friends did not come. I realized I was back on my own. That was fine with me; I had built my drug network once, and I could do it again.

My new drug operation in California was running smoothly by the time of my release. One of the key members I had added to my organization was someone I had met while at Eglin. Ismael, known simply as "the Arab," was a slim, dark-skinned man in his mid-twenties. He seemed to have a keen business sense, and he regarded loyalty as one of a man's highest virtues—my kind of guy.

To run our West Coast operation, I hired my former prison associate, Celestino Ruiz, following his release. My operation soon became remarkably streamlined. The Arab handled all the cocaine coming into Miami, transporting it to California, where Celestino made sure it was distributed to our contacts there. Soon we were pouring cocaine into California and making a ton of money. I sometimes flew to the West Coast to pick up payments, when the amount was large enough. Eventually I purchased my own King Air plane, as well as my own helicopter and a Hawker jet.

But the drug world had changed during the years I was in prison. A huge influx of merchandise had prompted a drop in prices. More important, the business had become much more violent. People were killing and being killed daily in the drug world, often the victims of senseless murders. It was clearer than ever that drug smuggling was not the "victimless crime" I believed it to be when I first entered the business. In those days Manny often told me, "Son, if you have to carry a gun to do a deal, that deal is not worth doing." Now I carried a gun everywhere, despite the fact that I was still on parole and the government no doubt had me under surveillance. I even slept with a gun under my pillow.

My ex-wife Luchy had remarried and was planning to move to Spain, taking our son with her, but I balked at that. I liked Luchy's husband and felt I could reason with him, so I instructed Big Eddie, one of my bodyguards, to bring Luchy's husband to see me. I made him a generous offer: If Jorgito stayed in America to live with Sherry and me, I would pay Luchy's travel expenses to return to the U.S. to visit her son; but if she took Jorgito out of the country, I would kill Luchy's husband. The man saw the wisdom of my plan, and Jorgito moved in with Sherry and me. Sherry did her best to be a good stepmother to Jorgito, trying to fill the void left by his mother's absence.

I purchased a home—a Mediterranean-style three-story villa with a boat dock in back—in an elite, gated community in Miami known as L'Hermitage. I struck a deal with the entrance-gate guards, paying them double their monthly salary to make sure that no one coming to visit me would be recorded in their logs. I also called an electronics genius I'd met in prison and paid him to outfit my house with the latest high-tech security equipment. I had an airtight secret room built, complete with a hidden door, in case I needed to hide while the house was being searched by police dogs. The room held a safe, a refrigerator stocked with food and water, and an oxygen tank.

I spared no amount of money in making our home at L'Hermitage as ornate as a fortress could be. The bedroom alone received more than $100,000 in remodeling work.

For further security, I never used my own name at L'Hermitage; my alias was Robert Jimenez, the name of a military officer whose personal identification papers I had managed to obtain, including his social security number and credit card numbers. Despite my meticulous security precautions, I rarely talked on the telephone from my home for fear that my lines were tapped. I established a practice of talking with business associates on cellular phones and then only in brief conversations.

By Christmas of 1984, with money flowing freely once more, I went on a car-buying binge. I bought a custom-designed Mercedes, white with gold trim for myself, a Z-28 for Sherry, and a Camaro for my sister. When the latest Corvettes came out, I couldn't decide which of three colors I liked best, so I bought one car in each color. Later I would purchase a $200,000 Porsche, a black convertible with a red top and a candy apple red interior. I also owned a series of trucks. One of the most difficult decisions I had to make each day was which car to drive.

As my personal aide, I hired a fellow named Chifo, a spark plug of a man who stood about five foot six and weighed three hundred pounds. Chifo was in charge of paying all my bills, taking Jorgito to school, picking up the maid, and making all the arrangements when I cheated on my wife. Whenever I wanted to get away from Sherry for a while, Chifo booked a hotel room, stocked it with a case of my favorite champagne, a videotape recorder, and a supply of pornographic movies.

After years in prison, I was sitting on top of the world again. So why was I so unhappy?

During this period of my life I started doing the unthinkable—using cocaine at my parties. Money, power, and women had not satisfied the yawning hunger within me; the only thing left to try was drugs.

I was discreet in my cocaine usage; I knew that if Manny found out in Colombia that I was using our product, it could jeopardize both my business and our friendship. "This is a business, and not something we use ourselves," Manny had so often said.

Though Sherry may not have realized the scope of my drug dealing, she saw that I had easy access to cocaine and joined me in using it. I told myself, "I can put this down any time I want to," but I discovered that this was easier said than done.

I partied with Sherry on the weekends, using cocaine two or three weekends each month. The coke was beginning to control me, because once I started to use it, I couldn't put it down. Nothing had ever controlled me, but now the curse I had inflicted on so many others was threatening my life as well, and I began to be scared.

At the same time, my obsession with pornography was becoming more blatant. I didn't even try to hide it from Sherry anymore. I had a video dealer deliver the latest porno movies directly to our home. At first I watched them only when we were partying, but soon they were a constant fare.

I decided that delivering videos could be a good front for my drug smuggling, as well as a strong moneymaking opportunity. I knew what sort of videos people didn't want to be seen picking up at a video store. How much better if we could deliver these directly to their homes, then pick them up on the due date. Private, discreet service—it was a sure thing. I purchased a few vans, refitting their interiors with shelves to hold the videos, and entered the porno flick delivery business with zeal. Of course we also carried a full line of popular, current movies and family videos, but I knew where the real money would be. It was one more instance of the drug and pornography businesses being in bed together.

A strange sadness struck me when I learned that more than seventy percent of our porno rentals were to housewives. But then, how dare I be critical of anyone else, when such perversity pervaded my own life?

I started seeking out porn stars to party with during my frequent trips to California, and one of them once asked me to finance a movie called *If Mother Only Knew*. As depraved as I had become, I considered doing it, and even thought about participating in the movie. Perhaps the title caused me to renege; I could only imagine how my involvement in such a thing would crush my own mother if she ever discovered it.

As I slid further into debauchery, Sherry suddenly turned spiritual on me. She had grown up in a Christian family, but from the earliest stages of our relationship, she had compromised her beliefs for my sake. Now, at the oddest moments, she reverted to her spiritual roots.

I had purchased a beach house at Fort Myers Beach, overlooking the Gulf of Mexico. One day I was lying in our Jacuzzi there, watching a porno movie, when Sherry came out carrying a Bible. She stood there, reading it to me. I had been high for an entire day, drinking champagne and doing cocaine, but strangely, when Sherry started reading the Bible, I suddenly sobered up. "Get that book away from me!" I yelled in anger.

Sherry kept her Bible hidden so I wouldn't throw it away, but she continued to read it and to speak to me about it often. At the time, this seemed like nothing but harassment—for some inexplicable reason, I felt guilty every time she did it.

In late spring of 1985, we got the news that Sherry was pregnant. To protect the baby, Sherry immediately cut out her cocaine use and also refused to drink alcohol. I watched my twenty-year-old wife, who had previously been a party animal, suddenly become virtuous. Since I had no intention of abandoning my party life, her decisions put a strain on our relationship.

To match my fortune in the drug business, I pursued fame in the world of show horses. Early in 1985 the Arab and I decided to buy a good stud as a strong breeding horse at the ranch. We decided we could spend $100,000 for the animal and traveled to Texas in search of the right horse. One day we were having lunch with a horse trainer in a small town north of Dallas, and he mentioned that he knew about a good deal on a stud that was available in the far north corner of the Texas panhandle.

I thought, *Hmm, a good deal? That must mean $100,000 to $150,000.* As I was eating my barbecue sandwich, I casually asked how much the horse was.

"A million dollars," the trainer responded matter-of-factly.

I nearly choked on my sandwich. "Can you believe that?" I asked the Arab. "A million dollars?" A kilo of coke was currently selling for about $25,000, and I measured most purchases by that standard. "Forty kilos of coke for a stud!"

Turning to the trainer, I shook my head. "No animal is worth a million dollars, on two legs or four legs."

Nevertheless I was intrigued. Why would a horse be valued so highly? I nudged the Arab. "Let's check out this horse."

We flew from Dallas to Amarillo, then rented a car and drove . . . and drove. We finally arrived at our destination at three o'clock in the morning. After coming that far, I wasn't going to wait around till daybreak to see the stud, so we knocked loudly on the front door of the ranch manager's house. Soon we were walking out to the stables, where I got my first glimpse of Tardee Impressive as the rancher led him out of his stall. *Impressive* was the right word! The dark, chestnut-colored horse stood more than fifteen hands tall and looked to be around thirteen hundred pounds. His disposition was as attractive as his physique. He was a pleasant, playful animal that any horse lover was bound to adore.

As the trainer walked the horse toward us, I couldn't help myself. "I'll buy him," I said aloud, adding to myself, *at any price.*

The Arab stared at me as though I'd lost my mind. But within a few months, the sale was completed at a price not far from a million dollars.

For our anniversary in October 1985, I bought Sherry a Lincoln Givenchi, for which I spent $35,000. I brought the car home for her and called Sherry outside, eager to see her response to such a gift.

"Is that it?" she said.

Few people could dream of owning such an expensive car, yet it wasn't good enough for her; she was disappointed that I hadn't bought her a Jaguar. Her response disgusted me.

Blinded by my own avarice, I didn't see that I had fostered Sherry's attitude. I didn't understand the deepest reason for my disgust: Sherry couldn't be satisfied with a Lincoln Givenchi because Jorge Valdés would not have been satisfied with a Lincoln Givenchi. I was sitting on top of the world, but my life was devoid of any true joy and contentment. No amount of material possessions brought more than a momentary ebb in the wave of dissatisfaction washing over my life.

■　　　■　　　■

The one place I found sheer joy was in an experience where I least expected it. On February 25, 1986, I rushed Sherry to the hospital to give birth to our baby. While the nurses prepared Sherry, I sat there with a cellular phone and called several of my colleagues in the horse business. I jokingly told them that my mare was about to have a foal. Sherry, not appreciating my humor, cursed me as she battled each contraction.

I put on a hospital gown and entered the birthing room with Sherry. As I watched the miracle of our beautiful baby being born, my mood changed from frivolity to absolute awe. Suddenly, there was a new life—a baby girl! Ten fingers, ten toes, her tiny features already indelibly etched in my heart and mind. I loved her from the moment I saw her. The doctor handed me a pair of scissors and told me to cut the umbilical cord. As I clipped the cord that connected our baby to Sherry's body, an equally strong tie wrapped itself around my heart.

Our daughter was the jewel of our lives, and we named her Krystle. At that moment, I could never have dreamed how God would use this little girl to shatter my world, bringing me to the point of complete anguish and despair, and how God would work through her to show me what really matters in life and how to find it.

But that was still in the future. The night before Sherry's release from the hospital, some horse trainers came to visit me. When they heard the news of our baby, one of them said, "Let's celebrate!" I told Big Eddie, my bodyguard, to line up a couple of women, and the Arab and I took the guys out to a strip club and bar. We partied for a few hours, but in the back of my mind I kept thinking about my baby.

At about three o'clock in the morning, I took the trainers back to the hotel, introduced them to the women, then left.

When I went to the hospital to bring home my wife and daughter, I was elated to see them, yet at the same time I felt dirty from being out watching naked women the night before. As we drove away from the hospital, I noticed the love with which Sherry looked at our baby. *Maybe this baby will bring Sherry and me closer together,* I thought.

With the California connection running strong, I jetted to the West Coast every few weeks to check the books, deal with any problems, and of course, pick up the money from the latest cocaine delivery. One morning, just as I was preparing to leave for a scheduled trip, I became extremely nauseated. I'd already made arrangements with my pilot to pick me up, but I felt so sick that I called in Big Eddie and told him to go on without me to check the books and bring back the money.

Later that day, Big Eddie called me from California. "Everything looks fine, Jorge. I'll be back home tomorrow."

The following day, three hours after the plane's scheduled departure from California, one of our pilots called to inform me that Big Eddie hadn't shown up. I was furious, thinking he'd stayed out partying the night before. I had warned Eddie not to use cocaine while doing business, but I suspected he sometimes disregarded my admonitions.

Three more hours passed without any word from Big Eddie. I started to worry. Unexpected problems were common in the drug business, and sometimes they required extra time—but not six hours.

Eddie had been dropped off at a hotel the previous evening, but our contacts could find no sign of him when they checked the hotel.

My associates and I racked our brains, trying to guess what might have happened to Eddie. Despite the obvious risks involved in big-time drug running, I never sacrificed my people for our product. We labored hard in planning even the smallest details of our runs to give us the best possible advantage and to protect my people from possible arrest or attack. No person was expendable.

Eddie's wife called repeatedly, and I assured her he was fine and would be coming home in a couple of days. But I couldn't sleep that night, wondering what had happened to Big Eddie—and to the money he would have been carrying.

The following morning, when there was still no word from him, I hired an investigator to find Big Eddie.

After three days, the investigator called. A body fitting Big Eddie's description was waiting to be identified in a California morgue. Big Eddie had been found on a roadside, shot through the head.

My mind raced: *Who murdered him? And why? What had gone wrong?*

Sitting at Big Eddie's funeral service, I couldn't even look at the casket. I stared blankly into space as if in a trance, my mind already making plans to get even with his killers.

Only the sweet voice of Eddie's little daughter brought me back to reality. Looking at me with all the innocence of childhood, she said, "My daddy went to be with Jesus."

Her words seared through me like electricity rushing through my veins. I couldn't help but wonder if one day Krystle or Jorgie would be looking into the eyes of a stranger, longingly, pleadingly asking where their daddy was. How long would it be before a drug-related bullet smashed through my skull, forever separating me from my children?

One day, not long after Big Eddie's funeral, Jorgito asked me, "Dad, where is Eddie?"

"Well, son," I answered, "Eddie died."

Jorgito looked disgusted. "I told him not to take any shortcuts, Dad."

Jorgie's words brought a bittersweet smile to my face. One of Jorgie's heroes was Hulk Hogan, the professional wrestler who constantly reminded his admirers, "Don't take shortcuts, take your vi ta mins, and say your prayers." For some reason, the slogan had connected with Jorgie, so I reiterated Hulk's words often to Jorgie—or at least the part about not taking shortcuts.

Now, when Jorgito reminded me of Hulk's words, I thought to myself, *How many shortcuts am I taking in life? How many shortcuts am I taking with other people's lives? And when will a shortcut spell the end of my life?*

Eddie's death crushed me. Day after day I tried to make sense of it, mentally sorting through the few details we had. We weren't certain who had pulled the trigger, but it seemed unlikely that a rival or a punk drug dealer had been involved; it was someone in my own organization.

How could someone I trusted—one of our own people—have perpetrated the gangland-style execution of one of my best friends? For what? Money? No, it couldn't have been for money alone.

Then the devastating truth hit me: *That bullet was meant for me. If I had gone as planned, I would be the one dead, not Eddie. I was the only one who knew how much money was owed. By killing me, they would have gotten away with the murder, the money, and the theft of the cocaine.*

My mind was in a daze, my stomach churning. I couldn't deal with the thought that Eddie had been murdered in my place and that for some reason my life had been spared.

On the other hand, why should I be shocked over what had happened? Why should I be surprised at the death and the deception? Wasn't it inevitable in the world I'd chosen to live in?

Twenty-Six

Death Closing In

After Big Eddie's death, I closed our office in California. I wanted nothing else to do with it. But we continued to expand our cocaine distri bu tion through Miami, which looked to be more profitable for us in the long run.

We were now bringing cocaine into the country along a new route, through Alabama. The Arab had introduced me to Bill Grist, a man with whom he had worked in the Bahamas. Bill had some tremendous connections whereby he could bring airplane loads of cocaine straight from Colombia to Alabama, after refueling in Belize in Central America. The coke was then driven from Alabama to Miami.

We entered a new dimension for our organization, as we received much larger amounts of cocaine per load. I was also dealing with new contacts in Colombia. Manny had just gotten out of prison but was awaiting extradition to the U.S. He wasn't getting involved in any new business for the time being, though his influence and prominence in the cartel and the drug world would long continue. My new contacts did not have the same aversion to violence that Manny and I did. Among the leaders of the new regime were Pablo Escobar, a powerful drug lord in his own right, and Gacha, a man with a particularly ruthless reputation. Gacha also was known as "the Mexican" because of his penchant for wearing Mexican hats.

Another of my new contacts, Victor, was one of the most feared Colombians of all, a man said to have killed hundreds of people. Victor had been raised on the streets of one of Colombia's worst neighborhoods. His general policy was "Hurt others before they hurt you." The bullet was the ultimate judge between right and wrong. Victor was a straightforward man; when he gave you his word, you could go to the bank on it—or to the grave.

I learned much from Victor. Since law-enforcement officials had become much more aware of how drug deals were conducted, Victor helped me set up a delivery system that was almost impossible to foil.

I learned quickly why all the cartel members wanted Victor to be their distributor in Florida: This was a man who believed in prep aration. When he came to my office, he carried a two-way radio, with which he kept in contact with two other cars in the area. One driver sat immediately outside my office, car engine running, ready for a quick getaway; the other car circled the area to keep Victor informed if someone was watching or if some potential threat was approaching.

As Victor and I prepared to complete our first deal, he gave me the keys for two separate cars. Each car contained secret compartments in the trunk. We loaded the cocaine in the compartments and delivered the vehicles to a nearby shopping center. Our drivers were then picked up, leaving the cars behind. At the time set by Victor, his drivers came along with their own keys, opened the delivery cars, and drove away. It was a clean, safe delivery plan.

Victor's strategy formed the basis of my own system, though I refined and tailored the details. Our procedure in Miami relied on cars with hidden compartments and duplicate keys, follow-up cars to watch for trouble, constant two-way radio communication, and staggered drop-offs and pick-ups in high-traffic areas. Through this method, we reduced our risks to the bare minimum. The customer never knew when or where the cocaine drop would be made, and if any problem developed at any stage of the delivery, our guys could easily abort the process.

Eventually my organization operated so efficiently that we sometimes delivered huge caches of cocaine right under the noses of federal agents or local police, yet we were never even stopped for a traffic violation. We ran most of our operations in broad daylight, during "banker's hours."

The Arab and I were now profiting more than a million dollars each per load. We were bringing in one load per month, although we once delivered three loads in one week—just to prove we could. But it was commonly known among the other cartel members that we kept only two-thirds of our profits. The other third I sent to Manny in Colombia. I was frequently questioned on this. "What can he do for you?" they would say. "He's not doing any deals." Apparently they resented the respect I continued to show Manny despite their rise to leadership within the cartel. To me, it was a matter of personal integrity and loyalty. Manny Garces had helped me get started, I loved him like my own father, and I wanted to repay him a portion of the financial prosperity I had reaped because of him.

By the middle of 1986, the Alabama connection was beginning to show signs of stress. That fall, while on a trip to Texas to look at some horses, I met with a former Colombian military officer whom Manny had encouraged me to contact. The officer wanted to talk to me about the possibility of bringing cocaine from Colombia to the United States through Mexico, where he had been living. The officer claimed that his partner, a man named Aurelio, had strong ties to the military in Mexico's Juarez region.

At this time, although the Mexicans did a brisk business in marijuana, no major drug lord was using Mexico as a route for cocaine. That made me even more excited—I liked new challenges.

A few weeks later, I met with the Colombian military officer again. This time his partner joined us. Aurelio was about my age and had been involved in the drug business in Colombia before moving to Mexico. I liked his proposal and especially his price—a mere $2,000 per kilo, with the freight cost another $1,500 per kilo. At $3,500 per kilo, that was $1,500 cheaper than the coke we were bringing in through Alabama, a significant difference in a load of 600 or 700 kilos. Better yet, a bigger plane would be used to bring the coke from Colombia to Mexico, which meant we could bring in 1,000 or possibly even 2,000 kilos per trip. The thought of bringing in a ton of cocaine made my mouth water.

After getting an okay from other trusted cartel members on this move, I gave my two new partners $100,000 to buy a farm in Mexico and begin our operations.

As my drug business became almost self-perpetuating, I turned my attention more and more to building my horse business. Now that I owned Tardee Impressive, the best stallion in the country, I wanted to acquire a herd of mares that was worthy of him. I crisscrossed the country with a million dollars in a suitcase, traveling to horse ranches and buying everyone's best mares—at up to $125,000 each.

When the Arab and I attended various horse shows in late 1985, flamboyantly flashing money in front of other owners, they had looked at us with raised eyebrows. Now everyone wanted to do business with us.

In October 1986, I showed horses for the first time in the All-American Quarter Horse Congress, the most prestigious and the largest horse show in the country. More than three thousand horses were competing in this two-week event in Columbus, Ohio.

The competition was fierce, but when the judges' final ballots were tallied, my two horses were highest on the list—the first time ever in the Congress that horses from a single owner had taken the two top places. In equestrian circles, this was equivalent to owning both teams playing in the Super Bowl.

We threw a big party to celebrate, spending more than $15,000 on champagne and a buffet. People poured into our hotel suites all night long, and things got pretty wild.

Sherry had come to Columbus with me, but we had just found out that she was pregnant with our second baby. She was doing her best to be sociable, but I could tell she was tired and fading fast. As we both worked the room, I occasionally caught her eye, then quickly diverted my gaze.

As I made my way through the crowd, a gorgeous young woman approached me and said, "Why don't you take me to bed?"

As I followed her out of the room, I caught a glimpse of Sherry, smiling and being nice to everyone. Trying to shrug off the unexpected feelings of guilt, I went to the young woman's hotel room and had a drink with her. As she peeled off her clothes, the guilt kept eating at me. I thought, *I can't do this.* I got up, walked out, and returned to the party.

With the birth of our second baby approaching, Sherry and I moved to a different house in Miami, where again I sent a work crew to build a secret room similar to the one I had at L'Hermitage. And I once more installed a battery of high-tech surveillance equipment in and around the house. Because this home was more open than L'Hermitage, I bought several houses in the neighborhood and moved some of my employees into them. I bought two German shepherds to be on watch, in addition to the bodyguards who patrolled the grounds perpetually. I had bars installed in all the windows and had the window behind our bed blocked by concrete reinforced with steel bars. I was becoming increasingly paranoid about security.

At the same time, Sherry's and my relationship continued to be strained. To my way of thinking, it was time for her to go back to partying again—after all, our first baby had been born healthy. But Sherry hadn't even taken a drink during the months she was breast-feeding Krystle, much less now that she was pregnant again. I tried to win her favor by getting up in the middle of the night to take care of Krystle, but even that became my twisted excuse for staying up all night and watching porno movies.

I was using cocaine more frequently on the weekends, enough to make life miserable for Sherry. The cocaine made my paranoia even more pronounced. I stayed awake for days at a time, staring at the security monitors, waiting for someone to break in and try to kill me. When I finally fell asleep, I slept with a nine-millimeter handgun under my pillow and an Uzi beside my bed. I'd often wake up screaming at Sherry, "Someone's outside in the trees!" I'd go out to search, carrying my loaded submachine gun.

Jorgie's bodyguards took him to school and sat in parked cars outside the school all day long, watching for anything unusual. Of course the only thing unusual at school most of the time was the carful of armed bodyguards sitting outside. Sherry complained that Jorgito couldn't even swim in our pool without the bodyguards patrolling the area with machine guns.

When I wasn't glued to the security cameras, I watched one of two television sets that I kept in the bedroom. One was tuned to X-rated cable channels; the other was hooked up to a VCR loaded with X-rated videos. While Sherry was lying in bed reading her Bible, I'd lie next to her and watch pornography.

Some nights I'd go out to a hotel room and meet two or three girls. At other times, I simply rode around Miami by myself for hours in the middle of the night, going from one topless bar to another. I was wearing $150,000 worth of jewelry and carrying as much as $40,000 cash in my pockets. I was a walking bankroll at a time when thugs wouldn't hesitate to kill someone while robbing a convenience store of $50. It would have been simple for any mugger hanging around those nightclubs to follow me, rob me, kill me, and score the biggest hit of his life. But nobody touched me. Apparently, the God who didn't exist was watching out for me.

My mind became increasingly cloudy and confused. When my friends asked, "How are you doing?" I'd sometimes reply, "Miserable. I hate every second of my life, and I don't know why."

They thought I was joking, so they'd laugh at me. But occasionally someone noticed I wasn't trying to be funny.

"How can you say that?" they would ask. "You have everything that everybody in the world wants. What more do you want?"

I didn't know the answer. The struggle raged within me, an inner torture was far worse than anything I had experienced in Panama.

As I had done so often before, I sought solace in the arms of another woman, this time one of Sherry's friends. Because of my obsession with security, I didn't like Sherry going out alone, not even to get her hair done or to go shopping, and she hated the intrusion of having a bodyguard accompany her. So I was pleased when Sherry hired an attractive manicurist named Margaret to come to our home to do Sherry's nails.

Margaret possessed a vibrant personality, upbeat and witty. Of Brazilian heritage, she combined a delicate Latin beauty with a sassy sensuality. As Margaret and Sherry forged a close friendship, she told Sherry that she had just moved to Miami from Michigan and needed all the work she could get.

One day Sherry told me that Margaret needed $8,000 to keep her car from being repossessed. I told Sherry to have Margaret stop by my office. When Margaret came to see me, she explained her predicament. Jokingly I asked, "How would you pay me back?" It was not a serious question, but Margaret misinterpreted my motives.

She smiled seductively. "I would do *anything* to pay you back."

I got the message. I asked Margaret out to dinner that night, and she consented. I instructed Chifo, my personal assistant, to rent a hotel suite and order a private dinner prepared in the room, complete with a bottle of champagne. I didn't take Margaret home that night until two in the morning.

Margaret continued doing Sherry's nails, and Sherry had no idea what was going on. In fact, Sherry confided more and more to her, and Margaret used the intimate information to undermine Sherry's and my relationship even further. Margaret conveyed to me how disgruntled Sherry was with me, subtly insinuating, "What more could that woman want?"

My thoughts exactly. Margaret's comments provided all the rationale I needed to let my relationship with my wife grow even colder.

In a way, my affair with Margaret seemed part of a much larger spirit of destruction at work within me. Death seemed to be closing in, like a self-fulfilling prophecy.

The Arab and I took another trip to Texas, and on the way there, I kept kidding our pilots, "Don't kill us; if you do, you'll be out of a job." We stayed in Texas for a week, seeing horses and meeting with Aurelio, our Mexican connection. We partied with some beauty pageant contestants, then returned to Miami. On the way back I asked Ed, one of my pilots, to meet me again in Miami in a few days, to fly my wife and kids to Walt Disney World. In the meantime, I told Ed to take the plane and go visit his daughter and grandchild.

On the appointed day, I had my family ready for the flight to Orlando, but Ed didn't show up. I called his home, and a woman who later identified herself as Ed's mother-in-law answered the phone.

"Who's calling?" she responded when I asked for Ed.

"I'm Jorge Valdés, Ed's boss."

"Do you mean you haven't heard?" she asked.

"Heard what? No, what happened?"

Ed's mother-in-law burst into tears as she said, "Ed was killed in a plane crash."

I nearly dropped the receiver. The weeping woman did her best to explain what had happened. While trying to land at the same airport in Ohio where he had learned to fly as a sixteen-year-old, Ed's plane encountered a wind shear and crashed.

It seemed that everyone around me was dying. At one time everything I touched turned into gold; now everything I touched seemed to vanish like ashes in the wind.

As I grieved the loss of another associate, I wondered, *When will my turn come?*

Twenty-Seven

Never, Never Again

Although my cocaine business was flourishing and the money was flowing, by 1987 everything seemed irrelevant. Not even money piqued my interest. One day as I worked at the desk in my office, I bumped my pager, dropping it behind the sofa. As I reached behind the couch, my hand touched a bag. I pulled out the bag, opened it, and found $700,000. I'd hidden it there weeks earlier, and I hadn't even missed it.

No matter what I did to try to regain a sense of purpose—or at least amusement—I was depressed and despondent. My marriage was falling apart, and I couldn't have cared less. The only bright spots in my life were my children.

Even my desire for revenge against the U.S. government was beginning to wane. I had nothing else to prove. I had rebuilt my drug empire from scratch after my release from prison. I had unleashed a cocaine blizzard that now blanketed the nation. I had proven that I could get away with it, often flaunting my ability to bring in cocaine right in front of the authorities without being caught. It was all a game, and I had won.

So why didn't I feel like celebrating?

■　　■　　■

One night, when I was lying in bed, watching TV with Sherry, I suddenly felt as if I was leaving my body. Certain I was dying, I could see myself floating away. I was trying to talk to Sherry, trying to get her to wake me up from this nightmare. When I snapped to, I was soaked with perspiration.

"Jorge! What's wrong?" Sherry cried.

"I don't know, but I think I just had a heart attack."

The next day I went to see a cardiologist in Miami, a specialist in such high demand that I had to donate $20,000 to the University of Miami Cardiology School just to get an appointment with him. After running a series of tests, he

153

concluded that I had experienced a mild heart attack—at only thirty-one years of age.

But worse than death's encroachment was my feeling of being dirty all the time. Sometimes when Krystle woke up in the night, I felt the need to scrub my hands vigorously before running to her crib. It was like starring in a bad version of *Macbeth;* I couldn't wash the guilt from my hands. Even when I talked to Krystle, I felt dirty. She was so pure and I was so . . . so utterly sinful.

As I looked at my cherubic little daughter in her sleep, I couldn't understand why I was unable to change my life for the better. Why was I in such despair? Krystle loved to chase me all over the house in her walker, and every so often I'd stop and just look at her. She and Jorgito were the loves of my life, yet I was gambling with their future.

One day while I was preparing to go to the ranch for the weekend, Margaret called, looking for Sherry.

Sherry was attending a shower for our baby that was due within weeks, but I lied to Margaret. "Sherry left me," I said. I told her I was depressed. "Do you want to spend the weekend with me at the beach house?" I quickly added, "Just as a friend?"

Margaret was now working as an airline flight attendant, and she told me that two of her coworkers were staying with her for the weekend. "Would you mind if my friends came along?"

"No problem," I replied.

I spent an enjoyable weekend with Margaret and her friends, partying in Fort Myers Beach and lounging around the pool at our beach house. On Sunday we had lunch on my boat before I took Margaret's friends to the airport. I talked Margaret into accompanying me on the drive back to Miami, so we went back to the beach house to pick up my things before leaving.

While Margaret freshened her makeup in the bathroom, I was sitting on the bed, talking by phone to my horse trainer. Suddenly a rock smashed through one of the glass panes in the French doors leading to the bedroom. At the explosion of sound, I jumped up from the bed, grabbed my gun, and cocked it. I inched my head outside the door. Just as I was ready to shoot, I saw my attacker. It was Sherry.

I started screaming at her. I was disturbed to realize how close I'd come to shooting my wife. To regain my composure, I went out to sit near the pool. Sherry began railing at me, claiming I was having an affair with another woman.

"No," I said, "I am not!"

Sherry slapped me so hard she knocked my glasses into the swimming pool. Still screaming, she began beating on me and kicking me in the groin. I yelled back at her, threatening to knock her out and throw her into the pool.

Margaret, meanwhile, had tried to make her escape, but ran smack into Sherry's mother, who had been waiting quietly in the front of the house. She led

Margaret back to us, and as they approached I heard Margaret crying, "I'm sorry, Sherry, I didn't do anything!"

Sherry took one look at Margaret, then realized that not only was her husband with another woman, but the woman was one of her best friends. Devastated, she broke down and wept.

I told Sherry that nothing had happened, that Margaret and I were just friends, but my words served only to reignite Sherry's fire. She slapped Margaret, dragged her by the hair, and threw her out of the house. Then she screamed again at me. "I'll turn you in to your parole officer," she threatened. "I'm gonna take everything you have!"

The next day Sherry called me at the ranch and said she was filing for divorce. "Fine," I answered.

For the next several months, Margaret and I were lovers. Meanwhile, Sherry was doing everything she could to make me feel even guiltier than I already felt. In the middle of the night when Krystle woke up crying, Sherry called me to say, "See what you've done! Your darling little girl is crying for you."

I was slowly dying a horrible death. Searching for relief, I partied even more, but that only made me feel worse.

Sherry and I engaged in the typical dance of divorcing couples, shuffling our children back and forth between households. Each week I trekked to Fort Walton Beach to pick up Krystle and bring her to the ranch to spend the weekend with Jorgito and me. Krystle was now nearly two years old, and it was the delight of my life to hear her call out to me, "Daddy! Daaad-dy."

One day in May 1987, Sherry called to tell me she was about to give birth to our second child. Despite our separation, I got on a plane that morning and arrived at the hospital in time for the birth of another precious baby girl, whom we named Jade, my second jewel. Because of Sherry's and my estrangement, being together at such an intimate time was awkward, but nothing could diminish the sense of awe and wonder I felt as I held my darling new daughter.

I spent that night in a hotel room with Krystle, wondering, *Where is my life going? How can I relate to this new baby?* Now I had two little girls whose smiles I would miss every day, daughters for whom I would most likely not be there at the important junctures in their lives. The way my life was headed, I probably wouldn't live long enough to see them graduate from high school.

The words of Big Eddie's daughter haunted me. "My daddy went to be with Jesus." I wondered: *When will Krystle or Jade look into a stranger's eyes and say something similar? Worse yet, will they tell someone their daddy went to hell?*

During the 1986 Quarter Horse Congress the previous fall, where my horses had finished in the top two places, a young man had approached me about buying his horse. "I have this nice yearling," he said. I wasn't really interested—I wanted only the best horses in this country. I kindly declined the kid's offer, but he persisted. I liked his hustle, so eventually I asked him what he wanted for the horse.

"Ten thousand dollars."

"Fine," I said. "I'll let you know in a couple of days."

After the Congress, I persuaded my dad to buy the horse, and he agreed.

Meanwhile I gave my horse trainer $400,000 and instructed him to canvass the country and buy the best two-year-old horses he could find, in preparation for the 1987 show season. By that spring, he had purchased five topnotch horses. Unfortunately, by late summer all five horses—one of which had cost more than $250,000—came up crippled or lame. There was no way they could compete, but I had been boasting to everyone that we would win the Congress again.

With Mom and Dad in Cuba, 1956. I was fifteen days old

The Valdés family, still in Cuba: Mom, Maria, J.C, me, and Dad

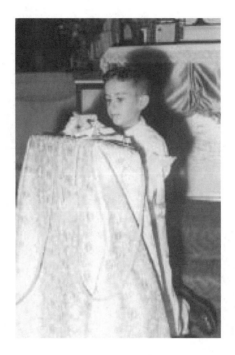

My first communion . . . but God would soon mean so little to me.

J.C. and me. My brother has been a faithful support to me all through life.

1956: The year before we fled my homeland.

After our arrival in Florida: J.C. and me in the Boy Scouts

At age seventeen, now working for the Federal
Reserve Bank in Miami.

A break from work on the banana boat in Stockton.

My soon-to-be-companion in prison and torture:
Harold Rosenthal, shortly before the plane crash in Panama.

With a partner and the Queen Air, our plane for taking cocaine out
of Bolivia. That's me on the right

From DEA file: A photo of our crashed Queen Air in Panama.

Jorge "Lino" Latinez as he interrogates us in his office in Panama.
This photo is also from DEA files.

DEA photo of cocaine found on our crashed plane.

Working in the dental clinic while a prisoner at Eglin.
I quickly learned how to get what I wanted in prison.

Six-year-old Jorgito visits father in prison at Eglin.

At Eglin in 1983, on the day I married Sherry.

My waiting Porsche, after my release from Eglin in 1984.

With Jorgito and Mom after my Eglin release.

On these pages: A few signs of the "good life," 1987;
but my life as a drug lord was emptier than ever.

Giving Krystle a ride at the ranch.

Krystle was too young to know how God would use her to end my
life as a drug lord.

A bold believer who got my attention:
Tim Brooks and his wife, Teruko.

With my mentor at Wheaton College, Dr. Walter Elwell.

God's amazing gift to me in my new life: Sujey in 1997.

My precious children, growing up so fast: Jorgito behind Krystle
(Left), Alex, and Jade.

More of God's amazing grace towards Sujey and me, our two precious
children, Estevan born in 1999 and our queen Isabela, born in 2002.

I asked our trainer what we should do.

"Well," he answered, "our only horse ready to compete is the one your dad bought from that kid last year."

"Let's enter him," I said. "If he shows badly, we can always pull him and say he was lame, and at least save face."

By the time the season was over, however, that cheap horse had won the 1987 Congress and every other major show. He was the highest earning two-year-old in the country. His name said it all—Heaven Sent.

By late 1987, I was struggling with a serious loss of passion for the drug business. The thrill was gone. To the cartel members in Colombia and other contacts, I constantly made up excuses about why it wasn't a good time to bring in the cocaine. Usually I said I was under surveillance—an assertion I could easily assume was true.

Making matters worse, Sherry reported to my parole officer that I had a private jet in which I was traveling all over the country—and each out-of-state trip represented a parole violation. But Sherry didn't reveal that I was involved in drug activities.

My parole officer started making my life miserable. Without warning she would call me and require my presence in her office in ninety minutes. To be late or to miss an appointment carried the potential penalty of going back to prison to complete my fifteen-year sentence in full. When the parole office called, I dropped everything and ran.

This went on for several months. Finally I'd had enough. The next time the parole officer called, I went to her office carrying a bag with a few clothes and said, "Lock me up. I can't take this anymore. I hate you, and I hate my wife. Just put me away."

The parole officer thought I was crazy. "I'll make a deal with you," she said. "If you agree to see a psychiatrist, I'll give you a break until he reports to me."

I agreed. The psychiatrist I was sent to see was a Christian named Fred Percetti, and although it was awkward, I began to open my life to him. I wasn't about to admit my involvement in anything illegal, but I dropped plenty of hints concerning my immoral lifestyle and the sense of guilt that I'd begun to experience. This was a major crack in my armor, and it caused me a great deal of consternation. *This is the ultimate weakness,* I thought, *needing someone to tell me how to straighten up my life.* Everybody in my world wanted to be like me, so what could be wrong with me?

I visited my mother and father often during this time, so much so that my bodyguards worried that my schedule was becoming too predictable for any foe who might be watching. Mom and Dad still lived in the home I had secretly helped purchase for them. They refused all my offers to move them to a bigger, nicer house, wanting nothing to do with tainted drug money. There was little use in trying to conceal anything from them, especially from Mom, who had sat through every moment of my trial.

Dad warned me frequently about the slippery slope I was traveling. "Son," he implored, "if you go back to prison, you're going to kill us."

I didn't deny that I was involved in the drug business again, but I assured him I was far removed from actually handling the merchandise. The business had become so sophisticated by now that all I needed to do was pick up the phone and tell the Colombians to send the coke. My subordinates handled everything from there. I was still making millions of dollars, but with less risk. At least that's what I thought.

Despite my lessening exposure to being caught, I nonetheless began contemplating how I could end my involvement with the drug business—something few individuals at my level had ever done. Nobody walked away from the money or the power. But I was disenchanted with both.

I could find only three reasons for remaining alive: Jade, Krystle, and Jorgito. My son was now approaching adolescence, and I wanted to be there for him as he went through those turbulent years. I was especially saddened for Jorgie when Sherry walked out of our lives. Sherry and Jorgie had grown extremely attached to each other. Now that she was gone, I wondered what my son thought about me. Not only had I divorced his mom, but now I'd broken up with his stepmom as well.

My appetite for pornography and perversion increased dramatically after Sherry's departure. One weekend when I had two women partying with me at the ranch, Sherry unexpectedly decided to drop Krystle off for an overnight stay. After Krystle went to sleep, the women and I resumed our drinking before ending up together in bed.

I awoke at about one-thirty, thinking I heard a knock on my bedroom door. At first I ignored the sound.

Tap, tap, tap. There it was again. I lifted my head off the pillow and listened intently. Just then, I heard a sound that haunts me to this day.

"Daddy. Daaad-dy?"

Instinctively, I jerked a bedsheet over my naked body. The women stirred next to me.

"Daddy? It's Krystle," I heard her tiny voice calling.

I shook the women violently, scaring them awake. "Get out," I said tersely. "Get out now!"

"Why? Jorge, what's wrong?"

"Shut up and go!" I whispered harshly. Quickly the women gathered their clothes and started toward the door.

"No, not that way! Out the window."

"Jorge, this is ridiculous."

"Go!" I shrieked hoarsely, glaring at them with a face that clearly convinced them to obey.

As the women scurried out the window, still wrapping themselves in their clothing, I pulled the bedcovers up around my neck.

Again the angelic voice called through the door. "Daddy! Daddy, it's Krystle. Please open the door. Daaad-dy! Please!"

I felt as though I'd touched the ends of a live electric wire. I began to perspire profusely; my body was trembling. The more my baby girl kept calling for me, the more I continued to sweat and shake.

I closed my eyes tightly, as if by blocking my vision I could somehow block out the sound. But just as I had experienced when the plane careened toward the earth in Panama, my life passed before my eyes. I blinked hard. I didn't want to see it.

Is this the end of my life?

Krystle's voice gradually diminished from a high-pitched call to a heartrending wail to a sniffling whimper. All the while, I clutched the covers around me, as if the bedclothes could cover my shame.

How could I be doing this to my little baby? *I've never been subjected to anything as horrible as what I'm doing to my precious daughter right now.* How could I be so evil? What had consumed me? If my guns had been close by at that moment, I wouldn't have hesitated to shoot myself.

Finally, I heard no more sounds from Krystle outside my door.

Only then did I stop trembling. Slowly, ever so quietly, I slipped out of bed. I was repulsed by myself, but it wasn't the perspiration glistening on my skin that made me feel so repugnant. Filth seemed to emanate from deep within me, seeping out, inexorably working its way to the surface.

I wanted to check on Krystle, but I was too dirty. I wanted to run to her, to hug her tightly, but I felt so filthy. She was so pure—and I was so corrupt, so vile. If I even touched my daughter, I would taint her forever.

I stumbled toward the shower, turned on the water as hot as I could stand, and tried washing away my foulness. Scrubbing my body roughly, over and over, until my skin was raw, I stayed in the shower until it felt that my flesh itself was going down the drain.

Finally I shut off the water and wrapped myself in a heavy terry-cloth robe.

I opened the bedroom door, and the image I saw was burned forever in my memory. My precious baby girl was lying on the floor crying, her face pressed against the doorjamb as if she was trying to catch any glimpse at all of her daddy.

She looked up at me through tear-filled eyes. "Daddy!" she cried.

I knelt beside Krystle and hugged her. Cataclysmic upheavals of emotion ripped through my body. I held Krystle tightly and promised, "Never, never again! Never again will I ever put you through this."

By now, it was three in the morning, but I called Mom anyway. I quickly allayed her fears about my early morning phone call. With Krystle still in my lap, I said, "Mom, I'm finished. I'm through with this kind of life."

I didn't need to say anything further. Mom knew exactly what I was talking about, and by the tone of my voice, she could tell I was serious.

I tried to talk to her, but the words caught in my throat. It didn't matter. Mom didn't need the details. Through her tears, she just kept thanking God, over and over, for answering her prayers.

I hung up the phone and suddenly realized that for the first time in my life, I felt a peace in my heart. I had no idea what was going to happen, but I knew I had to make a clean cut with my Colombian business partners. I couldn't go halfway. Intuitively, I knew that if this change stood a chance, it would require drastic action—all or nothing.

Not that my absence would impair the cartel's business for a moment. Nor was I worried about retaliation. If they wanted to kill me, let them do their worst. They couldn't hurt me.

Jorge Valdés, the king of cocaine, was already dead.

PART FOUR

1987-1995

Tim stepped closer. He planted his feet solidly in front of me, squared his dangerous body, and put his face less than an inch away from mine. I could see fire in his eyes and determination in the set of his jaw . . . .

"Let me tell you something," he said. "What I have to give you, you don't have enough money to buy."

Twenty-Eight

What Money Can't Buy

The next morning's light did not change my commitment. I had given my word to Krystle and my mom—and if I never broke a promise to drug dealers, I certainly wasn't going to renege on a promise to my family members who had loved me so deeply and unconditionally.

I called Manny and told him I had lost my will; I no longer had the courage to continue my business. I couldn't take it anymore, and I wanted out.

Though Manny regretted my desire to leave, he respected my decision. He knew I had never compromised my loyalty to the cartel. I had been tortured in Panama and gone to prison for them; through it all, I had never snitched on anyone. No one had ever served a day in prison because of information I had volunteered. None of the cartel's family members or closest friends had died at my hand or because of my directive. Manny knew that no one had anything against me.

Sherry moved back to Miami while I lived at the ranch, and we talked by telephone and occasionally spent time together at her townhouse when I went to pick up the children. My partner, the Arab, encouraged me to try to put my marriage back together, and gradually I allowed myself to entertain the possibility of being reconciled with Sherry.

But Margaret was keeping me company on the weekends while I worked through my depression. With her help, I had stopped doing cocaine. After the initial few weeks of flinching every time somebody slammed a door, my paranoia subsided, and before long I stopped worrying about somebody trying to kill me.

I continued my counseling sessions with Fred—I needed his wisdom now more than ever—and in November, when Sherry suggested we give our marriage another try for the sake of our kids, we both began going to Fred's office for counseling. By New Year's, I was occasionally staying overnight with Sherry at her townhouse.

Early in 1988, I told Margaret I was going to reconcile with Sherry. Margaret became extremely distraught, but I knew I had to do this. Sherry and I had been separated for more than seven months, but she was still the mother of two of my children, and I owed it to her, to our kids, and to myself to give our marriage another chance.

Sherry moved in with me at the ranch. We were still going to the counselor twice a week, and at times I thought we were making great progress. At other times I was convinced the sessions were a total waste of time. I couldn't understand why Sherry could not simply forgive and forget and move on. I had no idea how much unresolved hurt and resentment she still carried within her. Nor did I care to understand. Even though a slow metamorphosis had begun in my life, I still lived in a world where everything revolved around me. Other people were important only in relation to what they could do for me; I wanted them to understand my needs and cater to them. I was all that mattered.

■   ■   ■

Sherry and I were watching a karate movie on television one night when I said, "Why don't we hire an instructor to teach us karate?" Sherry liked the idea, and we soon visited a karate studio in Fort Myers, where we met Tim Brooks and his wife, Teruko. In his mid-forties, Tim was tough looking and solid as a rock, carrying two hundred pounds on his five-foot-nine frame. Originally from Ohio, Tim had grown up in Japan where his parents were missionaries. There he had met and fallen in love with Teruko.

Sherry and I observed one of Tim's classes. It was obvious the man knew his karate. Tim was a *shihan,* a master, with a seventh-degree black belt. I told Tim that I wanted to put in a karate studio in my home and asked if he would consider giving Sherry and me private lessons. Tim agreed to come out to the ranch to have a look.

After Tim gave me instructions on how to have the karate studio built and equipped, he agreed to come every weekday. I offered to pay him $150 for each two-hour lesson.

Sherry wasn't feeling well the day Tim came for our first lesson, so I met him at the studio alone, dressed in my new *ghi,* the white karate uniform. He was also dressed in his *ghi,* bedecked with a seventh-degree black belt.

Eager to begin, I started stretching and loosening up for my first lesson. "Before we get started, Jorge," Tim said, reaching into his gym bag, "I want to teach you about the sword."

I thought Tim must have brought some kind of compact sword—something he could press a button or squeeze to make it stretch to a full-size weapon. I could hardly wait to see what he pulled out of the bag. Instead of the switchblade-style sword I imagined, Tim pulled out a Bible.

Anger surged through me as I stared at the book. "Look," I said, "let me explain something to you. I don't believe in God. If you really want to know the truth, I *am* God, and I'm paying you a lot of money to teach me karate, so tomorrow leave this 'sword' at home."

Tim stepped closer. He planted his feet solidly in front of me, squared his dangerous body, and put his face less than an inch away from mine. I could see fire in his eyes and determination in the set of his jaw.

More than that, he had an undeniable lack of fear—something I hadn't seen in years, since most of my subordinates and partners regarded me with such fear and respect. Tim spoke calmly but with power and intensity. "Let me tell you something," he said. "What I have to give you, you don't have enough money to buy."

It was clear Tim wasn't about to back away from a fight. I wanted to kick myself for making him mad—this man with a seventh-degree black belt, who could whip me and toss me right through the windows. At the same time, a rush of exhilaration raced through me. This guy wasn't afraid of me and didn't try to elevate me. And he believed in something.

I decided to try lowering the tension level by inserting a little levity.

"Do you mean this isn't going to cost me anything? This isn't part of my lesson time?"

Tim relaxed slightly, but he didn't break a smile. "No," he replied.

"All right," I said, "I'll make a deal with you. When we're through with our karate lesson and waiting for the steam room to heat up, you can talk to me all you want about that Bible."

Tim smiled. "Deal," he said, as he reached out his hand and grasped mine.

Just as I had imagined, Tim was not only an expert karate practitioner but also an excellent teacher. Yet he was an enigma to me. Why was he willing to risk blowing $750 a week for only a few hours worth of work just because he felt convicted to tell me about the Bible? I was perplexed—and beginning to feel a little scared.

After the lesson, Tim told me about the Bible and how he had come to have a relationship with Jesus Christ. Eventually he also told me the reason he was so persistent in talking about this Jesus whom he served.

Karate was already the love of his life when one day, shortly after Tim and Teruko married, he approached a railroad crossing while driving home. He saw a train barreling right at him, but he thought he could beat the train. Tim tromped the gas pedal to the floor. The little Honda lurched past the first rail but never made it across the second. The train caught his car and cut it in half, tossing Tim about a hundred feet through the air.

By the time his wife arrived at the hospital, the doctors had given up hope of saving Tim's life. Even if he lived, she was told, he would be a vegetable the rest of his life.

Teruko refused to accept their prognosis. She alerted their family members and their Christian friends, and they formed a prayer vigil, asking God for a miracle. Teruko told the doctor, "Not only will my husband live, but he's going to walk out of here, and he's going to continue to teach karate."

Then she prayed, "Lord, I promise that if you save my husband, then everyone that he teaches karate to, he will tell about Jesus." God granted their request, and Tim held true to Teruko's promise.

As we sat in the steam room, Tim looked over at me and said, "So you see, Jorge, I have to tell you about Jesus, whether you want to listen or not."

I didn't say much, but somewhere deep within the recesses of my heart, I knew that one of the reasons God had performed a miracle for Teruko and Tim was so Tim could bring the gospel of Jesus Christ to me.

Not that I made it easy for him. In the beginning of our relationship, I did everything I could do to test Tim, to see how sincere he was about his conviction. I showed him my collection of pornographic movies and told him that many of the actresses were my friends. Tim never told me, "You're going to go to hell if you keep watching that stuff!" He just kept telling me about Jesus and, most important, allowing me to see Jesus through him.

Tim and Teruko began visiting often with Sherry and me at our beach house. We did normal fun things—hanging out around the pool or in the Jacuzzi, riding Wave Runners, or going out in our boats. Tim loved the ocean, and when he and Teruko visited, he and I rose early in the morning to practice karate on the beach as the sun came up.

Tim and Teruko's influence began to impact my life dramatically. I was healthier; I drank hardly any alcohol, and I wasn't doing any drugs at all. I was getting up early in the morning to do two hours of karate. I also began paying closer attention to my ranch business.

Although Sherry and I made great strides in our karate, the progress in our marriage relationship was nil. We slept in the same bed, but had no intimacy, not even to touch.

Meanwhile, I kept observing Tim and Teruko Brooks and wondering how they could be so happy. They seemed to love and appreciate each other so much. I noticed the little things they did for each other—the little touches they shared, the way Tim looked at his wife with such immense admiration, and the way they spoke to each other with such respect, though they had been married for more than fifteen years. I thought, *How can this be possible?* At times, I wondered if they were on drugs. Either that or they were just putting up a front for me.

That summer, their family and ours did all sorts of activities together. I enjoyed camping with them and doing other special things, but I noticed that their excitement and contentment didn't seem to stem from what they were doing or where they were. They could have a lot of fun with each other just drinking soft drinks. They didn't need promiscuous sex, alcohol, or drugs. The more I studied

Tim and Teruko's family in everyday settings, the more obsessed I became in discovering what was driv ing these people.

Tim introduced me to Jeff Pate, a fellow karate enthusiast. Jeff was the son of a wealthy businessman from Fort Myers. He had grown up in a broken home and had gone off to school in Boston, where he had lived the life of a playboy. As a young man, Jeff became an alcoholic. But then he began to take karate lessons from Tim, who talked to Jeff about Jesus. Jeff became a believer. He met and married Elaine, also a Christian, and together they were one of the most loving couples I had ever seen.

I watched Jeff and Elaine with the same interest as I did Tim and Teruko, trying to decide whether these people were for real. They were totally consistent. When Jeff came over to my ranch to watch a sporting event with me, he brought his nonalcoholic beer and had as much fun as anybody else.

These people bewildered me. *I know they say they're Christians, but there's got to be more to it,* I thought. I experienced something I hadn't felt since childhood—envy. I was envious that these people could have peace and contentment without all the money or power I had.

They invited me to their church, so Sherry and I went occasionally. Usually I made up excuses why I couldn't attend. Even though I was intrigued by these couples' lifestyles, I wanted no part of church.

I continued to suspect they were putting on an act. Yet I couldn't deny that Tim and Teruko, Jeff and Elaine, and their other Christian friends were different. They acted differently and talked differently. And their values were different from those of most people I knew—though they were strikingly similar to my mom's values.

Near the end of summer, we decided to attend a karate tournament together in Seattle. My friends made our flight reservations, and when Sherry and I arrived at the airport, I was surprised to discover that all our seats were in the coach section. At the time, it was a major adjustment in my life just to fly first-class on an airline rather than in my own private jet. Not wanting to be rude, I took my seat along with the others. Before long, we were having a tremendous time; Tim talked the flight attendants into giving us some apples, which we promptly karate-chopped into oblivion. We laughed all the way to Seattle. Almost against my will, I was enjoying myself.

I also discovered that it didn't take much money to make these people happy. We went whitewater rafting and did a host of other simple activities—and we always had a great time.

Never were my new Christian friends oppressive or rude in trying to convert me, but they weren't reluctant to talk about their faith. Their conversations about God didn't seem contrived. When they spoke about a relationship with Jesus being more than mere religion, it seemed almost second nature to them. Sometimes their talk about what God had done in their lives became a little too much for me, and I excused myself and left the room. Usually, though, I listened to what they were saying, wondering if it could be true, trying to analyze each of my friends, looking for the chinks in their armor.

I'm going to catch them, I told myself. *They can't fool me forever.* Sooner or later, they would let down their guard, and I would find out what was really going on.

Following the closing events of the tournament, we went out for the evening. We had dinner, danced, and laughed. Strangely, nobody expected me to pay for everything, which I was more than willing to do. These were, after all, my good friends, and I was used to paying for people around me to have a good time.

But these couples wanted to pay their own way. It was almost embarrassing to me as the couples pored over the restaurant bill, trying to figure how much each of them owed and tossing their tens and twenties onto the middle of the table. Despite my discomfort, I was impressed. I wasn't accustomed to people who wanted me around for more than my money.

That night, when we went back to our room, Sherry and I were especially affectionate. We hadn't been intimate with each other for some time, but as a result of that special evening, our precious son, Alex, was born nine months later.

Now that I was using my business acumen legitimately, my horse business flourished. Tardee Impressive virtually paid for himself with the huge stud fees he was commanding. Mom and Dad finally consented to spend more time with me at the ranch, so I built a house for them there, right next to mine. I enjoyed having Mom and Dad nearby, and we spent many evenings together, just talking or watching movies.

I had to cut down on my overhead; I didn't have the millions in cash coming in anymore, and it hadn't taken long to spend the cash I had on hand when I left the drug business. I had millions of dollars in assets, but I could no longer afford to blow $30,000 to $40,000 on a shopping spree, as I often did during my drug days.

But I was much happier than I'd been in years. I had a new zest for life, getting up early in the morning, working all day, and managing my business. My horse-breeding business developed many new clients. I spent long hours to keep up with the work, but I didn't mind. I enjoyed the fact that I was making something prosper legitimately, a business that gave other people a sense of pride and accomplishment rather than the white death I had been peddling.

The best part of my workday occurred each afternoon when, like clockwork, my private office phone rang at three o'clock. Without picking it up, I knew who was on the line.

"Daddy, horsy, horsy!" Krystle would say. That meant it was time to go riding with the kids. I dropped everything and met Jorgie, Krystle, and Jade at the stables to go horseback riding. Jorgie was now an accomplished rider and was able to ride one of the girls with him, while my other daughter rode with me. After an hour-long romp all over the ranch, we returned the horses to the barn and went swimming together. It was our afternoon ritual, and I felt that my children and I were growing closer together every day.

But I couldn't say the same thing about my relationship with Sherry.

Twenty-Nine

Disintegration

Sherry and I continued our counseling sessions with Fred, but we were making little progress. I criticized Sherry constantly, finding fault with almost everything she did. I never apologized for having an affair with her friend, nor did I make any attempt to be gentle and compassionate with her or to understand the pain she had experienced because of me. In my mind, I felt that I had come back to her, that I had made a major concession by even consenting to get back together.

I didn't know how to express love or even kindness and caring in the way Sherry wanted. All my life I'd used women as trinkets, simply for my own convenience, appearance, and wanton pleasure. I wasn't accustomed to giving love. A person couldn't survive for long in my former line of work by being soft and mushy.

As much as I tried, I really didn't have the ability on my own to straighten out my life or my marriage. I could change exterior circumstances, but my inner person remained callous and self-centered.

One day during a counseling session, Fred said, "I want to give you a trust test." Sherry and I stood with our faces toward the wall, and Fred moved behind me. "Now, just drop backward with your eyes closed," he instructed. I allowed myself to fall backward, and Fred quickly caught me. Then he instructed Sherry to do the same, and she also tipped backward into Fred's waiting arms.

Next, Fred asked me to stand behind Sherry and catch her when she fell. I stood behind her, but Sherry wouldn't allow herself to drop.

"Okay," Fred instructed. "Sherry, you get behind Jorge and catch him when he falls." I stood there for a moment, knowing that if I dropped back, Sherry either would not or could not catch me.

I turned around. "No, I don't think this is a good idea," I said.

We went back and sat down, Sherry on one side of Fred's desk and me on the other. Fred said, "I told you when you came to me that I would try to help you reconcile and reconstruct trust in your marriage. But sometimes—"

Sherry interrupted him. "I don't want to reconcile," she said. "I just want to punish him!"

Her comment caught me off guard. Anger welled within me, and I wanted to reach across Fred's desk, grab Sherry, and shake her—hard. After all, I was trying to be a better husband. I was trying to straighten out my life, disrupting my schedule to come to a counselor twice a week. And this woman wanted to punish me?

We talked further, and Sherry and I decided we would hang in there until the end of the year. If our relationship didn't improve by then, we would divorce.

Later that fall, during a business trip in Oklahoma, I bought a Chevy Suburban complete with a television, upscale stereo system, and seats that folded down into beds. I called home and told Sherry I would be driving the Suburban back, rather than flying.

"When will you be home?" Sherry asked.

"It should take me about three days to make the drive."

That night, as I was preparing for the trip, my ranch manager told me that his wife had called from Florida to tell him that Sherry had been at my office all day, photocopying documents. This was not good news. Sherry rarely went into my office when I was home, let alone when I was gone. I knew that nothing in the office could incriminate me, but I decided not to take any chances.

I told my ranch manager, "Drive the Suburban back. I'm taking a flight home, but don't tell anyone."

I flew back to Florida and took a taxi from the Fort Myers airport to the ranch. When I arrived, Sherry wasn't there, so I searched the house immediately. Nothing seemed unusual or out of place. I began to think that perhaps I'd overreacted, until I opened a closet and found a bag filled with copies of documents. I quickly scanned through the pile of paper.

Sherry had written a letter to the U.S. attorney telling him everything she knew about me. Although her information was sketchy at best and filled with conjecture, she was nonetheless informing the government about my Colombian godfather, Manny Garces, about my planes, and about the many shady characters around me. Sherry wrote that she suspected that I was heavily involved in narcotics.

Fury and fear surged through me as I read the dangerous revelations in her letter—not necessarily fear for myself, but fear for my children and my entire family. I thought, *How stupid are you, woman? You're not destroying just me; don't you realize that if this letter ever gets out, you're a dead person?* There was no way I could fully protect her from the people she was compromising, some of whom were ruthless killers. By her foolish attempt to defeat me, she was endangering the lives of her children, her parents, and herself.

I paced around the house, collecting all my guns as I went. I put them in a large sack and took them to my ranch manager's wife. "Just keep these," I said, "because I don't know what I might do if I have a gun right now."

When Sherry drove up to the ranch house, I grabbed her by the hand and pulled her inside. Picking up the bag full of copied documents, I threw it at her and roared, "Get out of this house before I kill you!"

She cried and screamed at me. I couldn't understand her pain, nor did I care to. She had betrayed me, and I knew that if she stayed there much longer, I might do something I would regret forever.

Sherry left the house, picked up the kids from school, and went to the hotel across the highway. When she called later that night, I told her to rent a U-Haul, call someone to help her pack, and get out of my life forever.

I hated putting my little girls through this. Jade was still a toddler, but Krystle was old enough to remember our previous time of separation. I tried to be strong, but every time I saw my daughter crying, I wondered what was going through her mind.

Sherry called frequently, arguing over various details of our divorce. As much as we both tried to shield our children from the ugliness, I'm sure they heard things that I will forever wish they hadn't.

My Christian karate friends, Tim and Teruko, came over to the ranch to console me. I told them I felt betrayed, but I didn't go into any details. They didn't take sides between Sherry and me or try to answer my questions or take away the hurt; they simply offered to pray with me. I wasn't in much of a praying mood. I felt that prayer was useless at this point, and that the God whom they served really must not exist. After all, I had been making an attempt to clean up my life, yet my relationship with Sherry had disintegrated anyway. Where was God in that?

In actuality, my attempt at going straight had been halfhearted at best. Although I acknowledged that something "spiritual" was happening in my life—something that Tim and Teruko and the others attributed to God—I was just as sinful as ever. I often felt convicted about what an evil person I was, but I still enjoyed watching my porno movies occasionally, and I still liked to party.

No, I couldn't say that I'd given God much of a chance to change my life. I had made a token effort, but I hadn't placed any faith in God, and I certainly hadn't committed myself to be a follower of Jesus Christ, whatever that meant.

Recognizing how disorientated my life had become, my brother, J.C., began making frequent trips to the ranch in an effort to encourage me. J.C. had battled alcoholism ever since my imprisonment in Panama. He blamed himself for being unable to rescue me from the torture I endured there. J.C. drank in a futile effort to forget and to avoid the demons that taunted him.

One day, driving from Miami to the ranch in a semi-inebriated condition, J.C. got into a severe auto accident. He survived the wreck and finally realized he needed help. He went into an alcohol rehabilitation center, and with their help and with a vibrant faith in the Lord, J.C. was able to break the control alcohol held on his life. He came to work at the ranch and eventually took over the finances. J.C. soon lowered our overhead drastically, increased our profit margins, and actually transformed the ranch from an expensive hobby into a moneymaking machine.

In contrast, my life was empty and miserable. I now had two broken homes, and I was separated from my children.

In July 1989, we entered the Hendry County courtroom to finalize our divorce. In that dreary setting I first saw our son, Alex, who had been born in April. Alex was handsome, but I didn't even want to look at him. My defense mechanism kicked in, and rather than suffer more pain of separation, I forced myself not to become attached to my baby boy.

Strangely, when I returned home following the divorce proceedings, I didn't feel that I had been freed from a bad relationship. For some reason, I felt as though I was imprisoned, held captive by some invisible force.

I spent most of my spare time going to the beach, visiting with Tim and Teruko Brooks, and practicing karate. Eventually I received my black belt in karate. Throughout that period, Tim and Teruko and Jeff and Elaine Pate continued to talk to me about spiritual matters, without pushing too hard. They just lived their Christian lives in front of me, loving me and supporting me with their encouragement. But I wasn't ready to give in yet.

In September of that year, I came down with a nasty flu bug. I used the illness as an excuse to call Margaret. Her response surprised me: "Jorge, I can't believe you're calling me again," she raged. "I've just barely gotten over you!" Then she hung up the phone.

I called her back and insisted that she come if she wanted to see me one last time, since I was dying. The flu made me sound weak and emaciated, which I was—relatively. Whether or not she believed me, Margaret came to the ranch later that day. Before long we were back in each other's arms. I apologized for the pain I had caused her, and I told her I was different now, that I didn't drink or do drugs.

Margaret seemed genuinely happy for me. She started coming over on weekends, and I introduced her to Tim and Teruko.

In December, less than six months after my divorce from Sherry, I gave Margaret an engagement ring. The next month we went skiing in Colorado, then visited Santa Fe, New Mexico. There we unexpectedly met Amado Peña, a famous southwestern artist whose paintings Margaret especially liked and who, it so happened, was a fan of my horse, Tardee Impressive.

I had known nothing about Amado Peña, but the beauty of his richly colored work impressed me. In his portraits I was struck by Peña's obvious belief that a person was the sum of his or her surroundings. No person could be separated from family, from the land, or from the work of his or her hands. The people depicted in Peña's paintings were products of their cultures, their sweat, and sometimes their blood. Peña chose to meld human features into figures that depicted the universal human struggle and to place them against the awesome backdrop of southwestern landscapes.

Amado radiated a warmth and sincerity as well as a concern and compassion for the people of Mexico and the American Southwest. I quickly understood why so many of his paintings portrayed such incredible power and pathos. We talked for four hours, and I bought four pieces of art from Amado.

When I learned that he planned to come to Miami soon for an exhibition of his works, I invited Amado to our ranch to see Tardee Impressive. He accepted with delight, and when he came, it was obvious that Amado was as equally at home caring for horses as he was in a studio creating his masterpieces.

Amado and I did not discuss spiritual matters, but he modeled many of the character traits espoused by my Christian friends. His morality and his concern for powerless people seemed to permeate everything he did. Though his work was prominently displayed in corporate boardrooms of numerous large companies as well as in museums, Amado did not buy into any ostentatious attitude. This intrigued me. Here was a man with whom I could identify, since he had climbed to the top in his chosen field. Amado was fabulously wealthy and highly esteemed by his peers, yet he was a humble and gracious man. Amado's life showed me that one need not flaunt success. Through Amado, together with Tim's example, God was showing me an entirely new way of living.

I bought numerous pieces of his work, and Amado gave me several more, so that I literally had a gallery of his work at the ranch. It eventually struck me that everything Amado's life stood for—all the beauty and culture he portrayed on canvas—was what I had been destroying. I had assaulted my land, my family, my children, and my heritage, giving precedence instead to my insatiable quest for money and power.

Thirty

Convicted

About two months after my trip with Margaret to Santa Fe, I sat alone in my room. The cumulative pain, despair, and misery of my life seemed to envelop me like a shroud. For no clear reason, I began to cry. I thought about God and about the many things Tim and my other Christian friends had told me about their relationship with Jesus Christ. I kept thinking about the happiness they possessed.

I was surrounded by wealth and was soon to be married—so why was I so miserable?

I thought of my sweet, innocent children, and I missed them terribly. I thought of the pain I had caused my parents and how my mother had aged. I thought of the anguish I had caused my brother. And I thought of the many people outside my family circle whose lives I had impacted negatively.

As I considered the concentric circles of shattered lives around me, the pain in my soul deepened. Before long, I was weeping uncontrollably.

I was convicted, convicted to the core of my being that Jorge Valdés was not God. I was nothing but a frail human being, lost and floundering on a sea of meaninglessness and in need of a Savior. At the same time, I was convicted by what I saw in my Christian friends. If Jesus and his goodness could do more for them than all my money, power, alcohol, cocaine, and promiscuity, he must be an amazing God! Yet I was also convinced that since he was so good and I was so evil, I stood little chance of making it into heaven.

In abject desperation, I fell to my knees beside my bed and looked up toward heaven. With tears streaming down my face, I cried out, "Jesus, I don't know if you are real or not. I don't know if what Tim has been telling me is true or not. And I know that if you are for real, you might look at me and think I have lived such a sordid life that you don't want me.

"But Jesus, there is something about these Christian people that I want. I want the peace and tranquillity they possess, and if you accept me, and if you will help me change and give me this peace and tranquillity, I'll give you my whole

---

heart, and I will serve you. And as much as I have lived for the devil in the past, I will do ten times as much for you, no matter what the price or the place."

It wasn't a fancy prayer. It wasn't replete with theology—but it was a genuine plea for help.

And God heard my cry.

A rush of peace flowed through my body, mind, and spirit. I was ebullient. I felt like a buoy bobbing peacefully in the ocean, with the wind blowing gently on my face, drying my tears. I couldn't explain it; I couldn't quantify it. Nothing in my experience had prepared me for this sort of feeling. My sense of tranquillity was deep and unfathomable.

I felt refreshed. And perhaps strangest of all, I felt *clean!* I felt clean on the inside—as though all the dirt of my life had suddenly been power-washed away.

■   ■   ■

My prayer didn't transform my life overnight, but I did notice subtle changes almost immediately.

With faith starting to blossom in my heart, I began to believe in God with a marvelous spiritual naiveté, despite my usually analytical approach to life. One day Tim and I were tending to a sick horse. The animal hadn't responded to medication, so Tim and I did a seemingly foolish thing: We placed our hands on the horse and prayed that God would touch it and make it well. The horse made an amazing turnaround and recovered.

Another consequence of my conversion was that I started feeling guilty about sleeping with Margaret. I tried to rationalize our relationship by the fact that we were engaged to be married and that the wedding ceremony was merely a formality. Yet deep inside, I knew that having sex outside of marriage was wrong.

I also felt guilty for the way I talked. In my lifestyle, profanity peppered almost every conversation. Now, however, I cringed as I occasionally paused and realized that my language was an indicator of the filth with which I had filled my life for so long. I was especially sensitive about the name of Jesus. If Jesus was who he claimed to be and had died for me, how could I use his name as a curse?

On the other hand, I believed that Jesus accepted me just as I was, so I talked to him as I would talk with any close friend. "Jesus," I told him, "if there's anything in me that isn't right, please help me change it, because I cannot change it on my own." I knew that if I could have changed my inner life under my own power, through some self-improvement program, then I didn't need Jesus. But in fact I could not change my heart attitudes, and that's where Christ was doing the deepest work in me.

I became increasingly conscious of the price Christ paid for my salvation. As a businessman, I understood costs; I understood sacrifice; I understood buying low and selling high. But Jesus turned my accounting system upside down. Why had he, the highest, suffered an excruciating death on a cross for me, the lowest?

I continued to grapple with the troublesome issues that had twisted my view of God in the past. Why had God allowed my family to experience such suffering when we had to flee our home in Cuba? Why did he allow all the hunger and suffering in the world?

Tim stood firm under my barrage of questions. When he didn't have an answer for me, he didn't make one up. Instead he encouraged me to keep searching the Scriptures, to keep seeking the Lord with all my heart, and to spend time in prayer, talking with God. "He will reveal whatever you need to know in due time," my friend assured me.

My parents, meanwhile, were overjoyed at news of my conversion. My dad wrote me a moving letter, expressing how glad he and Mom were that I had found God. He reminded me that faith was all a man needed to survive. Reading his letter helped me understand how God's presence sustained my parents through all the years of suffering after they left Cuba. I realized that God alone had given my parents the strength to endure the pain and shame of my conviction and my five years in prison.

In June of 1990, I attended my parole hearing. Ordinarily, by that time I should have been taken off parole automatically. But I was told that, because of an ongoing investigation in New Orleans, my parole was being extended. I would have to continue reporting to federal authorities until further notice.

I was peeved at the inconvenience, but I wasn't concerned about being implicated in the New Orleans investigation since I had never done business there.

■　　　■　　　■

Margaret and I planned to get married at the ranch in early September. Two weeks before the wedding date—after all the invitations had been mailed and we had ordered a massive wedding tent, plus all the food, beverages, and a huge wedding cake—Margaret and I had a big fight, and I threatened to cancel the wedding. Her father called and encouraged me to reconsider, assuring me that Margaret had just flown off the handle, that she really loved me.

I wasn't so certain, but I decided to go ahead with the marriage. That was a major mistake. The wedding went fine, but deep inside I had an uneasy feeling.

After the wedding, we stayed at the ranch overnight, then headed to California for a honeymoon. From California we traveled to Detroit to visit Margaret's brother. There we had another intense argument. We screamed at each other, and I cursed the day I had married this woman. We had been married less than a week, and already I regretted it.

While Margaret was happy about my newfound faith and the difference it was making in my life, I struggled with guilt about the sinful beginning of our relationship. Margaret, too, had trouble letting go of the fact that we were together because I had cheated on Sherry. When tensions were high, she brought up my past record; our life together was becoming a continuous fight.

From Detroit we headed out to the first big horse show of the season, in Springfield, Illinois. As we were driv ing from Chicago to Springfield, I looked in my mirror and saw flashing red lights.

I didn't think I'd been speeding. *Oh no! What now?* The state policeman pulled me over, asked for my license, then ordered us out of the car.

Without offering any explanation, he searched me, then searched Margaret. He went back to his car, and in a matter of minutes we were surrounded by five more squad cars, including a canine unit. The officers demanded that we open our suitcases, while the dog sniffed inside our car and through all our belongings. The officers inspected every article of our clothing, laying them out on the road, piece by piece.

Extremely irked by this interruption of our trip, I kept asking, "Did we do something wrong? Are you looking for something in particular? Perhaps I can help you."

The troopers simply grunted and refused to give us any information. They kept us standing along the side of the highway for several hours before finally telling us we could go.

Before we left, they asked once more where we were going.

"To a horse show in Springfield." I answered again.

Later that night, when we got to the horse show, I explained to my ranch manager why we were so late. He suggested that I return to the ranch immediately, but I shrugged off his concern. I would never have been so naive during my drug days. Back then, if I'd had such a close encounter with the authorities, the next day I would have been out of the country. But because I'd been retired from the cartel for a few years, my guard was down. Besides, I was a Christian now. I was a new person; why should I worry?

Nevertheless, I told my ranch manager that I'd be home the following afternoon rather than staying another couple of days in Springfield, as I had originally intended. Margaret and I had been gone nearly twenty days, most of which we had spent arguing with each other. Now that we were married, Margaret had suddenly developed a distaste for horse shows and the people who attended them. In fact, since the wedding, I was seeing many aspects of Margaret's personality that grated against mine.

The next morning, Margaret remained in our hotel room while I went to the show with friends. I noticed several people staring at me, people who didn't look like cowboys, and who seemed to have little interest in the horses. I passed it off, telling myself I was being paranoid because of our earlier encounter with the state troopers.

Our filly won the show, and as I was walking toward the stables with some friends, receiving accolades from well-wishers along the way, somebody tapped me on the shoulder. I turned to see a man in jeans and boots. "Are you Jorge Valdés?" he said.

"Who is asking?"

The fellow pulled out a badge, and said, "United States Marshal. You're under arrest."

"For what?" I asked. "I haven't done a thing."

The marshal didn't reply, but simply slapped a pair of handcuffs on me. "You don't need to do that," I said. "I'll go with you peaceably."

"Standard procedure," the officer replied. My friends stood there, mouths gaping. I turned to them. "Please call Margaret at the hotel and tell her I'm okay, so she won't be nervous."

But I wasn't okay. *How can this be happening?* I'd given my life to Christ, and I hadn't done anything illegal for years.

"Why am I being arrested?" I asked the agent.

"I can't tell you that," he replied, "but you'll go in front of a judge within an hour, and I'm sure you'll find out."

Shortly afterward, in a holding room at the Sangamon County Jail in Springfield, some officers asked me if there was anything I wanted to say.

"I have no idea what you're talking about," I answered. "I don't have a clue why I'm being arrested. Can I please make a phone call?"

I was led to a phone, where I called my mom. While waiting for the call to go through, I thought back to what I'd heard at my parole hearing in June about a New Orleans investigation. I knew that some people in the cocaine trade in Louisiana were working for Dickie Lynn, a man who had developed our Alabama connection for us. I had first teamed up with Dickie after meeting him while we were both in prison at Eglin.

I talked briefly to my mom, telling her there had obviously been some mistake. I could hear the worry in her voice, but she was trying to be strong. I also talked to J.C. and asked him to patch me through to the Arab. Not certain if we were being recorded, when the Arab came on the line I spoke tersely: "I've been arrested, and I think it has something to do with Dickie." Then I quickly hung up the phone.

At my request, my family contacted Alan Ross, the young Miami lawyer who had represented Oscar Nuñez in our drug trial in Macon. Alan had greatly impressed me back then—I still marveled at how he was able to get Oscar off on charges of selling me cocaine while I was convicted and sent to prison. I had stayed in contact with Alan over the years and had recommended many other potential clients to him. Alan's small practice had burgeoned, and he had become one of the leading criminal defense lawyers in the country.

Alan dispatched a local Springfield attorney to stand with me during my initial hearing. The attorney told me I had charges pending against me in Mobile, Alabama, for conspiracy to import narcotics. We went in front of the judge and I waived an extradition hearing, then was taken back to jail until I could be transferred to Mobile.

I called Margaret, who was in shock. Apparently the DEA had entered her hotel room without warning and searched everything. They found nothing suspicious, but it was enough to traumatize Margaret. She came to see me later that day, and I gave her my jewelry and my wallet. "Just leave with this and go back home," I told her. "I'll be okay."

Two days later I was taken to the Atlanta Penitentiary on my way to Mobile. In Atlanta I met with another lawyer who had investigated the charges against me.

"Jorge," he said, "you're facing fifteen life sentences without the possibility of parole."

Had somebody smacked me in the face with a shovel, I couldn't have been more surprised.

"Do you know Dickie Lynn?" the attorney asked.

"Yes."

"Well, he got eight life sentences, and from what I understand, he was only a worker."

I gulped hard. I went back to my cell, lay on the top bunk, and stared at the ceiling. "I don't understand all this, Lord," I prayed, "but I gave you my word that I would live for you. I just ask you for two things: Please save my children, and please give me the strength to go forward. You know that I walked away from the drug business of my own free will, so please help me."

I never questioned God. I never asked, "Why are you letting this happen to me?" I knew I had brought this upon myself.

And I knew in my heart that God had forgiven me. Tim Brooks had pointed me to Scriptures showing how God is the God of second chances, how Jesus restores a person's life, how everything would be different, everything would be better. But nowhere in the Bible did I recall reading that the consequences of my sins would be wiped away.

So I didn't ask God to deliver me from this trial; I knew I was guilty, and I knew I had to somehow pay for my crimes. And I truly wanted to do so, because I wanted to come clean.

Despite my experience of God's forgiveness, an overwhelming, horrendous sense of guilt over my drug dealings haunted me night and day. I was deeply troubled as I thought of all the harm I had done to people by bringing tons of cocaine into America.

Yes, God had forgiven me—but some people were dead because of me. How many thousands or even millions of lives had been hurt or destroyed because of me? Their most productive years squandered away in the insatiable quest for the white powder I had peddled? The effects of my cocaine sales had shattered untold numbers of marriages. And perhaps most devastating of all, countless numbers of teenagers, preteens, and even babies had been robbed of their childhood because of their addiction to cocaine or their parents' addiction.

And as for my rationalization that I was simply supplying pleasure to consenting adults, that I wasn't harming anyone, that my business wasn't dealing drugs to kids—it was a lie. It had been a devil's lie from the beginning, and I had bought it. I had easily justified the evil and sin in my life, but now that I'd finally come into a relationship with God, it was as if somebody had turned on a searchlight in my heart. I began to see things I'd never known were there. And so much of what I saw sickened me.

That night in Atlanta, I tossed and turned till dawn. In my mind I saw my dad in his rocking chair and heard his voice: "Son, if you go back to jail, you're going to kill us." My dad was now sixty-four years old, his health failing in a battle against cancer. My mother was a warrior; I knew she would hang in there, but I also knew this new ordeal would profoundly affect her.

The next day the marshals picked me up and drove me to Mobile. In the prison there I met some guys who had been arrested because of their involvement in drugs in the Miami area. One young man had been nothing but a "mule," a person paid by people like me to carry drugs across the border. I knew he would be serving a lot of time in prison. Again I was reminded of the ramifications of my drug business. *How many other kids are in prison because of me? How many moms and dads spend every ounce of energy they have, not to mention their financial resources, traveling to prisons to see their kids who are incarcerated because of the drugs I author ized to be sold?*

Several of the fellows in Mobile told me that they had become Christians, and I confessed that I, too, had committed my life to Jesus Christ. It was one of the first times I'd told anyone outside my family and close circle of friends what had happened to me.

I possessed a genuine faith, but my heart and mind were still plagued with questions. *I'm only thirty-four—is my life over? Will I spend the rest of my years in prison? Will I ever get to live with my children again? Will I be able to walk my daughters down the aisle at their weddings?*

I also questioned many of the things I'd heard about Christianity. I had sincerely trusted Jesus Christ; I believed he died on the cross to pay for my sins, and I truly wanted to live for him. And yes, I had known a peace that surpassed understanding. But instead of my life getting better, it had grown progressively worse. I felt I was at the lowest point in my life.

But in my darkest moment, God sent a light.

A group of Christian men and women came to conduct a service at the jail—which at the time did not particularly thrill me. I wasn't in the mood to listen to somebody preaching to me just then. But the leader of the group had such an infectious spirit, I couldn't be rude to him. The Spirit of God radiated from him. He introduced himself as Brother Emmett Philleau, pastor of Wings of Life, a ministry to Mobile's homeless people, drunkards, drug addicts, and prostitutes.

One of the women with Brother Emmett had been a missionary to Africa, and her story greatly inspired me. At the conclusion of the woman's testimony, Brother Emmett asked if I wanted to come and pray with them.

I really didn't. I was wallowing in my own despair and concentrating on my own inner turmoil. Nevertheless, out of courtesy and respect for the man, I agreed to pray with them. We all prayed, then I went back and sat in my chair. Afterward, one of the women in the group spoke to me. "Young man," she said, "while we were praying, the Lord told me that you are going to have a great ministry. You are going to impact many lives for Christ."

I thanked the woman kindly, but inside I chuckled. I was a businessman, not a preacher; what did I know about the Bible? And wouldn't being behind bars limit my impact just a little? Nevertheless, her words stayed in my heart. I was surprised that someone would say something like that to me. After all, neither she nor anyone else in the jail knew about my past as a drug lord and the amazing transformation that had recently taken place in my life.

The next night, Alan Ross came to see me. We were due in court the following day to state my plea. Alan said he was on good terms with the DEA agent handling my file, so he felt sure we could present a strong case.

But I had already purposed in my heart and mind that I wouldn't fight this case. I wouldn't try to claim innocence; I wasn't going to make excuses or try to find a scapegoat or legal loophole. Nor would I try to avoid punishment for my crimes. I felt I could not confess to be a Christian and purposely participate in lies.

This decision was not prompted by some fatalistic attitude, but because my life was truly different. God had begun to work in me. Though I was young in my faith, having been a Christian only a few months, I was growing in fervor and I wanted to do what was right—which meant I had to come clean with God, society, and myself.

Alan was a brilliant attorney, a straight shooter held in utmost respect by both prosecutors and defendants. He had a reputation for being incorruptible. And he would not sell out a client to the government; if Alan believed in his case, he would fight to the very end—and he usually won. I trusted Alan wholeheartedly, which was going to be important in light of what I planned to ask him to do.

Alan was telling me that our chances for winning had improved because he'd just found out that one of the pilots planning to testify against me had been killed in an airplane crash.

I shook my head. "Alan, you won't believe what I'm about to tell you," I said. "I can't go in that courtroom and say I'm innocent. I'm guilty. I just pray that I'll be charged only with what was my part in the conspiracy."

Alan was shocked. "Jorge, let me explain something to you," he said. Alan outlined the charges against me and carefully explained why they were far more serious than the charges I had been convicted on in Macon. When I was in the drug world, the maximum sentence a convicted drug seller could get was fifteen years in prison. This was known now as the "old law." Near the end of 1987, the laws had changed. For my type of crimes, the sentence for a convicted drug runner now carried a mandatory life sentence without possibility of parole.

Even though I had retired prior to the change in the law, Alan explained that the people with whom I had formerly "conspired"—which meant we had done business together—had continued their activities beyond 1987. Because of this, I was still considered part of their conspiracy and was therefore to be charged according to the current law.

"The bottom line," Alan said, "is that instead of a maximum of fifteen years, you're now facing a life sentence without the possibility of parole for each count on which you've been indicted—and you've been indicted on eight counts."

Alan paused to allow the awful reality of his to words sink in. Eight life sentences virtually precluded the possibility that a judge might be lenient.

They were going to put me away for a long, long time.

Alan looked at me as if to say, "Okay, Jorge; do you still want to talk about giving up without a fight?"

I took a deep breath and let it out very slowly. "Alan, I don't care what I'm facing," I said. "I have lived by one principle: My word is my bond. I've always believed that though you may not have control over being sick or healthy or having money or not, you always have absolute control of one thing, and that's your word. *You* control whether your word means something—whether you break it or keep it, whether you are a man of your word or you are a liar."

I had lived by that principle even when I was serving the devil. And it was that principle, when I was twenty years old, that allowed me to be trusted with hundreds of millions of dollars. The people I did business with knew that that twenty-year-old kid would die before he'd break his word.

I had learned that principle from my father and my mother, who drilled it into their children: "Your word is your bond. You don't need to have things written down in contracts and legal forms. When you say something, you live by that and you die by that."

It was this same principle that allowed me to hold my peace in Panama and to endure torture rather than implicate my partners.

"Alan," I continued, "you may not understand, but I've made a promise to God, and I'm not about to break that oath."

Alan was bewildered. He told me he thought my decision was a mistake, but he agreed to meet with the prosecutors and tell them what I wanted to do.

Later that day, Alan returned from his meeting with them.

"Jorge, it's very simple," Alan said somberly. "They want everything you have—all your money, all your property, all your horses, everything." That was to be the trade-off for the possibility of getting reduced time in prison.

My punishment boiled down to this: either lots of money and less time, or less money and lots of time.

"Alan," I responded, "I'm willing to give up everything I own."

I continued, "I live by a new principle now. I gave my word to follow Jesus, and I promised him I would do everything in my power not to tell a lie and to live a different life. Until the day I really confess it all, I feel I will never be cleansed of this evil I've done. I need to come clean and face the consequences of my evil life.

"I know God is the God of new beginnings, but that beginning doesn't start until I come clean with the past, so perhaps he'll give me the chance to start anew. And if not, he'll give me the strength wherever he sends me, and I'll tell others what I've been through, and that I'm a different person.

"I know I'm going to touch many lives. It might not be here, Alan, or in the streets or in prison, but one day I will have to face the Savior, the God who gave his life for me. Although there's no way I can adequately make up for all the evil I've done in the past, from now on I can do all I can to live by what he's taught me."

For one of the few times since I'd met him, Alan Ross was speechless. He sat staring at me, as though trying to connect all that he knew of the old Jorge with the words he heard coming from the new me.

Alan was a pro; he was the best of the best. He'd heard enough jailhouse conversion stories to choke a priest. He also was smart enough to know that most judges as well had heard their fill of prison conversions, and that this approach by defendants had long since lost its effectiveness—to the point that it was now considered an unwise, counterproductive approach, no matter how sincere.

Finally, Alan blinked hard, shook his head slightly, and said, "Okay, Jorge. Guilty as charged. You're coming clean."

Thirty-One

The One in Charge

Together with Alan, I soon met face to face with the federal prosecutor and the DEA agent in charge of my case.

The DEA agent was Ed Odom. Alan had informed me that Ed was a devout Christian who took his job seriously and strongly believed in getting drug dealers off the streets. He was a good cop, a person to whom the judge and prosecutor listened with respect.

The federal prosecutor was Gloria Bedwell, a strikingly beautiful woman with a reputation for being extremely intelligent—and extremely tough.

Once the perfunctory introductions were made, Gloria got down to business. She quizzed me concerning my plea, so I told her straight out, "This is the most difficult thing I've ever done in my life. But I need to come clean with God and the authorities."

Gloria told me she already knew most of the details regarding my drug operations in which Alabama had been used as a shipment point, because Bill Grist, our partner, had cooperated fully in this case. Dickie Lynn had already gone to trial and had been convicted, so Gloria wasn't looking to make a deal for information that might incriminate my partners.

I liked Gloria immediately. She was a no-nonsense woman, and I felt that she and I could find some common ground.

I also liked Ed Odom. Ed had been tracking me for several years and probably knew more about my drug business at that point than I did. He was tough, but he was a kind and straightforward person, and he didn't try to play the bad cop. I had heard that, even though he played a major part in Dickie's receiving so many life sentences, he was also the only person in the entire process that Dickie respected. Over time, as Ed did everything to keep his word to me and to facilitate my stay in Mobile, he and I became friends. I didn't look at Ed as the enemy, or as a government agent, but as a Christian brother.

I asked my interrogators if they knew how much money, property, and other assets I had available, and I quickly discovered that their information about me was frighteningly accurate. "I'm willing to give it all up," I told them. I wasn't playing a shell game with my interrogators. I wanted a new chance and a new life.

The prosecutors made it clear that in court they would not recommend any sentence for me; it was up to the judge to decide that. "The only thing I can do," Gloria told me, "is to ask that you be sentenced under the old law, which might avoid a life sentence." She emphasized that the judge would not be legally bound by any agreement the government made with me.

I thanked Gloria and Ed for being willing to concede even that much, then added, "I want you to know that I'll do as much time in prison as God deems I should do. He will use you and he will use the judge, but no one but God controls my life now."

Those were not idle words. I thoroughly believed them.

For the next three days, Gloria, Ed, and their associates grilled me on every aspect of my life in the drug business.

■　　■　　■

Meanwhile, Alan told me he'd discovered that I was also under investigation in Florida for drug activities in the Clewiston area. The Hendry County sheriff—with whom I had secretly arranged a deal for bringing drugs through Clewiston—was also being investigated. Alan warned me not to report anything about my drug activities involving the Clewiston people until he knew what sort of charges the Florida authorities would bring. I followed Alan's legal advice and didn't mention anything about the Clewiston group during my interrogation by the Alabama authorities.

A week later, I was called back to the Mobile County courthouse, where I was met by a group of law enforcement officials from Florida, representing the FBI, the DEA, the U.S. Customs Service, and the Internal Revenue Service. They began asking me why I hadn't mentioned anything about the Hendry County sheriff being on my payroll and why I hadn't confessed to my drug activities in the Clewiston area. Alan interceded and told the agents that he had advised me to remain silent on those issues.

Several days later, I called home to the ranch in Clewiston to talk with Margaret. A male voice answered the phone. "U.S. marshals," the man said curtly.

"This is Jorge Valdés," I said. "Is my wife there?"

"No, she is not. We own this place now."

An atomic bomb exploded in my heart and mind. I couldn't believe that the government agents in Florida would be so conniving as to confiscate my property while I was still arranging with the Alabama prosecutors for the voluntary forfeit of the property.

"Well, can I talk with my wife?" I asked, the exasperation obvious in my voice.

"No, call back later, and maybe you can talk with the agent in charge." Click. The agent hung up the phone—my phone, in my house, on my property, in the United States of America, the land of the free!

I was outraged. There was no need for a show of force such as this, since I had already promised to give up all my possessions.

I could easily have fought the government's seizure of my property; I had purchased the ranch prior to my first incarceration, and the statute of limitations had run out for confiscating that part of my possessions. But I had willingly offered to relinquish it all to the government without a fight. Now I felt betrayed and ripped off.

I went back to my cell in a daze, having gone from being a multimillionaire to having nothing almost overnight. The devil attacked my mind: "See, I told you so. You can't trust these people. Come back where you belong. You can fight this thing. You can be rich all over again. That would show them, wouldn't it?"

Shaking off the devil's taunts, I prayed, "God, please give me a word or a sign—something that lets me know you are in charge."

I opened my Bible and casually flipped the pages. Without consciously trying to do so, I let the pages fall open to Hebrews, chapter ten. I could hardly believe my eyes as I read about persecution, property confiscation, and perseverance:

"Remember those earlier days after you had received the light, when you stood your ground in a great contest in the face of suffering. Sometimes you were publicly exposed to insult and persecution; at other times you stood side by side with those who were so treated. You sympathized with those in prison and joyfully accepted the confiscation of your property, because you knew that you yourselves had better and lasting possessions.

"So do not throw away your confidence; it will be richly rewarded. You need to persevere so that when you have done the will of God, you will receive what he has promised. For in just a very little while, 'He who is coming will come and will not delay. But my righteous one will live by faith. And if he shrinks back, I will not be pleased with him.' But we are not of those who shrink back and are destroyed, but of those who believe and are saved" (Hebrews 10:32-39).

I got down on my knees in that jail cell and cried, "Thank you, Lord!" Tears flowed freely down my face as joy filled my heart. From that moment on, I knew that Jesus was going to walk with me through this situation.

This was the strongest confirmation I could have imagined. Again and again I read the words that mentioned joyfully accepting the confiscation of property, and as I did, I suddenly began to rejoice, singing out, "Hallelujah! Praise God!" right there in jail.

The other inmates looked at me as though I'd lost my mind, but I didn't care. I was free! And my freedom was not restricted by walls or steel bars. I now possessed a freedom far greater than I'd ever achieved when I was making millions of dollars and had an abundance of possessions, power, and prestige. I now had the freedom that came from knowing Jesus Christ and of knowing he would never leave me or forsake me. I was not alone. No matter how dark and bleak and ugly my cell looked, I had the joy of Christ.

I was awestruck. It had to have been God who led me to those verses in Hebrews. As a new believer, I didn't know the Bible well enough to have found that passage, let alone know what it said. Yet God directed my attention to words that spoke directly to my situation. A few years later, I'd hear Bible professors warn against casually opening the Bible and taking the first words you see as a divine revelation, a personal message. And maybe it's true that God doesn't work that way—but I know he did so at least once.

Ed Odom came to see me and told me how upset he and Gloria Bedwell were about what the Florida authorities had done.

"Ed, it doesn't matter anymore," I told him. With tears in my eyes, I told him about the passage in Hebrews and how God had spoken to me.

Ed was clearly touched. He and I hugged in the attorney's room. What a picture we must have made—two longtime mortal enemies, the DEA agent and the drug lord—now hugging, bonded together by the love of Jesus.

"You're going to be all right, Jorge," Ed told me as he brushed a tear from his own eye.

When Alan Ross learned what the Fort Myers prosecutors had done, he went ballistic and vowed to fight the seizure.

Eventually, Alan persuaded the Florida group to combine all charges against me into one case there in Mobile, though all my assets would remain confiscated. As it turned out, the only piece of Valdés property that remained was Heaven Sent—the $10,000 horse of my dad's that had won the 1987 Congress. The horse hadn't been at the ranch at the time of confiscation.

My dad voluntarily gave up the home I had built for him and Mom at the ranch, as well as more than $500,000 of his own money that he had invested in the ranch. He had the legal right to claim his portion of the proceeds when the ranch was sold, but he decided to give it all up, demonstrating his belief that money was nothing compared to family and honor. Dad talked to me by telephone and reminded me, "We came to this country from Cuba without a cent in our pockets, but we had our family and that's all that mattered. And that's all that matters now, son. Don't let money get in the way of your freedom."

As I thought of my father that day, I wondered, *How much have I hurt this man?* He'd worked hard all his life for what he had, but he was willing to give it all up for his son. A half million dollars meant nothing compared to his love for his son.

Over the years I had sometimes regarded my father and mother as losers. I couldn't understand why they would never accept the expensive homes or cars I wanted to buy for them, and how they could be so content with such a few material possessions.

But that day, as I talked to my dad by phone from the jail in Mobile, I realized what a giant of a man my father truly was. My dad wasn't a loser; neither was my mother. They knew what really mattered. They knew that family possessed a value far beyond silver or gold, and they were willing to sacrifice anything for it. I wondered, *Will I ever be even a small percentage of the person my parents have been?*

While I awaited sentencing in the Mobile County jail, I used the time to study the Bible. Several local preachers visited the jail, and a few became especially dear to me. One of them was Pastor Kenneth Libby, an elderly, white-haired, old-fashioned, country preacher. Brother Libby reminded me of Abe Lincoln's comment, "I like to hear a man preach like he is swatting bees!" I loved to hear Brother Libby preach, and I looked forward to his visits. He became a spiritual father to me. We'd talk for hours, and I'd ask him questions about the Bible. He and Brother Emmett were having a profound impact on my growing Christian life.

One day Brother Emmett told me, "If you really want to be free, read twenty chapters of the Bible every day." Amazingly, Brother Emmett could barely read a letter, yet he knew the Bible backward and forward. I figured that if Brother Emmett recommended twenty chapters a day, I'd do even better and read thirty—after all, I had plenty of time for reading. Soon I was devouring the Word of God. I sent away for a home-study Bible class and began taking lessons by correspondence. Amazingly, God began to renew my mind, replacing with his Word the filth with which I had filled my thoughts for years.

On another day, Brother Libby conducted a baptismal service in the jail. We didn't have a tub large enough for a baptistery, so Brother Libby baptized me in the shower.

At night I listened to *Unshackled,* one of the longest running Christian radio programs. Each evening, the program aired another exciting testimony of what Christ had done in someone's life, often someone who had been involved in a life of crime before meeting the Lord. I drew great encouragement from the real-life stories of God's power to transform lives. This program became a major source of my spiritual encouragement and growth, helping me make it through many lonely nights when I wondered if I'd ever again get to live in the outside world. As I wrestled with whether God had brought me to this point to punish me or to discipline and prepare me for something else, the stories on *Unshackled* helped me know that God still had a plan for my life. I didn't imagine then that one day, one of the real-life stories of transformation aired on *Unshackled* would be mine.

Margaret visited me often in Mobile during the first few months I was there. On one visit, she went out to dinner with the wife of a fellow inmate who had been incarcerated for many years. Later I learned that Margaret told the inmate's wife, "If Jorge is going to be in prison for a long time, I think I'll have to move on with my life."

I was deeply hurt, but not surprised, to hear of her comment. I had felt that Margaret would eventually leave me, especially if I received a long sentence. Worse yet, I wasn't sure whether I wanted her to leave or stay.

THIRTY-TWO

MAKING PEACE

Being incarcerated as a Christian was a different challenge than being imprisoned as a nonbeliever. In my previous experience, I went behind bars with the attitude that I would do whatever was necessary to survive—which included providing contraband to other inmates in exchange for whatever I needed done, challenging the guards, and even sneaking outside the prison at every opportunity. I'd learned that with enough money, it's possible to get almost anything in prison, including drugs, sex, alcohol, or roast pig.

But now I was a different person. Even if I'd had the money to wield that kind of power again, I had changed—but the prison system had not. Life on the inside was just as violent and corrupt as ever.

I knew that I would encounter many situations in which my newfound faith in Christ was sure to be tested. Jesus said, "Do not resist an evil person. If someone strikes you on the right cheek, turn to him the other also" (Matthew 5:39). How was I to apply that statement in a society where a man who didn't stand up for his rights would soon find them trampled upon?

I believed I was to be a peacemaker in prison. I had also believed that during my first time in prison; back then, however, my reputation as a powerful drug lord helped me maintain the peace. Could the power of the one true Lord be just as effective?

I was about to find out.

One day I was cleaning the cell while my cellmate, Jimmy, was nearby in the TV room, playing cards with several other inmates. Jimmy had given his life to the Lord as a result of attending a Bible study I was teaching in the jail. But he was a loud kid, and I knew that one day his mouth would him get into trouble.

As I was mopping our cell, I heard footsteps hurrying in my direction. Instinctively, I wedged a broomstick between the door and the doorframe. Just as I did, two guys who had been playing cards with Jimmy appeared in the cell doorway and attempted to push me back inside.

As I struggled against the two men trying to lock me in, I caught a glimpse of the commotion outside my cell. An inmate whom I knew had been charged with five murders was attempting to throw Jimmy over the rail—our cell was on the second floor, overlooking a concrete-floored common area below. I quickly realized that the two goons were trying to lock me in so I couldn't go to Jimmy's defense.

I broke free, pushed past them, and ran out to help my cellmate. Two men were pummeling Jimmy in the face and head. I grabbed one of the guys and locked my hands around his head, securing him in a headlock.

"Valdés, this is not your business!" he growled angrily

"It is my business," I yelled back. "Jimmy is my brother, and I'm not going to let you both jump on him!" I had my hands in a position to easily snap the guy's neck, but he was holding a shank—a makeshift knife he had fashioned from a toothbrush. His hands were free, and he could easily stab me with the shank.

Two voices dueled in my mind and heart. One voice was roaring, "Snap his neck! Snap his neck!" The other voice was restraining me.

Silently I prayed, *O Jesus, help me!* Here I was, trying to keep a guy from getting killed, and now I could easily have a murder charge on my hands for killing his attacker.

A guard heard the commotion and started into the corridor, but he stopped cold as he watched me struggling with the thugs. I screamed at the guard, "Come help me!"

But he refused. "Help is on the way!" he called from his safe distance.

"Just give me a hand," I pleaded. But the guard stood still.

I prayed, *Lord, please protect me.*

Finally the guards stormed into the jail, broke up the fight, grabbed Jimmy's attackers, and threw them on the floor. The officers handcuffed the inmates and took them out of the cellblock.

Jimmy began to cry as he thanked me for saving his life.

By now a group of inmates had gathered around us. "Jimmy," I said, "when you're real for Jesus and you make your confession, you gotta live that way. I don't know if you were doing anything wrong in that card game or not, but I can tell you one thing: You can't call yourself a Christian and act like a nonbeliever. That's the problem with Christianity—and it's what kept me away from being a Christian for so many years."

I knew my words were hitting home not just with Jimmy, but also with some of the others standing there.

"If you're going to live for Christ," I continued, "you've got to let people see Christ through you every day. You might be the only 'Bible' a person ever sees."

Following my "speech," most of the inmates remained rather subdued, and gradually the guys drifted off to their own cells.

That night, Jimmy lay in his bunk sobbing. After a while I climbed down from the top bunk and asked him if he wanted to pray. We knelt together in our cell and prayed that God would become a greater reality to him, that Jesus would reveal himself to Jimmy in the way he had to me, and that he would overtake every aspect of Jimmy's life and make him clean.

Ed Odom came to visit and introduced me to Ken Cole, the officer who was handling my presentence investigation. Ken was also a strong Christian. Ken and I talked about my case, but we also talked much about the Bible and my newfound relationship with God. Ken seemed convinced that the change in my life was not simply jailhouse religion but a genuine conversion experience. I wasn't trying to impress Ken or anyone else; I wasn't really concerned what anyone thought of me. I knew my relationship with Christ was real. I also knew that what God had done in my heart surpassed human understanding, so I didn't even try to explain it.

One day I got a call to go to the attorney's visiting room. When I walked in, an agent introduced himself as David Borah. David told me that for many years he had been investigating Sal and Willie, my former partners in Miami. He knew of my relationship with them and wanted information from me.

I told David how my family had been close friends with Sal's family since coming from Cuba and that his parents were like my own. I related that Sal and I had worked together prior to my previous arrest, but that after my release from prison I rebuilt my business by myself, apart from Sal and Willie. I really had nothing to tell David that he didn't already know.

This was the most difficult test I had faced in my newfound faith. I had given God my word to come clean, to answer honestly whatever questions were asked. Keeping my promise to God meant breaking my word to my good friend Sal, something I had never before done—even during the torture in Panama.

David communicated his understanding of how difficult it was for me to discuss my past with Sal because of our once-close relationship. When David Borah left that day, I felt that I had found another friend within the government system. Eventually I wrote a poem with David Borah and Ed Odom in mind, and titled it "My Enemy Became My Friend."

Two days later, one of the attorneys for Sal and Willie came to see me, to find out what I had told David Borah. Clearly the heat was being turned up on all the members of our former group, especially Sal and Willie, who had already been indicted on charges related to their cocaine smuggling. But there was little I could do to help them or any of our other former associates. I had made a promise to God that I would not lie about my drug dealings. That decision would create numerous awkward situations and tests of my character and my faith and would even endanger my life at times, but I refused to compromise that commitment.

After my arrest in September 1990, I lost all contact with my children. Luchy had returned to the country, and Jorgito went to live with her in Miami. Sherry had moved, taken the children with her, and left no way for anyone in my family to contact her. I tried to connect with her through Sherry's parents, but they refused to reveal her whereabouts.

The situation was nearly intolerable. Because I had forfeited all my money to the government, I didn't have the means to track down Sherry and the kids. Satan used this to attack my faith. *What type of God am I serving who would allow me to lose my children? How can he not allow me to know where my kids are—the same children I used to drive twelve hours each way to visit on the weekends?*

Even when I was caught up in the power of the drug business, my children held a special grip on my heart. Now, because of the changes God had brought in my life, I desperately longed to make up for lost time, to erase some of the terribly deceptive principles my lifestyle must have presented to them as truth. The unbearable pain of the situation frequently brought me to tears, and I fought in prayer to resist Satan's incessant attacks and endure this test of my faith.

My mom and dad had sent me pictures of the children, and I gave some of the photos to Pastor Emmett to help remind him to pray for them and to ask God to make a way for me to communicate with them. Brother Emmett carried the pictures with him everywhere.

One day, more than a year after my arrest, Brother Emmett came to me with good news. He had been preaching at a conference near Pensacola, and after the service, a middle-aged couple invited him out to eat. During the meal they asked about his ministry. He told them about his work in Mobile, including his ministry to prisoners.

His comment piqued the couple's interest. "Do you really believe prison can rehabilitate a person?" they asked Emmett. "Or are some people so bad that they're beyond redemption?"

"God's power is great enough to change anyone who is willing," Brother Emmett replied. He told them he knew of many inmates whose lives had genuinely changed. "Is there a specific reason why you're interested in that subject?" he asked them.

The couple revealed that their daughter had been married to someone who was now in jail. Brother Emmett asked for the name, so he could pray for the couple's former son-in-law.

"Jorge Valdés," they told him.

Brother Emmett reached inside his wallet, pulled out the pictures I had given him, and showed them to the couple.

A look of panic flashed across the couple's faces.

"Jorge is a changed man," Brother Emmett told Sherry's parents. He told them that I was teaching Bible studies in jail and taking Bible classes by correspondence. He also said that he and I had been praying for more than a year that God would provide a way that I could talk with my children. Brother Emmett encouraged Sherry's parents to do all they could to facilitate communication between my children and me.

Soon afterward, they sent Brother Emmett a telephone number in Houston where I could reach Sherry and the kids. When I talked with them for the first time since being arrested, Krystle asked innocently, "Daddy, why haven't you called in such a long time?" I couldn't hold back the tears. It struck me hard once again that despite the wonderful peace God had brought into my life, and the sense of fulfillment I had found through my relationship with Christ, the consequences of my sin were sure to bring torrents of tears to my life.

And I would have plenty of time to think about that. Alan Ross now informed me that all the legal work was done; it was time for my sentencing.

Thirty-Three

How Long?

It wasn't a question of whether or not I was going to prison. The only issue was for how long.

I was facing the possibility of eight life sentences and had entered a guilty plea with no guarantees regarding how much prison time the judge would demand.

I hadn't pleaded guilty and forfeited all my earthly possessions in hopes of getting a lighter sentence. I simply wanted to come clean before God, and I knew this required me to also come clean before man. Yet during the entire time I had been in jail at Mobile, for some reason the figure of ten years kept coming back to me. Although I knew I must be punished for my crimes, I had read Jesus' words in Mark 11:24: "Whatever you ask for in prayer, believe that you have received it, and it will be yours." Staking my claim on that verse and others like it, I dared to believe that the judge would sentence me to only ten years.

When my sentencing session began, Judge Charles Butler announced that he was rejecting the plea bargain I had struck with the prosecution and that he was not bound to any agreement I had made with the government. Judge Butler said he felt obligated to give me at least one life sentence.

Alan Ross flew into action, suggesting that the judge wasn't obligated to give me the mandatory sentence. The suggestion was preposterous, but the judge postponed the sentencing for fifteen days to allow Alan to present evidence showing how I could possibly qualify to receive a lesser sentence.

That fifteen-day period posed a serious test to my faith. I'd now heard from the judge's own mouth that he planned to give me a life sentence. The devil went on the attack, filling my mind with doubts: *Where is God when you need him? You should have stuck with me; I would never have let you go back to prison for the rest of your life.* How could I expect anything less than a life sentence?

When those thoughts came, I cast them out in the name of Jesus. I fell back on Mark 11:24 and believed it. Any time I felt doubtful or weak, I went back again to Scripture, where I was spending hours each day.

Fifteen days later, when I returned to court, Alan Ross presented a solid case to the judge, emphasizing that I was now a different person than the Jorge Valdés who had committed the crimes for which I had pleaded guilty. It was marvelous to sit there and listen to my Jewish lawyer argue so convincingly that I had been converted to Christianity.

Alan also called federal agents Ed Odom and David Borah to the stand. Both Ed and David testified that I had been forthright, truthful, and honest in my answers during all their interrogations, despite the fact that my admission of guilt countered everything I had struggled to achieve during my drug days. Both agents testified that they, too, believed I was a changed man.

Alan further argued that I had never contested the government's charges against me and that I had voluntarily forfeited millions of dollars worth of assets, holding nothing back.

When Alan completed his presentation, I held my breath as the judge looked at me and prepared to pass sentence.

"Jorge Valdés, I sentence you to ten years."

My heart nearly leaped out of my chest. Ten years! *Only* ten years! Just as I had prayed and believed. Ten years—not eight life sentences or ten or fifteen! I felt as though angels were all around me. Tears trickled from my eyes, and I didn't bother to swish them away. I would still be only in my mid-forties when I got out. And think of that! I *would* be getting out!

I hugged Alan Ross, and then I turned to the judge and thanked him. It wasn't money under the table that had changed the judge's mind. I knew that God had worked a miracle in Judge Butler's heart. Indeed, he was taking an enormous gamble by being willing to buck the norm. If he had sentenced me to life, it would have been easy for him to go home that night knowing he had done his job according to the letter of the law. The crimes with which I was charged had occurred while I was on parole, and the judge had every right to throw the book at me.

Moreover, if I were to get out of prison and return to my old lifestyle—as I had in fact done after my first incarceration—Judge Butler would go down in court annals as the federal judge foolish enough to let a convicted drug lord back on the streets. Judge Butler's ruling was more than a risk; it was a potentially career-ending blunder if I failed to follow through with my commitment to Christ. I will be eternally grateful to this man who was willing to look beyond the letter and see the Spirit.

In January 1992, I was transferred to the federal prison at Jesup, Georgia, about 250 miles southeast of Atlanta, where I tried to settle in as quickly as possible. I was going to be there for quite a long time.

During my first stint in prison, nobody had dared to mess with me because they knew I would fight anyone anytime. I never backed down. But what might happen now, if predators in the prison thought I was unable to defend myself? In prison, the strong prey upon the weak. As a Christian, what would I do if someone stole from me? How could I maintain my Christian testimony in this environment?

As these unsettling questions lingered in my mind, I did the only thing I could do: I turned them all over to the Lord and committed myself to him. I determined to focus on Christ's command to seek first the kingdom of God and his righteousness and on his promise that everything I needed would be given to me.

Did I really believe that? In my first days as a Christian, while still living the life of a millionaire, it was easy to believe God would take care of me. But did I believe that here in this place?

Yes, I decided, I did believe. If God cared about every flower and was concerned enough to provide food for the birds, he would take care of me. Still, I didn't expect prison life to be a Sunday school picnic.

The attitude and composition of the prison population had changed greatly since my first incarceration. Because inmates had longer sentences, many with no possibility of parole, the guards had little with which to threaten or motivate the convicts. How many life sentences can one person serve? When I served time in prison earlier, most inmates had incentives to obey and behave. Now, chaos was the rule. Many inmates simply laughed at the prison's disciplinary efforts. Prison in the 1990s was a whole different world—and the problems promised to get worse.

Because of Jesup's burgeoning Hispanic population and because of my background and education, I was assigned to work in the prison's education department, helping Hispanic inmates to pass the GED tests, the government equivalent of a high-school diploma.

Meanwhile, one of the first and most lasting friendships I forged at Jesup was with Gene Lawson, an African American from Fort Lauderdale. Gene had intelligence, good looks, and a great personality, but he had made the mistake of introducing an acquaintance to somebody who sold drugs. For that introduction, Gene would serve more than six years in prison. Now a devout Christian, he attended Bible studies with me at Jesup and wasn't afraid to admit his faith in Christ to anybody. He was a consistent witness who lived what he believed.

Gene and I decided to explore the possibility of college courses by correspondence, and soon we were both accepted for course work from Southeastern Bible College. Each morning at five-thirty, we got together to study during the last hour of quiet before most of the other inmates were up.

My first class from Southeastern was on the New Testament. I studied diligently, and when I scored one hundred percent on the first test, I experienced a feeling of elation, fulfillment, and achievement that I hadn't known in years. I knew God was calling me back to school. I had always been a good student, and I loved my teaching job in the prison's education department. I recognized that God had given me a gift to reach people who were considered hard to reach. This seemed to be the ministry God had for me.

One day my case manager told me I was being sent to Miami for a government-mandated appearance in court. Not knowing what was going on, I called David Borah, who explained that the situation involved Sal and Willie's case. The matter was actually about Marty Weinberg, who had been my attorney in the Macon trial years before and was now representing Sal and Willie. The government was trying to get Marty dismissed as their attorney.

This turn of events disturbed me greatly. My getting involved in the matter would give the appearance that I was testifying on behalf of the government, which in fact I was not. I didn't want the word getting around that I was testifying, which could put me in potential danger from other inmates. Yet I had no choice but to go to Florida for the hearing.

When I returned to Jesup, the authorities asked me if I wanted to go into protected custody rather than into the general population.

"Absolutely not," I answered. "I've done nothing wrong and have done nothing to hurt anybody, so I have nothing to fear." I knew I'd done nothing to compromise my commitment to truth or to harm Sal and Willie's case.

Three weeks later, just when I was finally regaining the confidence of my fellow inmates, I was summoned to Florida for another round of hearings.

This time I was irate. I called David Borah and everyone else who might be able or willing to keep me from getting involved in the case again. I told them my life would be endangered if I went. I even talked to the federal prosecutor for Sal and Willie's case. The prosecutor responded, "You're coming to Miami, and that is it!" Before leaving, I prayed a lot about it with my friend Gene.

On the way to Miami, I was taken for a few days to the federal penitentiary in Atlanta, where I realized that God was up to something. Since inmates in prison have to put their names on a sign-up list to make telephone calls, I quickly put my name on the list in Atlanta so I could call my children while I was there. As I scanned the sign-up list to see if I recognized any of the names, I saw one that sent my blood pressure skyrocketing.

Monti Cohen! My former lawyer, the man who had betrayed me, was there in the Atlanta Penitentiary.

Suddenly, I was reliving that moment nearly a decade earlier when I told Monti I was going to kill him one day. Fiery emotions overtook me, fueled by thoughts of how Monti had betrayed my confidence, and the excruciating, prolonged pain that every member of my family had suffered as a result of Monti's duplicity. Anger, resentment, and bitterness began to envelop me like a thick fog.

Then I sensed the Lord firmly reminding me, "It wasn't Monti Cohen's sin that brought these consequences on you or your family; it was *your* sin." Quickly I repented of my attitudes. It seemed that the Lord prompted me. "You've hurt many people, yet you know how much I have forgiven you. Now you need to forgive those who have hurt you." A peace rushed through me as I acknowledged the truth of what God was saying to me, and I resolved to obey.

I found out where Monti was, and at the first opportunity I made my way to his cell. When Monti saw me, a look of terror swept over his face.

"Monti Cohen!" I said with mock seriousness. My one-time lawyer and friend stood paralyzed as I walked over to him—and hugged him. Tears of joy came into Monti's eyes as he realized I hadn't come for revenge.

I told Monti how I had met Christ and that I was now a different person from the Jorge he used to know. "Monti, the past is history," I said. "It is forgiven and forgotten, and I'm still your friend."

I knew now that one of God's reasons for my extended trip away from Jesup had to do with my forgiving Monti and asking him to forgive me for the anger I had harbored against him all those years.

Thirty-Four

New Beginnings

Following my second appearance at the hearings in Miami, I was housed for almost a month in a state prison facility near Miami known as TGK. Here, and wherever I went within the prison system, I had my Bible with me and continued both my study and my teaching of God's Word. The Lord was using me to lead numerous inmates to a relationship with Christ, and I began to look at every encounter as a potential opportunity to tell somebody about Jesus and his power to change lives.

At TGK I met a guard named DeMilio who had a reputation for being a tough guy as well as a ladies' man.

One day as I passed by his desk and saw him reading, I said, "You should read the Bible; it's a lot more informative than those magazines and will do you a lot more good."

DeMilio looked at me quizzically. Because of my reputation, he was willing to listen to me. He asked about my story and wanted to know why I had turned to Christ when everyone knew I had been such a womanizer. I told him some of my background, and from then on we talked frequently. As far as it's possible for a guard and an inmate to become friends, we did.

Before I left TGK on my way back to Jesup, I told DeMilio, "You really should turn around and give your life to Jesus."

DeMilio smiled and said, "You keep praying for me, Jorge, and I just might."

Back at Jesup, my friend Gene Lawson and I prayed for DeMilio almost every night after the ten o'clock count—one of four times each day when inmates had to be accounted for. Each night I asked God to manifest himself in DeMilio's life, to convict him of his sin, and to bring him into a relationship with Christ.

Five months later, when I was transferred back to TGK, I spotted DeMilio again, sitting at his desk. But he wasn't reading magazines; he was reading the Bible!

He ran to me and hugged me like a long-lost brother. "Jorge," he said, "the strangest thing happened after you left. You gotta hear this story."

I listened eagerly. He told me that every night when his shift at the prison ended at nine-forty-five, he would begin his drive home, which took about twenty-five minutes. "Every night," DeMilio said, "I became so convicted about giving my life to Christ. Some nights I fought that feeling for all I was worth. On other nights, I'd say, 'Maybe I will, but some other time.' Then when I got into my house, I'd forget about it . . . until the drive home the next night, when the same thing would happen.

"One night when I got to my door, I was finally tired of the turmoil. I dropped to my knees and couldn't get up. I asked God to come into my life and to fill me with his Spirit."

DeMilio told me that he then quit drinking and sleeping around. He joined a church and began socializing with other Christians and reading the Bible.

"I can't contain all the happiness within me," he continued. "Now I'm a light to these inmates who see me reading the Bible. They see that I'm a different person, and everybody notices."

I told DeMilio about our praying for him at Jesup—at exactly the same time each night that he had experienced such spiritual turmoil—and I saw a tear slip from DeMilio's eye. What a tremendous joy to see this brother whom God had transformed in such a mighty way. I was reminded again, *He really is the God of new beginnings.*

DeMilio asked if we could study the Bible together, so each day, during DeMilio's breaks or after he got off work, I joined him. Imagine that: the guard and the inmate studying God's Word together in prison!

With only a ten-year sentence, I expected Margaret to hang on in our marriage. But by the end of 1993, we both knew the marriage was dead. Margaret came to see me for only ten minutes on Christmas and fifteen minutes on New Year's, which would be her last visit.

The divorce proceedings were amicable on the surface, but a battlefront in the spiritual realm. I found myself having to go to God repeatedly to repent of my anger toward Margaret and to seek his strength in standing strong against the devil. Satan must have seen an area of vulnerability in me, because he launched an all-out attack on my heart and mind, trying to get me to revert to my old ways, tempting me with ugly thoughts of how I could conduct a reprisal against Margaret. I continually laid the matter before the Lord and sought daily deliverance from destructive thoughts and attitudes stemming from our divorce.

I continued to stay busy finishing my coursework for a bachelor's degree from Southeastern Bible College. What a joyous moment it was when I received my diploma in 1993, with a perfect 4.0 grade-point average. But that accomplishment merely whetted my appetite for more advanced biblical studies. I decided to explore the possibilities of going to graduate school while serving the remainder of my time in prison.

I had been told that Wheaton College was one of the finest Christian colleges in the country. I didn't know much about it, but after receiving catalogs from several schools, looking over their master's degree programs, and then praying and asking God where he wanted me to go, I believed that Wheaton was the place for me.

After being accepted by Wheaton, I again launched into correspondence classes. My second class from Wheaton was a systematic theology course taught by Dr. Walter Elwell. I had signed up for the course with tremendous enthusiasm, but my ardor quickly faded when I discovered that one of the first assignments was to write a record of my spiritual journey, a personal history tracing how I came to know Christ.

Panic struck me. I wasn't bashful about sharing my story with inmates, but since becoming more familiar with Wheaton, I had learned that it was a very fine, conservative school. After all, Billy Graham was a Wheaton graduate! I feared that if I told the truth in my "spiritual journey" project—if these fine conservative Christians at Wheaton discovered my sordid background—it could jeopardize my chances to continue my studies, especially my chances to fulfill my dream of actually being a student someday on the Wheaton campus. How could I ever convince them that I had indeed been washed and saved by the same blood of the Lamb that had saved them? Yet I knew I had to be honest about my confession of faith. After all, my story wasn't about who I was, but about what God had done in this sinner's life.

I wrote the assignment, appalled at seeing my own past on paper. I thought jokingly that if the apostle Paul were to pen his epistles today, he would have to rewrite one verse to say, "I was the chief of sinners . . . until Jorge Valdés came around!" I had committed almost every sin in the book except murder, and in essence I had done that, too, indirectly murdering countless people through the drugs I'd brought into America—and all with no sense of conviction, no remorse or repentance, even when I got caught. Only when I became a Christian did I repent.

As delicately as I could, I described my sinful past and recounted my journey to faith. I prayed over the project and sent it off to Dr. Elwell, thinking that this might well be my last correspondence with Wheaton College.

Three weeks later, Dr. Elwell wrote to me after reviewing my project and said, "It's wonderful what God has done in your life. What a wonderful Savior we serve! Call me if you have any questions, I am here to help you in any way I can."

I was overwhelmed and couldn't wait to call him and thank him. The professor had no idea what he had just done for me. During our initial phone conversation,

Dr. Elwell was scholarly and professional, but also warm-hearted and friendly. I felt I could trust this man, so I began telling him about my fears of being judged and rejected because of my past.

Dr. Elwell interrupted me. "Jorge, anyone who would do that simply does not know the Bible very well. I thank God for your life."

One evening, during a phone call to my children, my five-year-old daughter, Jade, asked me what she needed to do to give her life to Jesus.

My feeling of incredible joy over Jade's desire was combined with apprehension—several inmates were in line behind me, waiting their turn to use the phone.

"Honey," I said, "when we hang up the phone, all you have to do is go into your room, ask Jesus to come into your life and to be your Lord, and thank him for dying for you."

"Daddy," Jade responded, "do I need to go into my room?"

She wasn't going to settle for easy answers. I glanced around at the other inmates. They all seemed to be looking at me.

My mind raced as I sought how to quickly wrap up the conversation and still minister to my daughter.

My voice cracked as I said, "No, honey, you don't have to go to your room, but after we hang up the phone, then you can ask Jesus to come into your life and ask him to be your Lord."

"Daddy," Jade replied insistently, "can't I give my life to Jesus with you right now?"

I couldn't hold back my tears. I prayed with Jade on the telephone and she asked Jesus to come into her life. Suddenly, I recalled my prayer three years earlier when I was first incarcerated as a Christian, when I asked God for only two things: to give me strength to make it and to save my children. I knew at that moment that God was answering both prayers.

I let the tears stream down my face and called out to the inmates, "My child just gave her heart to the Lord! My child is saved and going to heaven!"

Thirty-Five

Miracles

How could I—a convicted drug lord doing my second stint in prison—ever hope to be released ahead of time? It was a miracle that I was serving only ten years instead of life. Did I dare ask for less time? Could I possibly believe that God's plan for me involved an early release?

Yes, I could. Only God could give me such an audacious faith—and an incredibly bold lawyer, Alan Ross.

I had been transferred to another federal facility, this time in Michigan, where I continued my prison routine, including my studies toward my master's degree from Wheaton. I had completed four graduate-level extension courses and received straight *A*'s in all four. Wheaton's policy, however, allowed only four extension courses in their master's program; the remainder of the required courses had to be taken on campus.

That created a problem for me, since I still had the majority of my sentence to serve. Nevertheless, I believed it was God's will for me to pursue my master's degree. Although the parole board had already rejected my release, I encouraged Alan Ross to check on the possibility of having my sentence reduced by the judges who had imposed it.

This request was outrageous, considering the extremely light sentence I had received. But Alan loved a challenge, and had, in fact, kept in contact with the prosecutor in my case, hoping for an opportunity to get me out early.

The rationale behind our request was that the judge could reduce my sentence to time served, which was approaching five years, on the basis that I had been completely forthright in my court proceedings, had forfeited all my assets, and had shown clear signs of rehabilitation.

With help from David Borah and Ed Odom, Alan's first job was to convince Judge Wilber D. Owens, the judge who had presided over my original case in Macon. Then Judge Charles Butler in Mobile had to agree as well.

Late in 1994, Alan and David went to Judge Owens on my behalf. With them, and offering critical support for me, was U.S. Attorney Pat Sullivan, who had earlier won a celebrated drug conviction against Manuel Noriega of Panama. Alan presented our request to reduce my sentence to time served—which was no simple matter, since Judge Owens was the man who had accurately predicted that I would not benefit from the fifteen years to which he had sentenced me in my first case. After getting out of prison, I had indeed gone straight back to a life of drug smuggling, only on a much grander scale. Now Alan had to convince that same judge that I merited another chance.

Amazingly, Judge Owens agreed. I praised God for this miracle, which bolstered my faith to believe for another.

Next Alan approached Judge Butler, who had already gone out on a limb in granting me a ten-year sentence rather than a life sentence. I could easily imagine Judge Butler viewing our request as one of the most outrageous he had ever heard.

A devout Christian, Judge Butler was well aware of my cooperation since my arrest as well as of the spiritual change in my life. Nevertheless, many judges are particularly reluctant to adjust a sentence based upon a prisoner's spiritual conversion since many so-called jailhouse converts have ended up right back in prison, giving the judge a black eye for having had compassion on the inmate.

But God makes possible the unthinkable. While I prayed fervently and believed against all odds that God would make a way for me to go to Wheaton, Alan, along with my friends David Borah and Ed Odom, went to bat for me in front of Judge Butler.

The judge did not reduce my sentence to time served, but he did reduce it to five years, which was roughly equivalent, since I'd served only nine months less than that. And in most cases, parole is possible after serving eighty-five percent of a sentence. The judge's decision meant that I could be released!

But the devil doesn't give up that easily. Despite Judge Butler's decision, the Bureau of Prisons refused to release me, saying there had been a mistake in calculating the amount of time I had already served. The bureau contended that the sixteen months I had spent in the Mobile County jail while my case was being debated did not count toward the completion of my federal sentence. The delay was a confusing, frustrating tactic of the enemy, and the devil often taunted me: "Ha! You thought you were going to get out to go study the Bible! Think again. You're not going anywhere!"

I kept praying and believing. Counteracting a decision by any government bureaucracy is difficult, but for an inmate to contest a decision of the Bureau of Prisons was like an ant deciding to tunnel through a mountain.

Alan went back to Judge Butler and asked him to reconsider lowering my sentence to time served, which would eliminate the problem. But Judge Butler was adamant. He had correctly altered my sentence, he said, and the Bureau of Prisons was wrong!

Now I was caught in a battle between the court and the prison. Finally, Alan filed suit on my behalf against the Bureau of Prisons. For three months the calculations of my sentence were debated. At long last, Judge Butler's decision was upheld. On March 5, 1995, I was released on parole from federal prison. All totaled, I had served close to ten years—one fourth of my life—in prison.

When I walked out through the prison doors, the feeling of freedom overwhelmed me. I was ecstatic to be out, yet at the same time I felt weak, nervous, and confused.

Alan and his wife, Susan, were in the prison lobby waiting for me. As soon as I came through the door, we all hugged and laughed and cried.

"Thank you, Alan," I kept saying over and over, wiping tears from my eyes. "Thank you so much for what you've done for me." Then, without a bit of hesitation, I began praising God for using Alan to set me free.

I told Alan, "I just knew that Jesus would use another Jew to get me out of prison!"

Alan laughed heartily.

"You know, Alan," I told him, "my mission now is to one day make you realize that Jesus is the Messiah, the one you've been looking for."

Alan smiled at me. "I'll be waiting," he said, his eyes twinkling.

Alan and Susan drove me to my parents' house. I purposely had not told them I was getting out, so I could surprise them. What a wonderful, tearful reunion we had! We just kept hugging one another and crying. Mom, of course, had believed all along that God would not allow me to waste away in prison.

And now that I was out, she wasn't going to allow me to lose any more weight. She immediately set about preparing a huge Cuban dinner of black beans and rice—my favorites.

Epilogue

In the Hands of God

In December 1995, only nine months after my release from prison, I graduated from Wheaton College with a master's degree. Four years later I completed a doctorate in New Testament studies from Loyola University.

While at Wheaton, I asked Dr. Elwell to mentor me, and he agreed to do so. Dr. Elwell encouraged me not to squander what God had done in and for me or to lose sight of what he wanted to do through me. I promised Dr. Elwell that I would consult him about any major decisions.

Whenever anyone asked me to go preach or tell my story, I referred the invitation to Dr. Elwell. He did not want anyone exploiting my testimony; he also knew well the temptations I faced in retelling and reliving some of the sordid details of my life without Christ.

During the first few times I told my story, I found myself enjoying it too much. Afterward, awful guilt haunted me. I felt compelled to repent again, not just for my past, but for giving the devil too much ammunition to use against others and against me in the recounting of my spiritual journey.

Consequently, Dr. Elwell rejected most invitations for me to speak, and I happily abided by his decisions. "There will come a time, Jorge, when you'll be ready to share your story," he told me. "And when you do, Jesus will get the glory, not you, and certainly not the enemy."

One night I was busy studying when someone knocked on my door. It was Jason, a fellow student, who asked if he could borrow one of my books. I could tell he was discouraged and distraught, but I was surprised when he said, "Jorge, I'm almost ready to graduate, and I'm not even sure God exists. I've grown up in the church, yet I still question whether the things in the Bible are true and if God really cares about me."

As I listened to Jason talk about his questions and doubts, I felt compelled to tell him what God had done for me. I began telling him my story, how God had transformed me from an infamous drug lord into a person with a passion to serve Jesus Christ. Jason's eyes grew wider by the moment. I emphasized that I didn't give my life to Christ because I got caught, but because I discovered that Jesus was the only true satisfaction in life.

When I finished, Jason and I prayed together that God would revolutionize his life and use him to point others to Christ.

While I hoped that this was encouraging to Jason, for me it became a milestone in my Christian walk. For the first time I realized that God could use my life as a means to help not just hardened criminals in prison, but hardened Christians in churches as well.

One passage of Scripture was particularly encouraging to me in this regard. In recounting his early spiritual training following his salvation experience, the apostle Paul wrote, "I was personally unknown to the churches of Judea that are in Christ. They only heard the report: 'The man who formerly persecuted us is now preaching the faith he once tried to destroy.' And they praised God because of me" (Galatians 1:22-24). The last part of that passage really spoke to my heart. Studying the passage in Greek, I realized that Paul was saying, "It wasn't because of how good or how bad I had been, but God was glorified because of the work he had done in me." This was my desire, that the work God had done in my life would bring him honor and glory.

Although I didn't advertise the fact that I was a former inmate and a convicted drug lord, I could not avoid reminders of my past. God brought this truth home to me in a powerful way.

Shortly after I went to Wheaton, in one of the first church services I attended, the pastor and several other members of the congregation asked us to pray with them over a baby whom I guessed to be about three months old. I gladly consented, and we gathered around the mother and sick child.

The little boy looked malnourished, gaunt, and emaciated, his eyes staring blankly into space. It was then I realized that he was a crack baby, a child born to a mother who had used crack cocaine, a child who might never experience a normal life. I broke down crying, asking God to forgive me. As I looked at that little baby, who had done no harm to anyone on earth, it hit me that he had been born addicted because of the sins of his parents and the sins of Jorge Valdés. I couldn't help wondering how many other children I had affected this way.

I prayed silently, *O God! Am I going to be reminded of the consequences of my sins for the rest of my life?* And I believe God's answer to that prayer was, "Yes. Although you are forgiven, you will encounter consequences to your former lifestyle."

To this day, I still struggle with questions. I pray, *O God! Why have you been so good to me? Why have you spared my children and protected them when I have impacted so many other parents' children for evil?*

I have no answer, but I know that God is good and his grace is sufficient. Yes, sadly, I will encounter reminders of my past, but thanks to what Jesus has done for me, I know that my past no longer has a hold on me.

And I know that, despite the darkness of my past, the brightness of my future is in the hands of God.

In God's hands also—which I was to learn in a surprising way—was someone who came into my life as the completion of who I am today and as the strongest proof to me that God in his grace has given me a new beginning, a new chance to make up for all the years I wasted.

Sujey Adarve was a young Wheaton undergraduate from Medellin, Colombia, whom I got to know while tutoring her in Greek—I was her instructor's teaching assistant. I was impressed with Sujey's vibrant energy and the passion she possessed for her country and her Hispanic heritage. We spoke to each other almost exclusively in Spanish—not to conceal our conversation from our companions, but simply because we relished being able to communicate in our native tongue.

Sujey was with a group of my friends one evening when I talked with them for more than an hour about my past. She was not put off by my story; in fact, she seemed genuinely amazed and thankful for what the Lord had done in my life. Coming from Medellin, she knew well how the cocaine industry had exploded within Colombia, and although she did not yet know the extent of my involvement, she knew it was a miracle that I'd been able to walk away from the cartel and the cocaine business.

Sujey and I got together often to study Greek or just to talk, and before long we became good friends. But one Sunday after church, Sujey told me that some of her friends were saying she was spending too much time with me, especially since I was nearly twice as old as she was.

The more I thought about it, the more pained and angry I became. I viewed Sujey simply as a friend, and I thought her other friends must be unfairly judging me, particularly for my past—after all, earlier that same year I was still in prison. But I shook off my hurt and told Sujey I didn't think she and I should see each other again. After saying good-bye to her that afternoon, I honestly believed I would never see her again outside of class. I had been praying about Sujey's and my friendship every day for more than a month, so I thought this was God's way of answering my prayers. Maybe this was for the best.

The following morning, Sujey telephoned to ask if she could get together with me one more time to talk. I sensed urgency in her voice, so I agreed to take her to breakfast that morning. When we sat down in the cafeteria, Sujey got straight to the point. "Jorge, I have been praying about this," she said, pausing to wipe the tears trickling down her face. "I believe that . . . I am . . . I am in love with you, and that God has revealed to me that he has put me in your life for a special purpose."

Her words hit me like a bomb. Sujey continued, "I'm willing to see where God leads in our relationship. However, if you're uncomfortable with that, we can go our separate ways."

I sat there dumbfounded, not knowing what to say. As astounded as I was, I reached across the table, held Sujey's hands in mine, and to my amazement, I heard myself say, "Okay, but I want to talk to Dr. Elwell, because I promised him that I would run any critical decisions in my life by him so we could pray about them together." To myself I thought, *And this will be a critical decision!*

I had been meeting regularly with Dr. Elwell since my earliest days at Wheaton. Besides the intellectual challenge, our weekly meetings were an opportunity for me to be accountable to someone for my spiritual life. Dr. Elwell always listened calmly to my heart cries concerning God's will for my life and encouraged me to continue seeking God and believing that he had me at Wheaton for a purpose. We rarely talked about my social life, except once when I mentioned to him that I thought I might become a monk. He had smiled and replied, "Don't worry, Jorge. You will know what God wants you to do. Look how far he has brought you. You can trust him to totally direct your life in this area as well."

Now I was bursting with anticipation as we met again. We usually began our meetings with prayer, but this time Dr. Elwell said, "Jorge, there's something I need to talk to you about. The other day, as I was working in my yard, a thought came into my mind." Dr. Elwell paused and looked at me kindly. "Have you ever thought about starting a relationship with Sujey Adarve?"

Tears came at once to my eyes. I was in awe of God's direction in my life.

With guidance from Dr. Elwell, Sujey and I drew up a plan for our relationship. We decided we would "date" for at least a year while we continued seeking God's will in our lives. We would become engaged only after we were both absolutely sure this was God's will, and even then, we would set a wedding date no sooner than six months after our engagement began. That would give us approximately two years to allow our relationship to mature, our love to grow, and our commitment to each other to be certain and irrevocable. And if the process lasted longer, fine. We were committed to take as much time as necessary for God to reveal his will to us.

In the meantime, we vowed to each other and before God that we would conduct our relationship in purity, which meant no sexual contact or anything else that would compromise our spiritual lives. We knew we couldn't disobey God in these areas and still expect his blessing in others. Our love was to be grounded in God's love, not simply in mere physical attraction. Most importantly, we asked God for his wisdom, his guidance, and his power.

Sujey and I studied together constantly, which because of our class load and work schedules was about the only time we had to spend with each other. We also worked together in a ministry at a Hispanic church in Wheaton. Most of our dates revolved around some form of ministry. Slowly but surely, our love deepened. The most marvelous part about the love we shared was that it originated in Jesus Christ. He was at the center of our relationship, and as a result we developed an unconditional love rather than a love based on what Sujey could do for me or give to me or what I could provide for her. It was a love that grew out of mutual acceptance, based on the truth that God had accepted us because of Christ's blood.

Finally, I had found true love.

Sujey and I became engaged on Thanksgiving Day in 1996, but the months leading up to our wedding were bittersweet for my family. My dad's health was deteriorating rapidly from his fight with cancer, and he was nearing the end of the time period the doctors had told us we might expect him to live.

At the same time, I accepted a position at Wheaton College as an adjunct professor, teaching Hispanic-Latino theology. Once again, I was reminded of God's grace and goodness toward me. *What a God we serve*, I thought, *who can transform a drug lord into a professor of theology at one of the world's leading Christian schools.*

I also continued pursuing my Ph.D. from nearby Loyola University. Part of my reason for pressing on in academic studies while my dad was dying was that I knew he was so proud of me. After wasting so much time, money, and energy, I was finally fulfilling the dream Dad and Mom had for me when they fled Cuba.

Sujey and I were together at my parents' home in Miami on the early summer day in 1997 when I held Dad in my arms as he breathed his last. Only the night before, J.C. and I had been at his bedside, preparing to pray together for him, when suddenly Dad spoke up. "No," he said in an unexpectedly strong voice, "it's *my* time for prayer." J.C. and I looked at each other in surprise. We had never heard our father pray aloud, but now we heard him pray with the voice of an angel: "Jesus, if it is my time to go, I welcome it. Please receive me into your kingdom. Please forgive me for all of my sins. I thank you for the life you have given me. I thank you for my wife and children, my family and my friends. Please take care of them. Amen." Then Dad shut his eyes and went back to sleep.

Now, while getting ready for Dad's funeral, I cried out to God, "Why did you take him? Couldn't you have allowed Dad to stay here just a little longer so he could see me finish my degree and watch Sujey and me get married?"

Then my mind flashed back to the angel's words to the women at the tomb following the resurrection of Jesus: "Why are you searching for the living among the dead?" I realized that my dad was not dead, but very much alive in heaven, and he no longer had cancer! He would indeed see me get my degree and watch Sujey and me get married—and he'd have the best view in the house.

Later that summer, as Sujey and I pledged our marriage vows to each other, it meant more to me than any commitment I'd ever made, except my commitment to follow Jesus Christ. As I thanked the Lord for the beautiful, loving woman of God he had placed at my side, I could not help but thank him again for how far he had brought me.

Sujey was also at my side in the storefront-style church in the Blue Island section of inner-city Chicago on the night I addressed the rowdy crowd of hardened gang members and told them, "I was everything you have ever wanted to be . . . and never will be. I've had everything you're looking for. I've achieved everything you're dreaming about. And I've also experienced your worst nightmares. But today my life is filled with more love than I ever thought possible."

After I spoke, dozens from the crowd walked forward for prayer. Among them were two boys about ten years old, wearing gang jackets. They were holding hands and crying more intensely than I had ever seen anyone cry. Others in the crowd were staring at them. Their profound weeping was sure to be considered a mark of weakness by their fellow gang members. They were risking the gang's rejection and perhaps even their lives.

After hearing of the pain God had released me from, the boys confessed tearfully their own painful lack of meaning in life. I told them that Jesus could provide that meaning and purpose for them. I joined Sujey in prayer with them, and they asked Jesus to come into their lives, to save them, and to change them by the same power with which he had changed me.

Then and there I realized anew that I had been called to give kids like these a message of hope: If God could save Jorge Valdés, then no one else's sin can possibly be too big to be forgiven, and no life is too dirty to be made clean.

My Thanks

To my father and best friend, Bebo: *Papi,* through your example I now understand what you meant when you said, "You will never know what it is to be a father until you have children." I pray that as you stand next to Jesus today you are smiling down upon me.

To my mom, Teresa: *Mami,* because of your prayers I now live. You taught me to dream and believe in God's ability to accomplish my dreams. *Sin ti no soy nadien.*

To my brother, J.C., who sacrificed it all for his family: *Mi hermano,* you are the living example of what Jesus calls a servant. I would not be half the person I am without you.

To my wife, Sujey: *Mi amor,* you have taught me what it really means to love as Jesus loves us. I am a full person because God gave you to me.

To my children—Jorge, Krystle, Jade, Alex, and Estevan: *Mis hijos,* I thank God so much for you all. I thank God for the manner in which he has used each of you to show me where to find real happiness and meaning in life. There is no greater joy than to walk with you as you walk through life with Christ.

To Hector: *Mi hijito,* thanks so much for being a true brother and always being there for my dad. I love you.

To *El Viejo: Te quiero como un padre.*

To Dr. Don Manuel: *Mi obispo,* I have seen Jesus in your humility and love. Your friendship has honored me beyond understanding.

To Dr. Justo Gonzalez: *Excelentísimo.* You have shown me what it is to sacrifice it all for others. I will always be indebted to you and H.T.I. for supporting me in this difficult journey.

To Roberto: *Mi compatriota,* thanks for being there for me during the most difficult time in my life. I love our people more because of you.

To David: *Compadre,* your encouragement has allowed me to be the scholar I am. You have impacted my life in more ways than you can imagine.

To the many professors at Wheaton and Loyola: Julius, Doug, Scott, Andy, Wendy, John. You had patience with me and allowed me to grow as a scholar. You taught me that I did not have to compromise my faith to be a serious scholar.

There are many others to whom I owe much, many who believed in me and always supported me, including Alan and Susan, Brother Libby, and Brother Emmett. Many others took great risks in believing me: David, Ed, Gloria, Jane, Chris, Pat, Judge Butler, Judge Owens, and Judge Highsmith. I am where I am today because of the risks you took.

My thanks would not be complete unless I recognize four important people in my walk with Christ: Tim and Teruko, when the world had given up on me, you were obedient. Through your living example of Jesus, I now know him. Walter Elwell, you mentored me through my most difficult times in my Christian life. As my professor, you taught me that, when the semester is over, the most important thing we have taught our students is not how to solve any critical theological issues, but how to be closer to Jesus. I will never forget all our lunches when you patiently helped me work through my crises. And my mentor, Manny Mill, your living example of what it is to be an effective Christian is my model. I love you, Barbara, and all the others at *Koinonia*. Your examples have kept me focused on the gospel.

So many people are responsible for bringing this book to completion. My appreciation goes to Mark Fretz at Doubleday for being a friend. I thank you for believing in this story and guiding me to the right people. To Greg Johnson, my agent and friend, whose guidance, focus, and belief in my dream are largely responsible for *Coming Clean*. To my publisher, Dan Rich: You believed in this book from the first day we met. You took a risk and showed me that a true Christian must be a risktaker for Christ. To WaterBrook Press editors Thomas Womack and Laura Barker: You patiently allowed the Holy Spirit to help you swim through a very difficult ocean. To the entire WaterBrook staff: Your smiles, support, and love for Christ allowed this difficult experience to be a joyful one. To my brother and associate, Ken Abraham: You lived with this story for a long time. You became part of the story, and you allowed Jesus to guide you in sculpting this story into a manuscript. Ken, I love you and I pray that together we will impact many for Christ.

Finally, to the many Christian brothers and sisters in prisons around the world, I urge you to place your faith in the One who cares and is able.